"We'll leave at two P.M.," Lieutenant Greely announced. It was 10 A.M., August 9, 1883. The commander of the Lady Franklin Bay Expedition had concluded he could not wait another day in hope of the relief ship's reaching his little band of men in the Far North. Summer was passing. New ice might close the harbor and trap them. They had to leave and leave quickly.

This was the beginning of the retreat of the Lady Franklin Bay Expedition—twenty-five men under the command of Lieutenant Adolphus A. Greely, who had been sent by the United States in 1879 to study the Arctic phenomena. From a scientific standpoint, their expedition had been successful, but before their mission was over, disaster was to strike again and again.

THE LONG RESCUE tells the terrible, suspenseful drama of the heroic attempt of Greely and his men to escape from the treacherous North. Fighting not only against the unpredictable forces of the Arctic, where a sudden shift in wind could take them miles off their course or move a gigantic ice floe in their path, but against time—for Greely knew that a few hours' delay could destroy any chance of reaching the relief ship—the expedition had to meet and conquer elements of nature unknown to most men. But the sinister Arctic was to strike a deathblow to their hopes of reaching the rescue ship on time, and they were to find themselves a prisoner of the North for a third long winter.

The story of the desperate fight for survival of the Greely expedition is an adventure story of almost unbearable dramatic suspense. It is also an epic of the courage and leadership of the men responsible for this heroic task—many of whom gave their lives for the winning of the *Farthest North*.

THE LONG RESCUE

THE LONG RESCUE

by Theodore Powell

DOUBLEDAY & COMPANY, INC., GARDEN CITY, NEW YORK

1960

Library of Congress Catalog Card Number 60-11389
Copyright © 1960 by Theodore Powell
All Rights Reserved
Printed in the United States of America
First Edition

Design: Charles Kaplan

A PATHFINDER BOOK REPRINT EDITION
Complete and Unabridged

Printed in the United States of America

ISBN: 979-8-8691-3367-0

ROSTER, THE LADY FRANKLIN BAY EXPEDITION

First Lieut. Adolphus W. Greely, Fifth Cavalry

Second Lieut. Frederick F. Kislingbury, Eleventh Infantry
Second Lieut. James B. Lockwood, Twenty-third Infantry

Sgt. David L. Brainard, Second Cavalry, Orderly Sergeant
Sgt. George W. Rice, Signal Corps, Photographer
Sgt. Edward Israel, Signal Corps, Astronomer
Sgt. Winfield S. Jewell, Signal Corps, Meteorologist
Sgt. David C. Ralston, Signal Corps, Meteorologist
Sgt. Hampden S. Gardiner, Signal Corps, Meteorologist
Sgt. William S. Cross, General Service, Engineer
Sgt. David Linn, Second Cavalry

Cpl. Nicholas Salor, Second Cavalry
Cpl. Joseph Elison, Tenth Infantry

Pvt. Roderick R. Schneider, First Artillery
Pvt. Charles B. Henry (true name: Charles Henry Buck),
    Fifth Cavalry
Pvt. Maurice Connell, Third Cavalry
Pvt. Jacob Bender (true name: George C. Leyerzopf),
    Ninth Infantry
Pvt. Francis Long, Ninth Infantry
Pvt. William Whisler, Ninth Infantry

Pvt. Henry Biederbick, Seventeenth Infantry, Acting Hospital Steward
Pvt. Julius Frederick, Second Cavalry
Pvt. William A. Ellis, Second Cavalry

Dr. Octave Pavy joined the expedition at Disko, Greenland, by contract as Acting Assistant Surgeon.

Mr. Henry Clay also joined the expedition at Disko as a military employee. He accompanied the expedition to Lady Franklin Bay and returned to the United States on the ship that carried the expedition north.

Jens Edward, Eskimo, sledge driver
Frederik Thorlip Christiansen, Eskimo, sledge driver

CONTENTS

INTRODUCTION

The history of the Lady Franklin Bay Expedition is one of the great adventure stories of all time. Today, less than eighty years later, it is all but forgotten. The full achievements of the expedition were not generally recognized even in the time of their accomplishment. They were shadowed by the dramatic story of the miraculous rescue of the survivors.

Unbelievable hardships were suffered by that small group of men at the top of the world. Such hardships brought forth some conduct that was shameful and more that was noble.

THE CIRCUMPOLAR STATIONS

The Lady Franklin Bay Expedition, or the Greely Expedition as it later came to be called, was but one part of an extensive scientific examination of arctic phenomena. In this international project the different participating nations each assumed responsibility for maintaining one or two observation stations around the Arctic Circle. (Two stations were established near the Antarctic Circle.) A program for all of the stations prepared by the International Polar Commission included meteorological, magnetic, and auroral observations to be made hourly throughout the year. Suggestions were made for other observations such as study of solar radiation, earth currents, ice, tides, and all peculiar local natural phenomena. It was clearly an ambitious and laudable endeavor in international co-operation for scientific purposes.

The United States already had in preparation in 1880 a scheme known as Polar Colonization. This was a program for a colony to be established as far north as possible to stay for three years and wait for a favorable chance to make a dash for the North Pole. This fever to reach the North Pole which gripped the United States and other nations in the latter part of the nineteenth century may be compared with the later desire to conquer Everest. There was little purpose in it. But it was an opportunity for heroic achievement in response to a challenge of extraordinary danger and difficulty.

Lady Franklin Bay was selected as the site for the Polar Colonization project because it was so far north and it was near a coal seam which would provide much needed fuel. It was in this bay that the British expedition in the *Discovery* commanded by Sir George Nares spent the winter of 1875–76. For the purposes of the International Polar Commission there was no need to go so far north. In fact, it was intended that the observation stations should be located in accessible places. Lady Franklin Bay, as events developed, proved to be certainly not easily accessible.

The Lady Franklin Bay Expedition, under the command of Lieutenant Adolphus W. Greely, sailed from St. John's, Newfoundland, in the *Proteus* on July 7, 1881. The sky was blue and the wind was favorable but the departure could not be called auspicious by anyone sensitive to the traditions of the sea. The new Commander in Chief, President James A. Garfield, in Washington's Union Station had been shot down by a political fanatic on July 2. The President was desperately trying to hang onto life but the specter of death hung over the nation. The presence of that specter was felt on board the *Proteus* as the expedition left for its extended vigil in the Arctic.

The Greely Expedition reached Discovery Harbor in Lady Franklin Bay the afternoon of August 11, 1881. The *Proteus,* a barkentine rigged steamer, had made the trip north with little delay. The waters between Greenland and Ellesmere Island were exceptionally free from ice that summer. The easy voyage north in 1881 was to foster an attitude that was to take two years and two successive failures of relief efforts to dispel—that it was an easy task to push a ship across Melville Bay past Smith Sound, Kane Basin, and on up Kennedy Channel in July and August. The *Neptune* in 1882 and the *Proteus* in 1883 could not reach the men at Lady Franklin Bay.

The Greely Expedition did very well in carrying out its mission. All observations were carefully made and recorded, extensive exploration and mapping was accomplished. Collections were made of vegetable and animal life. Many sledge parties were sent out, and although none reached the North Pole, one of them traveled around the northern shore of Greenland to a point farther north than man had ever been before. It was the first time in three hundred years that any nation but England held the honor of the "Farthest North."

The sledge parties also searched for signs of the *Jeannette* expedition. That expedition under the command of George W. DeLong had sailed into the Arctic through Bering Strait in 1879. Greely's men found no sign of the *Jeannette.* Not until they reached Cape Sabine were they to learn that the *Jeannette* had been crushed off the coast of Siberia and most of the expedition had perished in the delta of the Lena River.

The relief ship which was supposed to visit the Lady Franklin Bay Expedition in 1882 never arrived. The party had supplies for three years and was well housed at the building named Fort Conger (after the Michigan Senator who had sponsored the project in Congress). The barrack had been erected quickly by the use of a technique new in 1881—pre-cut lumber. This double-walled house, with a one-foot air space between the walls for insulation, provided for the enlisted men a large common room with double-decker bunks, tables, and stoves, and for the three officers and Dr. Pavy a smaller room. Between the two rooms was a galley and a bathroom. This arctic home proved comfortable and sturdy. (Indeed, twenty years later, Peary, on his attempts to reach the North Pole, was to make use of the house and find it still in good condition.)

After two years of strenuous arctic life, the members of the party were in generally good health. Not all of them were satisfied. There were seeds of discontent. But the commanding officer could justifiably feel that he and his men had fully accomplished their mission. When, in July 1883, the second relief ship did not arrive, Lieutenant Greely prepared for withdrawal to the south in their small boats.

Throughout their extended tour of duty, they had done well. The work was completed but the greatest trials were just beginning.

The writing of this book really began in a talk with Hal Rein about true adventure stories. After he had initiated my interest, there were a great many other people who helped me along the way. The staff of the public libraries in Manchester and Hartford, Connecticut, provided assistance with the initial research. Further research was done at that vast treasure trove on Fifth Avenue and Forty-second Street, the New York Public Library.

The richest discoveries were made in the National Archives Building, Washington, D.C. For anyone sensitive to the history of the United States, it is a most thrilling and awesome experience to walk through the aisles of records and know that so much of the real story of America is collected within those walls. The staff members seem conscious of the priceless quality of the material they deal with and are prompt, courteous, and efficient in responding to the requests of a researcher.

This writer trembled with delight and anticipation as he opened the boxes stored in the Archives containing the records of the Lady Franklin Bay Expedition and copies of the diaries kept by the men. My anticipation was more than fulfilled, and in the end I found myself with an embarrassment of riches. There was so much material available, intimate and detailed. The richness and abundance of the material in the Archives changed the problem from research to selection.

Major General John N. Greely (the son of the commander of the Lady Franklin Bay Expedition) and his wife added some family details to this story. While visiting with them in their Washington home, I was thrilled to hold in my hand a claw from the bear killed at such a critical point in the life of the expedition. It made those distant, dramatic days at Cape Sabine seem so much closer.

The author is indebted to a number of others. John and Elaine Mrosek gave encouragement, criticism, and practical help. Mrs. Dorothy Ferrell, good friend and neighbor, sped the work on its way and made the writer's task very much easier by swift, efficient typing of the manuscript. To the late Ellen F. Goodsell, the author owes more than he can say.

No apology is adequate for the sacrifices required of the author's wife and children while this work was in progress. His wife's enthusiasm for the story never failed, but the children grew impatient with a father who spent so much time at the typewriter in the basement. He hopes that someday they will come to feel the time was well spent.

To my editor, Harold Kuebler, the writer is deeply grateful for his understanding and for his skilled and sensitive criticism.

A word about technique. This is a work of history, journalistic history. Literary devices have been employed to round out the story revealed by the record, the diaries, and the reports of the survivors. The author has created dialogue. He has not created facts. As much as possible, the conversations of the participants are based on some written record. All of the events reported did happen in reality and are presented as fully and as faithfully as the records permit.

I am aware of the danger of writing about an area where

I have never been. I can offer no credentials at all as an authority on the Arctic. Gross errors have been avoided, I hope, by relying upon the statements of those who lived this story.

Theodore Powell
Manchester, Connecticut
April 1960

CHAPTER ONE

RETREAT TO THE SOUTH

August and September, 1883

"We'll leave at two P.M.," Lieutenant Greely announced. It was 10 A.M., August 9, 1883. The commander of the Lady Franklin Bay Expedition had concluded he could not wait another day in hope of the relief ship's reaching his little band of men in the Far North. Summer was passing. New ice might close the harbor and trap them. They had to leave and leave quickly.

There was an excitement racing through the party that moved the men to perform their duties with extra energy. They were going home after two years stationed in the Arctic at the top of Ellesmere Island. They were going home.

The significance of the occasion was underlined by the commanding officer, who appeared dressed for their retreat in full-dress uniform with his saber and revolver at his side and wearing his shoulder knots and helmet cord. He was an army officer leading his small command on what could be a dangerous mission. Two years of unbroken arctic service had erased some but not all of the formality of military life. Greely knew that the retreat to the south in hope of meeting their rescue ship would provide a number of severe tests of his leadership. He felt it appropriate, therefore, to emphasize his position as leader by donning his dress uniform for the retreat. The saber, revolver, shoulder knots, and helmet cord were the symbols of his authority and responsibility. He was the commanding officer. Neither he nor anyone else would forget it.

"Sergeant Brainard," Lieutenant Greely said, "you, Sergeant Jewell, and Private Long will work here at the station with me. Lieutenant Lockwood will take the rest of the party down to Dutch Island and load the launch and the boats."

Peering through his eyeglasses, the tall, thin, commanding officer, with his bushy electric beard and unsmiling, rather formal manner, made a sharp contrast with the rest of the party dressed in the haphazard fashion they had developed during their arctic service. (Greely's beard, fashionable enough for army officers of that day, served to hide a scar made at Antietam. A Confederate rifle bullet had cut through his cheek, broken his jawbone, and knocked out two teeth.)

Lieutenant Lockwood took his detail off to Dutch Island to load the remaining supplies and equipment on the launch and the other small boats. Lieutenant Greely, with Brainard, Jewell, and Long, returned to the barrack they called Fort Conger to take care of the last necessary duties in closing the station.

In their two years in the Arctic, Greely and his men had become accustomed to extended sledge journeys. They had traveled far and wide, staying away from the station for weeks and months, living on the bare supplies and equipment their sledge could carry. During roaring gales and in subzero temperatures they had slept protected only by the meager shelter of a sleeping bag. When storms had prevented use of their little stove on the trail, they had eaten frozen pemmican or had gone without food and water for fifteen or twenty hours and longer. They had traveled unknown lands—unknown to them and unknown to mankind. They had lived the life of arctic explorers for two years with extraordinary success. They were undaunted now by a trip southward of 260 miles. They were going south. Traveling conditions would improve as they progressed. The route was known to them, and they had the strength of their entire party on this journey.

They had ample food and most of the necessary equipment. The launch was loaded with five thousand pounds of coal mined from the coal seam nearby. They had four rifles with a thousand cartridges, two shotguns and ample ammunition for them. The surgeon for the party, Dr. Octave Pavy, had made a selection from their ample medical supplies which had been carefully packed by Hospital Steward Henry Biederbick. Their sergeant engineer, William S. Cross, and his assistant, Private Julius Frederick, had loaded sledges, tools, and other equipment on the boats.

Their major deficiency in supply was a lack of clothing and footgear. Their clothes and boots had received heavy wear in the severe arctic weather. The expedition was to have been resupplied by the ship which had failed to arrive the previous year. By the diligent efforts of Shorty Frederick, who made serviceable boots from sealskin and heavy stockings, every man was supplied with a new pair of boots for the retreat.

They faced a difficult sentimental problem in leaving their sledge dogs. Those faithful animals could not be taken along in the launch and the three little boats that would be carrying twenty-five men and thousands of pounds of equipment and supplies. While closing up the barrack Greely ordered Brainard to break open the remaining barrels of seal blubber, pork, beef, and bread so that the dogs would have food for some time. Greely's order was not merely sentimental. He knew they had all the food loaded on their boats that they could carry. They could not carry the dogs along with them. However (and Greely saw no need to announce this), they would need the dogs if they were unable to break through Kennedy Channel and were forced to return to Fort Conger for a third winter.

Their means of travel was limited. Their only power (other than their own muscles) would be supplied by the twenty-seven-foot navy launch, the *Lady Greely* (so christened by Lieutenant Lockwood). Lockwood would be in charge of the launch with a crew of six, including engineer Cross and Frederick, serving as fireman. Greely and Lieutenant Kislingbury would also travel on the launch. Three boats would be in tow: a whaleboat, an English iceboat, and a jolly boat. A small two-man boat would be carried on the launch.

As protection against loss of any of the vessels, Greely arranged that the records of the expedition, the provisions, the coal and other supplies be distributed among all four boats. They were carrying more than forty days' rations. There were also more than twenty days' rations cached along the route to the south. Greely ordered that a complete suit of canvas be taken for the boats. It might, he knew, be thought foolish to expect to move by sail in these ice bound waters, but he was looking ahead to the possibility that they might reach open water and not find their relief ship. If they should be in such a situation and not have canvas, Greely would not forgive himself.

MOVING OUT

Fort Conger had been established on the eastern shore of Discovery Harbor. The mouth of the harbor, which led into Lady Franklin Bay, was bordered by two capes,

Proteus Point on the east and Sun Cape on the west. Between the two, lay Bellot Island.

As Greely surveyed the condition of Discovery Harbor about two o'clock, he could see that heavy, closely packed ice extended across the eastern passage out of the harbor. That passage was too dangerous for their launch and small boats, so he decided they would leave by the western passage between Sun Cape and Bellot Island. Taking the tide at the flood, the launch with the three boats in tow moved away from Dutch Island out toward the western passage.

The launch and the boats, heavily laden with men and supplies, moved slowly away from shore. The sledge dogs stood like sentinels on the rise watching their masters depart. The dogs watched in curious silence for some minutes; then one of them raced down toward the shore, across the ice, and leaped into the water. The men, watching from the departing boats, could not be sure which dog it was. Private Roderick Schneider, who had assumed principal responsibility for training the sled dogs, said, "I think it's Flipper."

Flipper was one of the dogs born at the station the year before. Schneider had raised, fed, and trained him with great care and attention.

The men stole glances at the commanding officer. Greely was busy in the bow of the launch, calling directions to the helmsman. He showed no awareness of the distant dog striving vainly to catch up with them.

The men watched the dog in silence. The steam launch puffed along through the ice floes with the boats trailing behind. In the distance Flipper, if it was he, struggled valiantly to swim through the icy water. His head was angled above the water, arrow-straight, and pointed toward the retreating boats in somber, eloquent plea. The men could see that the dog was dropping behind and was having trouble. A few minutes later the small head disappeared abruptly beneath the water.

The silence among the men was broken as someone gasped, "He's gone." They looked at Schneider, who was still gazing at the point where he had last seen Flipper. There was nothing to be seen now but the cold, dark water and the shifting ice floes.

The convoy moved on, threading its way along the open lanes of water close to the shore. The steam launch and the boats, fully loaded, could not move fast enough, however, to keep up with the ebbing tide. Soon the boats were in low water and progress became more difficult. Hour after hour the convoy pushed forward toward Sun Cape.

Taking Sergeant Brainard with him, Lieutenant Greely stepped ashore and went to high ground to reconnoiter. From a summit above the western passage he could see, just one mile away from the launch, clear water across Lady Franklin Bay leading out to Hall Basin and Kennedy Channel. A little more effort, and they could be in open water. Greely and Brainard hurried back to the party.

"All right, let's move," Lieutenant Greely said, "let's move. There's open water just a mile ahead of us."

The men hustled back on their boats, hastily loading the cookstove and equipment and carrying in their hands the food that was only partially eaten.

Greely took his post at the bow of the launch. Sergeant George W. Rice was at the helm. Rice was actually the photographer for the party, but he had also displayed ability as a boat handler. He was a man of great energy and enthusiasm, and possessed a seemingly endless variety of skills. He had grown up in Nova Scotia and had adapted readily to life in the Arctic.

They were delayed by shallow water because of the fast ebbing tide but Greely urged them forward, taking advantage of every lead he could find through the ice-packed harbor. After they had moved forward a short distance some of the men thought they saw open water a few hundred yards ahead off the starboard bow.

"No," Greely said, "not that direction, Sergeant. I think there's a good lead about fifty yards off the port bow."

He adjusted his eyeglasses and gazed intently. Greely then left the launch and moved across the ice to get a better view of what looked to him like a good lead.

While Greely was reconnoitering, the tide seemed to ebb even faster and the ice began to move to the south. Greely had directed the launch into a small space of open water between one floe several hundred yards across and another floe that seemed to be miles wide. As the ice moved with the tide the launch was pinched between these two floes. The ice closed with considerable speed and in a few moments the men saw that the launch was in serious danger of being turned over. The small boats were likely to be crushed. The men in the small boats, acting quickly, leaped to the larger floe and hauled the boats up on the ice.

The launch crew also moved swiftly; several of them started unloading supplies and equipment from the launch to the larger floe. A dozen others jumped to the starboard side and threw themselves against the launch to prevent the boat's toppling over. The pressure of the ice mounted.

The situation was desperate. The men holding the launch upright yelled for assistance. Others of the party quickly ran to their side to help hold the launch in position. Watching the movement of the ice carefully the launch party slowly worked her into a safe, natural dock.

While this was happening Greely was running back across the ice to the boats, yelling orders. The men, desperately trying to save the boats and the launch, paid no attention to their frantic commander as he ran toward them, his sword flopping wildly at his side. By the time Greely reached the scene the small boats were safely on the ice floe and the launch had been moved out of danger.

Greely, looking around at their new situation, said that it was obviously impossible to attempt any further movement until the ice opened again. Several of the men grunted to indicate they had reached that conclusion long ago. They were all aware of the serious danger in which their commander had placed them by moving into the narrow lead between the two large floes. If they lost the launch they were deprived of their only source of power. They would be reduced to rowing or drifting in the smaller boats, or they would have to attempt to travel over impossible terrain, pulling their equipment and supplies on sledges.

The narrow escape, as much as the long day of labor, seemed to have exhausted the party. It was now 3 A.M. and Greely, after assigning sentry duties, allowed the men to turn into their sleeping bags for the sleep they so desperately needed. He took time for his first food in twenty hours, and then got some rest himself.

Greely could congratulate himself that because of his planning and preparations of previous months, it was possible for them to be starting on their retreat so well prepared. There were formidable obstacles in front of them. They had to reach Cape Sabine by September 15. His message to the Signal Office (sent back on the *Proteus*, the ship which had brought his expedition to Lady Franklin Bay) had stated that if the relief ship of 1882 failed to reach them, the second relief ship of 1883 should not leave Cape Sabine before September 15, if it, too, were unable to make its way through the ice of the waters above that point. Greely was now proceeding on the assumption that the Signal Office was following these directions. Greely assumed (correctly) that the relief ship of 1882 had been blocked by ice above Smith Sound and that the relief ship this year was similarly blocked.

It would take careful navigation through ice-packed waters, courage, hard work, and good fortune for the party of twenty-five men to make its way in small boats 260 miles to the south. It was now August 10. They had five weeks to complete their journey, to arrive there before the relief ship left. At first, Greely thought this was ample time. But the ice was so close and heavy . . . However, even if they were delayed beyond September 15 in reaching Cape Sabine, they could expect assistance from the party the relief ship would leave at Littleton Island. In his letter to General Hazen, Greely had written:

The party should then proceed [after the departure of the relief ship sometime after September 15] to establish a winter station at Polaris winter quarters, Lifeboat Cove [Littleton Island] where their main duty would be to keep their telescope on Cape Sabine and the land to the northward. They should have lumber enough for house and observatory, fifty tons of coal and complete meteorological and magnetic outfit. Being furnished with dogs, sledges and a native driver a party of at least six (6) men should proceed when practicable to Cape Sabine whence a sledge party northward of two best fitted men should reach Cape Hawks, if not Cape Collinson. Such action from advice, experience and observation seems to me all that can be done to insure our safety. No deviation from these instructions should be permitted. Latitude of action should not be given to a relief party, who, on a known coast, are searching for men who know their plans and orders.

I am respectfully yours,

A. W. Greely, 1st Lt., 5th Cavalry, A.S.O.
and Ass't, Commanding Expedition

Greely knew his plans and orders. He was taking his party south to Cape Sabine on the firm assumption that if they arrived there before September 15 a relief ship would be waiting for them. If they arrived later, a relief party would be established on Littleton Island.

Greely was worried about the time. He was glad he had not delayed their retreat any longer. He worried now if perhaps he had waited a week too long. In a few weeks the temperature would drop and new ice would be forming. The arctic night was approaching. They would soon lose the continuous twenty-four hours of daylight. They must press southward as quickly as possible. They could not lose time. They could not be caught in the Arctic for a third winter.

After several hours' sleep Greely and his men were up again hopefully looking for an opportunity to move on. The commanding officer was now wearing his usual arctic clothing. It was the second day of their retreat, and they were not yet out of Lady Franklin Bay. At the turn of the tide, the ice loosened. They were able to break through and steam across the bay to Cape Baird at the entrance to Kennedy Channel. While they were making this passage during the late morning of August 10, a gale began to blow. By 2 P.M. the storm became so severe they had to put to shore at Cape Baird. Here they checked the loads and equipment, putting everything in order.

The boats had been loaded with all the supplies and equipment that could be carried. In addition they were carrying the records, field journals, and sealed diaries of the members of the party packed in three metal, waterproof boxes weighing a total of fifty pounds. (Before departure for the Arctic each man had been given a diary by the Army with orders to maintain it during his stay in the Arctic. At the end of the stay at Fort Conger, the diaries were sealed, addressed to the Chief Signal Officer, and packed.) The large heavy pendulum, so essential to their studies of gravity, had been placed in a metal case and then loaded in a wooden box.

Because of the heavy load being carried by each boat, Greely ordered that each enlisted man and the two Eskimos, Jens and Frederik, would be limited to eight pounds of personal baggage and officers would be limited to sixteen. This advantage for officers was usual in the Army, but it must have offended some of the men in these circumstances. They may have expected that two years of unbroken arctic service would have erased such artificial distinctions. But for their commanding officer, the Army was the Army, whether in Washington or in the Arctic.

At Cape Baird Greely decided to erect a cairn. He was conscious that the relief ship coming after them, if it reached this far north, might have as much trouble as they were now experiencing. In the cairn he left a message about his plan to proceed to Cape Sabine, Littleton Island, or possibly the Cary Islands. He also left maps showing what exploration had been done by his party and reported that the party's original records and collection of natural history specimens were packed and stored, ready for shipping, in the building at Fort Conger.

The gale continued through the day but diminished about 9 P.M. The men were then resting in their sleeping bags on shore. When Greely saw the strength of the storm waning he rose to his feet and shouted, "All right, let's go, let's go. We're moving out, we're moving out."

It seemed to the commanding officer that some of the men did not move with sufficient speed. He moved around ordering several of them to perform specific duties and kept after them to move as quickly as possible. They had lost too much time, they must be moving.

Having learned the day before the critical situations they might face working their way through the arctic ice, Greely assigned a man to the towline at the bow of each of the three boats trailing behind the launch. In a crisis the towline could be cast free immediately and each boat could be moved independently. Like a hen with three chicks trailing after her the launch steamed past the floebergs caught on the shore at Cape Baird and moved out toward the channel.

Their progress was slow and Greely grew impatient under the continued delay. Sergeant Brainard was now at the tiller and was proving to be not quite as skillful as Sergeant Rice. Greely was at the bow of the launch looking ahead for the more favorable leads and shouting directions over his shoulder to Brainard at the stern. Some small crisis suddenly provoked the commander to an intense fit of temper. He had been on the go for twenty hours the day before and, after five hours' sleep, he had been up again to hustle all day long to keep his party moving south. Now, at midnight, it was to be expected that his temper might be quick. Some action of his most responsible noncom, Sergeant Brainard, displeased him. He expended on poor Brainard much of the fury that he felt toward the ice that was frustrating their progress. The sergeant could only endure the tongue lashing and in the privacy of his diary, plaintively record:

"As we pulled out from Cape Baird Lieutenant Greely

became much excited and used language toward me which my conduct did not deserve. We were all surprised by his extensive vocabulary and the fluent and forceful manner in which he delivered himself. In a moment, though, he calmed down."

It tells us much about Greely that men could serve under him for two years in the most arduous and dangerous duty and then be surprised to learn that their commander had a temper. Clearly, Brainard bore no grudge, although he was offended and surprised.

Brainard, a young man, twenty-eight years old, but a veteran of service on the Indian frontier, was a loyal and competent, orderly sergeant (first sergeant).

A native of Elmira, New York, and a graduate of the Cortland Normal School, Brainard had joined the Army on impulse. Alone on a visit to New York City, he had taken a ferry ride to the Statue of Liberty. The signs warning against pickpockets had moved him to tuck away his last ten-dollar bill. After the visit to the Statue of Liberty, he could not find the ten dollars. He found himself alone in the great city without friends and without money. He was too ashamed to write home for funds. When he saw the poster and the recruiting sergeant, it seemed the only thing to do. Later, when he was changing his civilian clothes for army uniform, he found the ten-dollar bill buttoned in a shirt pocket, but he was in the Army then.

Brainard went West to serve with the cavalry in Montana for five years. He was twice wounded fighting the Sioux Indians. His enlistment had only one more year to run and he had concluded that he would not re-enlist. When the call came for volunteers to go on an arctic expedition, it struck him as possible adventure. Rather on impulse he submitted his name.

In the Arctic Brainard proved to be the first sergeant

in more than title. He accompanied Lieutenant Lockwood on extended sledge journeys to the east, north, and west. They had discovered hundreds of square miles of new land, and they had won the most significant achievement for the expedition on a lengthy, weeks-long sledge journey around the northern coast of Greenland. They had reached the "Farthest North."

In their two years together in the Arctic, Greely had learned that he could rely on Brainard as a man who had the respect of the enlisted men and as a sergeant who would loyally carry out the orders of the commanding officer. Brainard felt he had earned a right to the commander's confidence, so he was especially hurt by Lieutenant Greely's tirade over a minor point.

Turning Cape Baird, the launch moved out into the deeper open water of Kennedy Channel and headed south. Somewhere down there should be the relief ship coming to take them away from the frozen wilderness which had been their home for so long.

The wind had been blowing from the south and had pushed many floebergs northward above Cape Baird. Now it shifted and began to blow from the northeast. The floes drifted rapidly southward, forcing the boats against the western shore before they had reached Cape Craycroft. Adding to the troubles of the little band, fog set in and light snow began to fall. Soon everything unprotected was wet. Greely ordered the men to throw up tents on the shore and get some rest.

The next morning the sentry awakened Greely at 7 A.M. to report that the snow had stopped and the ice was moving south. Greely immediately climbed a cliff to view Kennedy Channel. While he was reconnoitering, the party prepared breakfast. He returned while they were in the middle of breakfast to report that open water was but one mile away beyond a belt of packed ice. They would move immediately.

"All right, let's go, let's go," Lieutenant Greely said. "There's open water ahead. Everybody on the boats, we're moving out."

Once more the equipment was hastily loaded and food was carried in hand aboard the boats. The men climbed aboard grumbling and asking, "What the hell is the hurry?"

The men were quickly on board but the launch was slow in getting started. The engineer, Sergeant Cross, below in the engine room seemed to have some trouble getting under way. Greely uneasily watched the ice belt grow wider. His impatience grew and he was about to shout at Cross asking what the trouble was when the launch began to move and the convoy started south again. Greely ordered Rice, who was at the tiller, to follow the open water close to the shore.

"Lieutenant," Sergeant Ellis said, "I think there's open water farther out."

Greely was irritated by this seeming contradiction of the order he had just given to Sergeant Rice.

"Sergeant Ellis," he said, "I don't want interference with my orders. I just gave an order and I want my orders obeyed."

In the confusion of the departure Sergeant Rice had not heard Greely's order to stay close to shore, so he looked uncertainly forward while Greely and Ellis were having their spat.

Rice looked at the commanding officer on the bow and asked, "Lieutenant, what course should we follow?"

Greely realized that the contention was getting out of hand. The first thing to do was to show that he had control of himself. He called calmly to Sergeant Rice:

"Sergeant, I want you to follow the lead close to shore."

Sergeant Rice looked at the narrow opening between the foot ice and the heavy floes close to shore and then stole a quick glance out toward the center of the channel at the open water Ellis had referred to. Lieutenant Greely was taking them into a very narrow lead.

"Well," Rice thought, "he's the commander."

They moved in through the narrow lead and followed that for some time until they reached more open water and were able to move away from the shore. After about two hours they reached Cape Craycroft.

The year before, Greely had sent a sledge party here to deposit a cache of one hundred pounds of corned beef and a barrel of bread. Unwilling to risk moving in with the launch and boats in tow through the heavy moving ice along the shore, Greely sent in two men in the small boat they carried on the launch. The small boat made the trip with no trouble, and the men brought back the meat and the bread to add to their supplies.

They were passing Cape Defosse at noon August 11 when they ran into fog and had to slow down to half speed. Moving through the fog, they blew their boat horns regularly. They did not want to miss their rescue vessel by not seeing it in the fog. The fog continued through the afternoon. A little after 3 P.M. they ran ashore to cook a meal and wait for clearer weather. The fog cleared about 6 P.M. and they moved south again. About midnight they ran into fog and heavy ice again, so they ran ashore for sleep.

A few weeks before the expedition left Fort Conger, Brainard had recorded in his diary:

A certain member of this expedition requires a guardian. Whether he purloins his stimulating beverages from the bottles of natural history specimens or whether they come into his possession honestly, he is a nuisance from the effects and should be in the guard house.

This kind of misbehavior at Fort Conger could properly be described as a "nuisance." During the hectic, desperate days the expedition was to face, such behavior could only be regarded as criminal.

The launch was anchored in a little cove and the boats were hauled up on shore. Sergeant Cross, engineer for the launch, said he had work to do on her and would take the watch. Greely awoke the next morning at 7 A.M. to see that the bow of the launch had been allowed to ground with the ebbing tide. If they had to wait for another tide to get it in the water, it would mean losing eight to ten hours.

"Sergeant Brainard, Sergeant Brainard," he called, "get the men up. We must move the launch. We must get the launch into the water."

In moments the men were out of their sleeping bags, hurriedly dressed, and pushing on the bow of the launch to get her off the shore.

Greely then realized that Sergeant Cross was on the launch and called, "Cross, are you in there? Go into the bow and lighten the launch. Move anything you can to the rear of the boat."

Cross was in the boiler room moving around but seemed to be taking no particular action. In a minute or two Greely called out, "Cross, goddamn your soul, come out here so I can see you when I want you."

Sergeant Cross emerged from the launch covering in a drunken stupor. "You didn't tell me to come outside," Cross said in a thick voice. The commander, on shore, looked at his drunken engineer in the launch. This was not the first time Cross had taken advantage of his position to appropriate some of the fuel alcohol. Now this irresponsible drunk was adding insolence to his misbehavior.

"Shut up," Greely shouted, "or I'll put a bullet through you."

"All right, go ahead and do it," Cross mumbled.

Greely was furious at Cross's behavior, but his fury was curbed by the knowledge that the party might be further imperiled if it were necessary to replace Cross with an inexperienced man.

Greely cut short the argument to urge the men to push the launch into the water.

Cross's drunken lapse cost them two hours spent in freeing the launch and reorganizing for continuing their journey. The morning of August 12 was spent moving slowly through loose, heavy ice. It was a time for alertness and skillful boat handling but Cross, sullen or hung over, was repeatedly slow in responding to orders. Several times the launch was almost nipped in the ice. By 2 P.M. the route was more open. Greely sent Cross to bed and Private Frederick was given the engineer's duties. Frederick had filled this post on occasions before and he filled it ably now. The handling of the engine-room duties was much improved and they made better progress.

When Cross had slept off the effects of his drunk, he was returned to his post. Frederick resumed his duties as fireman. The weather cleared, and the expedition moved as far south as Carl Ritter Bay. On the way north in the *Proteus* in 1881, Greely had stopped here to deposit a cache of two hundred rations. Now he silently congratulated himself for his forethought. These rations were another welcome addition to their diminishing supply of food.

Greely was not satisfied with their progress and he could sense impatience among the men. He decided to strike directly across the mouth of Carl Ritter Bay running directly for Cape von Buch on the southern side. Lieutenant Kislingbury tried to persuade Greely to be more cautious. "It would be better," Kislingbury contended, "to follow the shore line all around the bay." Greely disagreed. The ice would be heavier inside the bay and the distance would be much greater. Greely rejected Kislingbury's suggestion and ordered the launch to move due south across the bay.

Contention between Greely and Kislingbury was not new. Their disagreements had begun on the trip north in 1881. Greely was precise and insistent upon all matters of discipline. Lieutenant Kislingbury saw no need to observe such strict rules while aboard ship in a situation that really was garrison duty. He was casual about attending to his few responsibilities. He did not observe the reveille that Greely established for all members of the expedition. Several times Greely had brought these laxities to Kislingbury's attention with increasing emphasis. Kislingbury viewed Greely's behavior as unreasonable. His resentment burst into open opposition after their arrival at Lady Franklin Bay.

Kislingbury had served under Greely back in the States, helping to build government telegraph lines. He had been eager to go along when it was learned that Greely would lead an expedition to the Arctic. Greely was glad to accept Kislingbury's offer of services, but now life in the Arctic seemed likely to be different from life on the frontier. Kislingbury was certain that he would be unable to serve under an officer who was so meticulous.

"Lieutenant Greely," Kislingbury had said, "I have concluded that I cannot remain with the expedition and serve under you. I wish to offer my resignation and return on the *Proteus* to the United States."

The ship was still standing in the harbor waiting for an opportunity to break out through the ice. Kislingbury had waited until the last moment to resign.

Greely was not entirely surprised by Kislingbury's actions and was icily formal.

"Very well, Lieutenant Kislingbury. If you will submit your resignation to me in writing I will accept it."

Kislingbury then sat down and wrote out his formal resignation. When he had completed it, he submitted it to Greely in silence. Greely read the letter and then said, "Lieutenant Kislingbury, your resignation is accepted. I will write you a letter of acceptance and orders for you to return to the United States."

While this cold drama was going on, the ice in the harbor was breaking and the *Proteus* prepared to move. As soon as Lieutenant Greely had written the letter of acceptance Lieutenant Kislingbury loaded his belongings on a dog sled and raced across the snow toward the distant ship. But a lane had opened, and the ship moved away from the harbor and slowly sailed out of sight.

Thus Kislingbury was left with the expedition in the status of a guest rather than an officer of the party. During the two years at Fort Conger, Kislingbury never asked for reinstatement as a member of the expedition. Greely just as doggedly never placed any official responsibilities on him. They were two strong-minded men. Kislingbury was an excellent shot and went on successful hunting trips. He also accompanied several sledging parties. He took part in the social life of the expedition. He lived in the barrack room reserved for officers' quarters with Lieutenant Lockwood, Lieutenant Greely, and Dr. Pavy, but throughout the time they stayed there Kislingbury's relations with Greely were formal and never friendly. The four men paired off. Lieutenant Greely and Lieutenant

Lockwood were close to each other both officially and personally. Dr. Pavy, who also found it difficult to get along with the commanding officer, developed a friendship with Lieutenant Kislingbury. This division among the officers was, of course, apparent to the men.

Kislingbury had frequently been offended by Greely's aloofness. Greely seemed incapable of listening to advice. This latest rejection was only renewed evidence of what Kislingbury had objected to from the very beginning.

Greely was not handling their retreat well, Kislingbury believed. They had been almost nipped repeatedly. Their safety was dependent almost entirely on the launch; yet Greely was willing to take risks that might mean the destruction of the launch in the ice. To Kislingbury this seemed in keeping with the arrogance and pomposity of Greely's leadership.

The degree of risk Greely was willing to take to keep them moving south as quickly as possible was dramatically tested on August 13.

On Greely's order they had moved directly south across the mouth of Carl Ritter Bay, meeting no serious obstruction. They went on meeting only sailing ice until they were about ten miles south of Cape von Buch. At two in the morning on August 13, they were faced with what was apparently an unpassable mass of ice floes. Most imposing was an immense floeberg which was grounded about one mile from the shore. It rose in cold, forbidding grandeur about sixty feet above the water. They could not tell how far out it extended, but it seemed that the entire channel was choked. Another smaller floe ran from the edge of the floeberg to the shore. They were blocked.

It had been snowing and the men were damp, cramped, and chilled. A bitter gale blowing from the south into their faces added to their discomfort. Greely ordered the boats to make for the shore. Luckily they found a small protected harbor. They hauled the smaller boats up on the disintegrating ice foot and brought the launch into protection close to shore.

Their miserable condition was not much improved by the change from boats to the shore. The only room for camp was a small patch of rock-covered ground slanting up out of the water to the foot of a cliff. Before the men crawled into their sleeping bags spread out on the unrelenting stone, Greely issued the first allowance of rum for the party. It was little solace for them.

In the morning spirits were improved by a warm breakfast. Greely sent Lieutenant Lockwood and Eskimo Jens to reconnoiter. They walked along the ice foot to a cliff about two miles to the south. After climbing the cliff they could see farther south. The ice appeared to be unbroken as far as they could see. They returned and gave the discouraging report to the commanding officer.

"There must be a way through," Greely thought. "We have to get farther south. The relief ship will never find us here."

When the tide changed, Greely sent Sergeant Brainard out in the small boat to examine the giant floeberg to see if there was any hope of getting past it. Brainard returned to report that a slight change in the position of the berg would open a passage for them.

Once more the boats were hurriedly loaded and the little expedition moved out, seeking to make its way south. But the passage between the berg and the smaller floe was not wide enough for the launch.

Greely ordered the launch to steam farther out into the channel. They soon discovered that the giant floeberg when it grounded had split and separated. This small continent of ice had probably taken centuries to form farther north in the polar sea. Over the years this floeberg, millions of cubic feet of solid ice, had moved majestically to the south. It had grounded here in Kennedy Channel. This impenetrable mass under the pressure of its own weight and the strain of other lesser floes had snapped in two like a bar of soap. There was now a water passage about twelve feet wide. On either side of this ribbon of water a cliff of ice extended skyward for sixty feet.

The passage through the berg was only about one hundred yards long. They could steam through in a couple of minutes, yet the great risk was obvious. If the split berg should move together during their passage they would be sealed in ice like so many beetles in a cake of amber.

At the bow of the launch Greely gazed at the passage and at the cliffs of ice extending overhead, then turned to the helmsman and said casually, "All right, take her through."

Kislingbury looked at the commanding officer as though he were a madman. Did Greely have no sense of caution at all?

The little string of boats moved through the narrow passage with everyone in almost breathless silence. They stared up at the sheer cliffs of ice on either side in awe and wonder. The cliffs seemed to reach toward each other near the top so that there was only a thin strip of sky visible beyond. The only sound was the puffing of the launch's engine and the ripple of the waves made by the prow of the boat. The waves seemed to strike against the ice on either side with unusual loudness and force and then rebound against the sides of the boats trailing behind. The curl of dark smoke streamed out of the smokestack and trailed overhead behind them.

The men did not speak but gazed from side to side and up above them. It was as though they were in some weird, blue-white cathedral. They were in solemn communion, receiving unforgettable knowledge of the terrible, wondrous power of nature.

The launch puffed steadily ahead. At last they came to the end of the passage and broke out into open water. They were clear. Their spirits lifted. They had come through and could move on to the south.

They made good progress for a short while; then they ran into bad weather again. The wind began to blow and a heavy snow started to fall. The ice, pressing in very thickly from the southeast, forced them closer to the shore. Along the shore the ice foot grew higher as they moved south until it loomed ten or twelve feet above the boats. About noon they reached a small indentation which provided a little protection for the launch and just enough room for them to make camp.

The men, once more soaked and chilled to the bone, were ordered into their sleeping bags to get some rest. The wind blew stronger and the ice moved in heavily against the shore. Greely sent one man up on a hill to watch for any movement of the ice pack while he and another man watched the ice near the boats. Greely was determined to move at the first opportunity to some safer point farther south.

They waited through the afternoon watching the tide and the wind threatening to move the ice against the shore and destroy the boats. About 4:30 P.M. Whisler, watching from the hill, yelled that the ice was loosening and a lead had opened to the south.

"All right, everybody up. Let's go, let's go," said Greely. Again they hurried aboard the boats, loading quickly and moving away from the shore. They had very heavy going, trying to move across the little bay. The ice was thick, and they struggled to take advantage of every bit of open water.

During this run engineer Cross let his resentment burst forth in verbal abuse directed at no one in particular and everything in general.

"This goddamn engine ain't ever going to run right. We'll never get the hell out of the Arctic," he said. "I don't know where the hell we are or where the hell we're going. I don't think anyone else does, either."

He banged around in the little engine room beneath the launch covering. His voice was clearly heard by Greely and others on the launch. It was apparent to all that Cross was taking this device to hit back at the commanding officer.

"Things being run the way they are," Cross groused, "I'll bet we'll all wind up at the bottom. It's too bad there isn't somebody who knows what the hell he's doing. I'm getting pretty damn tired of following damnfool orders that will just get us into more trouble."

While Cross was spewing forth this abusive language, Greely tried to ignore it; but when Cross meddled with the engine and almost caused it to stop, Greely reprimanded him sharply.

"Cross, damn you, your bungling is endangering the lives of all of us. Stop yelling and start doing your job."

Greely was pushing the launch to its utmost and taking chances that required alertness and energy in avoiding or warding off ice floes that might damage the vessel. Rice, at the tiller, was doing his usual skillful job, but the burden of an insubordinate engineer infuriated Greely. He knew that he needed Cross's services, however, and the commanding officer tried to keep his tongue in check.

By 7 P.M. of August 14 they had almost crossed the bay and were within a few hundred yards of the southern cape when the wind changed to the southeast, blowing the ice pack in against the shore and blocking any further advance. During the crossing Lieutenant Kislingbury shot a seal, so they had fresh meat for supper that evening. The men were learning to like seal meat. They ate with gusto.

During the night of August 14–15 the temperature dropped to a surprising low of twenty-one degrees. Greely could not sleep for worrying about the new ice that was forming because of the sharp cold. He was up early the following morning, stirring the men to quick movement to get away from shore and out toward the ice moving in the channel. He was afraid that if they stayed close to shore they would be trapped in the heavy, new ice and have to abandon the launch.

The movement of the launch and the boats in tow was much like their experience of the day before. Once again Cross was cursing everything that came to his mind.

"Goddamn engine never wants to work," grumbled Cross. "Nothing on this whole damn trip is going right."

His language became more and more abusive and his response to Greely's orders were more and more delayed. Greely's fury mounted. At last Greely said, "Sergeant Brainard, go below and see what's wrong down there with the engine."

Sergeant Brainard ducked below the launch covering into the engine room and returned in a moment to say, "Lieutenant Greely, I'm afraid Cross is drunk again."

"Now, how in the hell could he steal that alcohol again?" Greely asked. "That man has a positive genius for getting himself in trouble. All right, enough is enough. Sergeant Brainard, I want Cross out of the engine room and off this launch. Put him in one of the boats in the rear. Frederick will be in charge of the engine room, and Cross is not to be anywhere near him."

After Cross had been transferred to one of the boats,

Frederick went into the engine room and they moved on. By working strenuously until three-thirty in the afternoon, they moved the launch to within about four hundred yards of the moving ice in a small harbor protected by grounded floebergs. The temperature rose very little during the day and never went above the freezing point.

Everyone in the party was concerned about the possibility of entrapment in the ice. Some questioning began about the best course for them to follow. Sergeant Brainard went to the commanding officer and said, "Lieutenant Greely, may I have permission to go on ahead to Cape Lawrence? Some of the men think there might be a rescue ship in Rawlings Bay."

"No, Sergeant," said Lieutenant Greely. "No, I don't think we should do that right now."

Although Greely did not say so, he appreciated Brainard's effort to help. However, the commanding officer thought it was not wise for anyone to be separated from the party right then. The men on the launch, hearing Brainard's offer rejected, thought that this was only another example of Greely's refusal to take advice from anyone.

Later, talking to Lockwood, Greely said, "You know, Lockwood, it might not be bad if we were trapped in the ice. I think we could make better progress if we boarded a large floe and drifted south with it. This would mean we would leave the launch but we could keep the smaller boats and the sledges. When we were as far south as Cape Sabine or Littleton Island, we could move to shore by sled if the pack were closed or by the small boats if we had to cross open water."

"I think you're right, Lieutenant Greely," Lockwood said. "I certainly would be willing to try it. I think we would make better progress."

Lockwood was always daring and impatient. He was willing to take almost any chance to move rather than wait for openings.

To the rest of the men Greely's suggestion of traveling on an ice floe seemed nothing less than suicide. Lieutenant Kislingbury, talking to Dr. Pavy later in the day said, "He was serious about it. He seriously proposed that we should abandon the launch and board an ice floe. The man must be mad."

Dr. Pavy grinned and said slyly, "Of course that is a medical question, Lieutenant."

Kislingbury looked puzzled for a moment and said, "What do you mean, Doctor?"

"To determine whether a man is in his right mind or not," said Dr. Pavy. "That is a medical question, is it not?"

They looked at each other.

Dr. Pavy had joined the Lady Franklin Bay Expedition when it arrived at the port of Godhavn in Greenland. Dr. Pavy and Henry Clay had been sent to Greenland the year before in the unseaworthy ship, the *Gulnare*. That ship had reached Godhavn and was ordered to return to the United States because of its poor condition. Dr. Pavy and Henry Clay had stayed behind in Greenland. Perhaps the year together in that small settlement contributed to an antipathy between the two men. The antipathy grew severe aboard the *Proteus* as it moved north toward Lady Franklin Bay. By the time the expedition reached its destination the bitter feeling was apparent. Clay told Greely that he believed the best interest of the expedition would be served if he, Clay, returned to the United States on the *Proteus*. Greely reluctantly agreed. He liked Clay. He found this grandson of the early nineteenth-century statesman to be a congenial gentleman. It would have been pleasant to have such a sociable member added to their party. Greely, however, recognized that the services of Dr. Pavy were essential to the success of his mission. Despite Pavy's irritability and disorderly nature (which Greely attributed to the influence of a checkered and bohemian career), the leader of the party knew that he must keep the doctor and send Clay home.

This disagreement only forecast the difficulties Greely was to experience with the doctor later on.

The month before their departure for this retreat, Dr. Pavy placed himself outside the military command. His contract as surgeon for the expedition expired on July 20, 1883. He had stated that he would not renew his contract.

On July 19 when Lieutenant Lockwood, in accordance with the War Department instructions, was collecting the diaries from members of the expedition to be sealed and addressed to the Chief Signal Officer, Dr. Pavy refused to turn in his diary. After some argument about the matter, the doctor gave Lockwood a written statement declaring that his diary consisted of nothing but personal letters.

Lockwood said he would speak to the commanding officer about Dr. Pavy's statement. Greely told Lockwood to bring in Pavy. Lockwood went outside and told the doctor that the commanding officer wanted to see him in the officers' room in the barrack. When the doctor came in, Greely said, "Doctor, you are to turn in your diary as all of us are required to do by orders of the War Department."

"But I explained to Lieutenant Lockwood," Dr. Pavy said, "that there is nothing in my diary but personal letters."

"I give you until six o'clock," Greely said coldly, "to turn in your journal or consider yourself under arrest."

"It is not necessary," Dr. Pavy said. "I told you in this letter that . . ."

"Very well," Greely said, "you remain in the service and I place you under arrest."

"I do not consider myself in the service," Dr. Pavy said, "and I do not accept arrest."

"You do not accept arrest?" Greely said. "Then call Sergeant Brainard, Lockwood."

"Oh, I want to say physically I submit," Dr. Pavy said, "but morally I do not accept. I will obey all the rules and regulations and if some accident happens, well, then I will not be responsible for it."

"You are under arrest, Dr. Pavy," Greely said, "and you will not move outside a one-mile range of this hut."

Greely faced a dilemma. Dr. Pavy insisted he was not in military service and therefore not subject to Greely's orders. Greely felt he could not permit open defiance of his authority. Still the expedition needed the services that only the doctor could provide. The doctor was under arrest with permission to take necessary exercise within one mile of their house. It was a rather futile effort to keep up the appearance of military discipline impartially applied. Dr. Pavy shortly demonstrated his defiance by going beyond the one-mile limit of his parole, knowing that Greely would take no disciplinary action.

The day after the doctor was placed under arrest his status was put to a practical test when Bender became sick. Sergeant Brainard notified Greely of Bender's illness.

"Well, Sergeant," said Greely, "no medical assistance can be provided Bender. Dr. Pavy is no longer on duty with the expedition. When he was placed under arrest, the doctor made it clear that he would refuse to provide medical treatment any longer."

"Well, that seems like a terrible situation, Lieutenant," said the sergeant.

Brainard regarded the contention between Greely and

Pavy as rather childish, but like a good first sergeant, he discreetly led his commanding officer to suggest a compromise that would save face for both Greely and Dr. Pavy. Bender was called in, and Greely spoke to him.

"Bender, Dr. Pavy is no longer on duty with the expedition. In fact, he is under arrest for insubordination. However, you are free to ask the doctor for medical treatment, although I cannot order him to give you such treatment."

Accordingly, Bender went to see Dr. Pavy and received prompt treatment of his illness. Pavy was not a soldier, but he was a doctor.

Pavy thus had an intense dislike for the commanding officer and watched his behavior on the retreat with rising discontent.

The break between Greely and Pavy had led to a closer relationship between Pavy and Kislingbury. Now, when Kislingbury had casually said that Greely sounded like a madman, Pavy felt secure enough with Kislingbury to hint at a plan that had been forming in his mind for some time.

"It is a medical responsibility and within the authority of the Articles of War," Dr. Pavy said, "for the medical officer to determine when a soldier or an officer is mentally unfit for duty."

Kislingbury thought for a brief moment and then said slowly, "Yes, Doctor, I understand you now."

"Of course," Dr. Pavy continued, "if the commanding officer were not fit for duty, you as the next senior officer would have to accept that responsibility."

Kislingbury reflected a moment longer.

"It would be most important," he said, "to first learn how the men feel about this. I know there are some we can count on."

Kislingbury ran over the names of the men in his mind. Cross, certainly. Henry, probably. Henry, that strange, big, strong man with the large droopy mustache. Joe Elison would probably be happy to see a change. It was no secret how he felt about Greely. Dave Linn might also go along with them. He had experienced Greely's wrath, having been reduced from a sergeant to a private. Kislingbury could not go beyond those few names.

"Doctor, if this thing is to succeed, we will have to have Sergeant Brainard and Sergeant Rice with us."

"Surely," Dr. Pavy said, "Sergeant Brainard and Sergeant Rice know that Greely is not doing the right things. They know that he is not leading this expedition properly."

Kislingbury recalled that Brainard had taken some abuse from Greely just a few days earlier. Rice, who was their best boat handler, had been continually frustrated by Greely's mishandling of the navigation of the launch.

"I will talk to George Rice and see how he feels," Kislingbury said. Rice, Brainard, and the other sergeants had been friendly and cordial with Kislingbury during the stay in the Arctic. They recognized his awkward position and sympathized with him. Kislingbury, for his part, was cut off from the company of his fellow officers, Greely and Lockwood. He was friendly with Dr. Pavy who also shared officers' quarters. But the somewhat eccentric doctor was not entirely satisfactory company, so Kislingbury frequently sought out the companionship of the sergeants. He felt especially close to Rice and Brainard. Now he thought he could talk to them with understanding.

Kislingbury later talked to Rice privately.

"George, I'm seriously worried about our situation."

"We certainly seem to be having a bad time of it," Rice replied.

"At this rate we'll never get down to Littleton Island," Kislingbury said.

"He just can't see," Rice said.

"I know," Kislingbury said. "He can't see and he won't listen. He couldn't see anything I tried to tell him."

"No," Rice said. "I mean he really can't see. He stands there at the head of the boat looking for leads but his eyes are weak and his glasses aren't good enough. He really can't see where we should be going."

This added a thought to Kislingbury's indictment against Greely's leadership.

"The doctor says that he believes Greely is medically not fit to be leading us right now," Kislingbury said. He watched Rice's face.

"Really?" Rice said. He paused and then added, "If only he'd let me run the launch, I could get us out of here."

Kislingbury continued, "The doctor believes Greely is mentally unfit and is ready to sign a medical certificate."

"What would that mean?" Rice asked.

"Greely would be ordered under medical care for the rest of the journey and as next senior officer I would assume command," Kislingbury said. He waited while Rice thought about it.

"It would be a good thing," Rice said. "Yes, it would be a good thing."

"You know, George," Kislingbury said, "if Greely keeps on, I'm afraid he's going to kill us all."

"He does some strange things," Rice agreed.

"If you and Brainard agree," Kislingbury said, "we will tell Greely and then the doctor will make the announcement to the men."

"Have you talked to Brainard yet?" Rice asked.

"No," Kislingbury said, "I wanted to talk to you first."

"Well, I'm with you," Rice said. "Let's talk to Brainard."

Kislingbury clapped his hands together. "Good," he said, "good. We'll come out of this right side up yet, George. We'll come out of it all right."

There remained now only to talk to Brainard privately, win his agreement, and the expedition would have a new commander.

CHAPTER TWO

BESET

~~~~~~

Kislingbury waited until Greely was asleep and Lockwood was busy talking with Private Frederick about the engine on the launch. Kislingbury put his arm on Brainard's shoulder and said, "I would like to talk to you a minute, Dave."

Brainard was a little puzzled by the confidential tone Kislingbury used but replied promptly, "Sure, Lieutenant."

Kislingbury walked off for a little distance on the floeberg to which the launch was anchored, over to where Dr. Pavy was talking with Sergeant Rice. Brainard followed him.

Kislingbury began the conversation after a moment's uncomfortable pause.

"Dave, Dr. Pavy and I and George have been talking about our situation here. You know we're in a pretty serious state."

There was a long pause, then Brainard said, "Yes."

Kislingbury looked at the doctor and Dr. Pavy spoke.

"It is obvious to me and to the others that our commanding officer is not really qualified to lead us now. You can see that he is overwrought by the responsibilities he is carrying. Lieutenant Kislingbury said that Lieutenant Greely seriously proposed that we ride a floeberg instead of the launch. Perhaps you have heard the commanding officer say this, Sergeant Brainard. Lieutenant Greely really thinks we should abandon the launch and ride a floeberg to Cape Sabine. It is obvious to me," Dr. Pavy
~~~~~~

said, coming to the point, "that our commanding officer has been working too hard. This journey has been too much for him, and he is no longer really capable of command. This is my opinion, Sergeant Brainard. Lieutenant Greely is not in a condition to continue in a position of command."

Sergeant Brainard, his face hardened in a dark frown, stared intently at Dr. Pavy. Lieutenant Kislingbury looked at Brainard and then looked at the doctor. It was obvious the doctor was not going to continue. Kislingbury broke in.

"The doctor means to say, Dave, that it is his medical opinion that Lieutenant Greely is, well a —mentally unfit to continue as commanding officer."

Brainard turned his gaze from the doctor to Lieutenant Kislingbury. He still said nothing and Kislingbury continued.

"It seems obvious that if we continue as we have been that Lieutenant Greely is likely to get us into more impossible situations. He will likely lose the launch and we'll never reach Littleton Island or Cape Sabine. George has pointed out that Lieutenant Greely cannot see very well and yet, as you know, he insists upon commanding every move the launch makes. We all know we would be much better off if he would let George handle the boat without all these confusing orders."

Kislingbury paused for some reaction from Sergeant Brainard. Brainard said nothing.

"What we propose to do, Dave, is simply this. The doctor will tell Lieutenant Greely that it is his medical opinion that Lieutenant Greely should take some rest, that he has been overexhausted by the responsibilities of command, that medically he is in no condition to continue as commanding officer. Under the Articles of War, therefore, the doctor is ordering him to be relieved. As next senior officer, I will assume command of the expedition."

"And you want me to agree with you?" Brainard exclaimed. "Do you really think you could get away with this? Nobody is going to believe the doctor's story. You know that most of the men will be against any attempt to relieve Lieutenant Greely of command. Maybe some of them would be in favor of it, but I can tell you I would be opposed to it, and most of the men would be opposed to it. Then what would you have? The expedition would be divided. It would never work," Brainard concluded; "it would never work."

Brainard might have added that aside from the audacious and incredible nature of the scheme, there was a second weakness—Kislingbury was not an official member of the expedition. Lockwood was the ranking officer—indeed, the only officer other than Greely.

Brainard's concluding words, "It wouldn't work," were said with a firmness that invited no further argument. Rice looked at Kislingbury but said nothing. Dr. Pavy opened his mouth to speak and closed it again. Kislingbury gazed at Brainard for a moment, then gazed down at the ice beneath their feet. They had been standing there only for a few moments, but it was getting very cold.

"All right, Dave," Kislingbury said, "if that's the way you see it."

They turned and walked back to the launch.

The next three days were spent in cold, anxious waiting. It was the middle of August, but the temperature remained below freezing. The men were cramped in the boats with no chance to move. Some began to complain that they should not have left the shore. Greely was thankful, however, they had moved out from the shore, for the new ice now packing the bay would have prevented any

escape for the launch. On the first day of their entrapment
Greely began issuing a half gill of rum to each man. It
helped a little to warm them and lift their spirits.

The first day, August 15, a storm with a northeasterly
wind whirled about them, but the next day the sky
cleared and the wind died down. The cold continued, and
the ice around them grew thicker. On the morning of
August 18 Greely directed that the boats in tow be moved
over the ice ahead of the launch and nearer to the moving
pack in the channel. They were placed in a seemingly safe
position next to a grounded floeberg.

At 3 P.M. the floeberg suddenly split in two with a roar.
The men were startled, and there was a brief panic. Fortunately the boats were not damaged. Greely took advantage of the stir it caused among the men. He announced
they were going to cut through the ice to move the launch
into open water. This was greeted with some open resentment and some disbelief. The commanding officer insisted,
however, that they couldn't remain trapped, they had to
break free. He doggedly urged the men to hack away at
the ice in front of the launch. They worked for more than
two hours under his direction. They made little head-
way, and the men were almost falling with exhaustion
before Greely called a halt for supper.

Following supper, Greely put them to work again to
force a breakthrough for the launch. Many of the men
were muttering and throwing dark glances at the lieutenant. Sergeant Brainard was sent out to reconnoiter the
ice to the south. He returned shortly to say that there was
no hope of advancing in that direction.

They kept working their way out to the east. They would
cut the ice in front of the launch, then it would back off and
charge the ice. When it had been forced into the ice as
far as it would go, men would stand on either side, rock

it from side to side so that it broke the ice that encased it. Despite their exhaustion and much to their surprise they began to make progress. Hour after hour Greely kept them at it. As they saw their advance, the men's appetites for the work increased and they put more effort into it. To their great joy they broke into an open lead through the ice at 10:30 P.M. Hastily the smaller boats were brought up and taken in tow again. By 11 P.M. they were on their way moving south again.

They moved along rapidly for more than four hours. Then about three-thirty the tide changed and the ice began to move with incredible speed. A tumbling, heavy mass seemed to come at them like an express train. They quickly turned the launch for the safety of the shore. They were able to make harbor between grounded floebergs barely in time to escape having their boats ground to bits by the angry, roaring ice.

They were blocked for a full day by the frozen pack. Greely sent Sergeant Brainard and Eskimo Frederik down along the shore to search out a lead to the south. They had accompanied Lieutenant Lockwood on the momentous trip to the "Farthest North." The sergeant and the Eskimo were a good team and worked well together. Dr. Pavy asked for permission to go along and Greely assented. Perhaps the doctor was getting tired of being cooped up in the little boat. It was Sunday, August 19, so before the reconnaissance party left, the Psalms were read.

Greely had been very much concerned about the spiritual life of his men since their arrival at Lady Franklin Bay two years earlier. While they were separated from the usual religious and moral influences of civilization, some substitute would have to be provided. His command included men with differing religious affiliation and, therefore, he felt "that any regulations should rest on the broadest and most liberal basis." Indeed, the composition of the expedition resembled what might be called the "classic American platoon." They were men from various stations of life and with a variety of national backgrounds, native Americans, immigrants and sons of immigrants; they were mostly Protestant, but at least one was a Catholic, one was a Jew, and one apparently held no religious belief. Greely himself was the son of New England Baptists who traced their ancestry back to earliest colonial days. In adult life Greely became a Unitarian.

The first Sunday after their barrack, Fort Conger, had been constructed, Greely announced that Sunday was to be a day of rest and religious observance. There would be no games but it would be permissible to hunt or to leave the station. Each Sunday morning the commanding officer would read a selection from the Psalms, "and it was expected that every member of the expedition should be present, unless he had conscientious scruples against listening to the reading of the Bible." At their first Sabbath observance, Greely had read the 133d Psalm beginning:

> Behold, how good and pleasant it is
> For brethren to dwell together in unity

This was the text for many later pleas that the commanding officer was to make. This was the result that he hoped would be fostered, even adrift in arctic waters, by reminding his men of their spiritual heritage. He did not look to God for a miracle to save them, but he hoped that the Divine Word would provide them strength to meet their ordeal.

Before the reconnaissance party left, Greely told Brainard that if an opening developed, the launch and boats would move south and pick up the advance party along the way. After Brainard's group left, the rest of them settled down to wait and hope the ice would open.

At 4 A.M., August 20, a lead did open. Greely was quick to take advantage of it. The launch and boats moved south. A southwest wind slowed their movement but held the ice away from the shore. Brainard's party was picked up on its way back from Cape Lawrence. They had gone to the summit at Cape Lawrence for observation and had seen no break in the pack. The ice seemed to extend all the way across Kennedy Channel with no opening. The report was discouraging.

Greely ordered the boats halted and breakfast prepared. While that was being done, he went to the summit above Cape Lawrence to make his own observation. He saw broad lanes opening to the south and the southeast. He hurried back to the camp.

Kislingbury could tell from Greely's frantic manner as he approached that once more their breakfast would be interrupted by an order to board the boats. Kislingbury's prediction to himself was proved correct in a few minutes when Greely hastened into camp and said, "There are leads to the south and southeast. Let's move. We're moving out, load the boats, we're moving out."

The men were getting used to their hasty departures now. They hurriedly boarded the boats and were soon moving south.

For the next several days they made southerly advances each day. On August 22 at Cape Collinson they stopped to pick up the provisions cached there by Nares in 1875. Unfortunately the cache had been broken into, probably by polar bears. The bread, tobacco, sugar, and tea were missing. The rum cask had been placed with the bung on the bottom. The bung had been faulty and the rum was gone. They took up the remainder of the supplies however

—240 rations of meat, salt, pepper, onion powder; 120 rations of bread and also some fuel.

The broken cache was a forerunner of a series of hardships that were to seem unending.

On the night of August 22–23 a mixture of wet snow and rain fell, soaking their clothing, their sleeping bags, and other property. They were all cold, wet, and miserable.

Greely was growing intensely worried about their slow progress and the failure of the rescue ship to arrive. The ship should have been able to get this far north by the middle of August. Perhaps it was at Cape Hawks, he thought. They would have to push on south as fast as they could. They could count on their relief ship's remaining at Cape Sabine only until September 15. That left them just about three weeks to reach there.

Kislingbury, Pavy, and even Lockwood made it clear to the commanding officer that they thought it wiser to follow the safer course along the coast line rather than risk being nipped in the ice as it shifted back and forth out in the channel. The roar of the ice was terrifying when the strong change of tide brought floes crashing together. Small ranges of white mountains formed along the line of impact. If their boats were caught in such a collision, it was clear they would be destroyed. The massive ice floes moving together would crack their little launch like a walnut in the arms of a nutcracker. If their boats were not crushed, they might well be trapped in the ice and carried along with the floe past Littleton Island and Cape Sabine out into the vast waters of Baffin Bay, there to find the floe disintegrate beneath them.

Greely's repeated references to his proposal of riding a large floe to the south impressed most of the men as a wild, reckless scheme. The commanding officer saw the possibility of being trapped at some point north of Cape Sabine or Littleton Island as the far greater danger. They would not be found by the rescue ship. They would have no more than a few weeks' rations. They would stand little chance of obtaining food by hunting during the long arctic night. If they did not get farther south they would have little chance of escaping the Arctic. Greely felt it was essential to take every chance that would move them south faster. He was not afraid of being trapped on a floeberg if it would carry them to the south.

On August 24 and 25 they made some progress, but they felt little satisfaction. The ice pack, as they moved farther south, did not seem to be opening at all. In fact, the formation of new ice was making travel more difficult and bad weather was adding to that difficulty. Rain fell almost continuously on August 24. Everything was wet through.

Fortune turned a little in their favor. The rain stopped, the ice opened, and they proceeded as far south as Gould Bay beyond Cape Frazier. Eskimo Frederik shot a small seal, and the sun made a brief appearance in the morning. Their spirits lifted. The sun had a very strong influence on their outlook. Its appearance warmed body and soul, but its stay this time was all too short. Soon the fog closed in around them again, and their world was gray.

They pressed on toward Cape Hawks through the fog. Schneider, stationed in the bow of the *Valorous*, blew the foghorn every two minutes. It would be so easy and so terrible for the relief ship to miss them in the fog.

They reached Cape Hawks on Sunday, August 26. They searched for and found the cache of English provisions, including 168 pounds of dried potatoes, three gallons of rum, and a keg of onion pickles. Greely sent Sergeant Rice to Washington Irving Island to examine a cairn where

Greely had left a message on his way north in 1881. Rice found the cairn untouched and left a message reporting the actions of the expedition and the plans of the commanding officer.

From the summit of Washington Irving Island, Rice searched the horizon. There was no ship in sight, but as far as he could see the water was open or the ice was so free as to be of no hindrance to a strong ship pushing northward. Why did the ship not appear?

Lieutenant Greely felt their situation was critical. They had but sixty days' food supply. The temperature was now permanently below the freezing point and new ice was forming all the time. They were only fifty miles from Cape Sabine. They could cover that fifty miles by boat only if windstorms kept breaking up the ice so as to permit passage of the little convoy. They would have to move, and move boldly. If it meant taking a risk of being trapped in the ice pack, they would have to take that risk Greely believed. They had sledges and boats. They could take a chance on being able to escape from the ice by sledge if the ice were solid or by boat if it were not.

They moved away from Cape Hawks at 4 P.M. Sunday, August 26. Sergeant Rice again was assigned to the tiller of the launch. Greely now recognized him as a man of excellent judgment, and the best navigator in the crew.

The job of operating the tiller of the launch was an exhausting and demanding one. Rice had repeatedly shown that he had both the skill and the stamina. In steering the boat he had to stand on a platform above the stern. This platform was both narrow and slippery. Several times the boat had been struck forcibly by a strong piece of ice. The shock knocked Rice off his feet and into the water. The irrepressible fellow came up smiling every time, scrambled back on board the launch, swiftly stripped himself to the skin and put on dry clothes. Once his clothes were changed, he again took his place at the tiller as though nothing had happened. The only part of the experience that troubled him was trying to get his clothes dry before he was knocked into the water again. The wet clothes were strung on a line over the boiler. Lieutenant Kislingbury and others were quick to volunteer their clothing to help their unsinkable "water fowl" as they dubbed Rice. Kislingbury thought, "I would willingly strip myself and crawl into my sleeping bag rather than have him do so because he is without doubt the most indispensable man we have."

The boats moved out from the shore and made straight for Cape Sabine. As they moved toward the channel they found the water more open. Cape Sabine was now in sight and they had high hopes. There was open water around the cape and north of it. They had only about one mile of ice pack between the boats and the open water. If they could just break through that one mile of pack to the open water, they could reach Cape Sabine in about one day's journey.

The temperature dropped, however, and new ice formed faster than they could fight their way through the pack. The cold hand of the Arctic stopped them in sight of their destination.

They were, in the language of the arctic navigators, "beset."

They anchored the launch to a small floe and hauled the smaller boats onto the floe. Now they would have to wait to see what the ice and the tide would do with them.

The arctic forces had a grand jest in store.

The temperature during their first night in the ice dropped to eighteen degrees. The new ice grew thicker.

The commanding officer ordered a tripod observation

post erected on the floe. It stood about fifteen feet high and provided an excellent lookout. A flag was also erected in hope of signaling the ever-expected relief ship.

Greely was growing more worried about their situation. He was also concerned about the morale of his party. He decided to call the men together and explain his view of their present situation. At 8 P.M., August 27, Lieutenant Greely said, "Sergeant Brainard, call the men together. I wish to speak to them."

The men assembled on the ice floe around the launch and Greely, standing on the bow of the launch, said:

"Men, I wanted you to know that I purposely came out here into the pack. I was afraid to stay close to the shore, for there was greater chance of being frozen in. Nares, the English explorer, who was up here in 1875, spoke of fresh water coming from the glacier into Princess Marie Bay. I expected that the temperature would fall as it did last night and this, of course, would mean that the fresh water in the bay would freeze faster than the salt water out here. If we had stayed close to shore, we would have been in a worse condition.

"I think we now have a fair chance of getting through to Cape Sabine. We have left enough coal and wood for one day's steaming. We will remain at this floe and wait for the ice to open so we can make that run. If the ice should close in around us, the natural drift of the floe in the course of time will carry us between Cape Sabine and the Greenland shore. Within the next thirty days we can expect to drift into Smith Sound. We will then be within eight or ten miles of the coast. At that time we will try to reach whatever shore is nearest.

"I know that we have been through some bad times. We will probably face more difficult days before we are through, but I know you will not forget that we are all soldiers in the United States Army and that we will face those dangers and difficulties with the courage and fortitude that is expected of American soldiers."

It was really a dismal outlook that the commanding officer described for his men. Still it seemed to Brainard that the obstacles in front of them had not dismayed the men. He wrote, "Adversity in its worse form would not dampen the spirits of our men. Our situation is desperate. At any moment this ice may crumble from beneath us and swallow the entire party. Still, while exercising this evening, they danced and sang as merrily as if they were in their own homes."

For the next several days they drifted slowly to the south averaging less than two miles a day. Brainard suggested to Greely that they save food by reducing the daily ration. Greely disapproved. Such action, he thought, would depress spirits too much and weaken the men. They might need every bit of strength in the future.

Temperatures began to drop very low. On the night of August 30 the thermometer dropped below twelve degrees. The lowest August temperature ever recorded by any polar party, Greely noted.

Greely consulted with Lockwood privately. They agreed that as soon as the ice was strong enough they should start with sledges and the small iceboat for Littleton Island. They would abandon on the floe everything not essential. Lockwood suggested that at least two boats should be taken. Greely then advised Brainard of his plan.

On the evening of August 31 it rained, and Greely tried to lift spirits by ordering an issue of rum. This attempt was aided by Sergeant Israel's report that in the previous twenty-four hours they had drifted south three miles.

Greely valued the services of his excellent astronomer, Sergeant Edward Israel. A graduate of the University of

Michigan, Israel had proved to be a very competent and diligent astronomer during his service with the expedition. Slight of build, Israel had a handsome face and sensitive eyes. Always considerate and gentle in manner, he gained a place as one of the favorites in the party. All of them liked and respected Sergeant Israel. He was a man who knew his job and did it quietly and effectively. In the days immediately ahead Sergeant Israel's work was to become of crucial importance in the progress of the expedition.

The next day, September 1, they continued their slow drift to the south. In the early afternoon another crisis occurred. Experience had taught them to expect the great rush of the ice floes with the changing tide, but often the pack moved with such speed that they were caught surprised. In the afternoon as the tide changed there were great roars and crashes; the pack moved swiftly and floes crashed together. Other floes smashed into the large floe to which the launch and boats were tied; the edges crumbled and wide cracks opened in the floe. As the ice pressed against the launch, it started to rise slowly out of the water.

Greely cried, "Save the launch, save the launch!"

Most of the men, however, ignored their commander's cry and moved first to haul the small boats out of the water and onto the floe.

Kislingbury looked on with cynical amusement as he saw the men ignoring Greely's orders and doing the obvious and necessary things to save their boats, supplies, and equipment. In a few moments of swift action the men did their work and saved the boats. The launch was nipped, but did not crumble under the pressure of the ice. Rather, it rose in the air as the ice, moving together beneath it, formed a cradle. When the tide changed later in the day, the pressure was eased and the launch settled back into the water.

The day was brightened by the hunting success of Eskimo Jens and Eskimo Frederik. Each of them killed a harbor seal which would provide the expedition with two meals. They were rewarded by Lieutenant Greely with a half gill of rum. The men were learning to appreciate seal meat and even seal blood. Brainard recorded, "If drunk when warm it is very palatable—not unlike raw eggs in flavor."

During the night the launch was lifted out of the water several times by the pressure of the pack. Lieutenant Lockwood was the only one sleeping in the launch. He preferred the comfort and danger of the boat to the discomfort of sleeping on the ice floe. At the time of the first nip he rose to watch what was happening but familiarity bred the usual contempt even of this extraordinary danger and later nips did not arouse him.

James B. Lockwood was a second lieutenant serving with the Twenty-third Infantry at the time he volunteered to go to the Arctic with the Lady Franklin Bay Expedition. Although a young man in his late twenties, he had had eight years of army experience, most of it on the frontier, and had earned a reputation as an officer of high merit. Lockwood had performed extraordinary service for the expedition. Indeed, the explorations carried out by Lockwood and Brainard were possibly the outstanding accomplishment of the expedition. At the base, in the shadow of his commanding officer, Lieutenant Lockwood was a reserved, self-contained personality. But on the trail Brainard had found him to be an exuberant and daring leader. The long days spent together following a dog team and a sled, the many dangers they had faced jointly, had made Brainard and Lockwood close companions. To the rest of the men, Lockwood was a likable officer but a quiet man and one they felt they did not know well.

During these first days on the ice floe, the time was spent in reading, eating, and sleeping. The sergeants were assigned in turn the duty of watching the movements of the ice. The rest of the men took turns serving as cooks. Tedium was nothing new to them after two winters in the Arctic. But they had long ago exhausted means of relieving what Brainard poetically called "the treadmill existence of our darkest days."

The change in their spirits is contrasted sharply by Brainard's comment on January 21, 1882, and the same day one year later.

"Checkers are all the rage now," Brainard wrote, "having a greater run than the fifteen puzzle. But nothing lasts like the long, loud arguments. Today the windy subject was concerned with the relative merits of the fire departments of Chicago and New York. . . ." One year later checkers had lost their charm but arguments were still entertaining. "As usual on the Sabbath, Dutch arguments are above par. Oh well, even if most of the arguments are senseless, the men seem to enjoy the excitement and I believe it must do them good. It's exercise. As usual, the man with the strongest lungs won the debate. . . ."

The capacity of the men for talk and frequent contention was not accepted as calmly by the commanding officer. In his appeals for unity he had warned against the strains that the monotony of arctic life would place on them. He had asked that each of them try not to prolong any controversy but by conciliation end contention and resolve differences. However, on the ice floe talk was about the only way to pass time. And it precipitated a serious crisis.

Sunday, September 2, was cloudy and mild and the ice floe seemed to be drifting along a little faster. There was a Bible reading by Lieutenant Greely. Later, the party went to work moving the launch and boats about two hundred yards to the west to a larger floe that seemed safer. This larger floe was in the shape of a rough square about a half mile on each side.

About noon on Monday, September 3, the sun was out and shining brightly. The appearance of the sun generally improved the spirits of the party but Greely was worried. It was only twelve days until September 15, the last day they could count on their relief ship's remaining at Cape Sabine. Twelve days. So little time.

After about an hour Greely arose from his sleeping bag and told Lieutenant Lockwood that he wanted to speak to him, Lieutenant Kislingbury, Dr. Pavy, Sergeant Brainard, and Sergeant Rice. The commanding officer was calling a council. For the first time in the history of the Lady Franklin Bay Expedition, Lieutenant Greely was calling together his officers and principal noncoms to discuss their future plans.

CHAPTER THREE

THE DISTANT SHORE

It was late in the afternoon of September 3 when Lieutenant Greely gathered his council of two officers, his surgeon, and two noncoms in the rear of the launch.

"I have called you together," Greely began, "because of the seriousness of our position. I don't believe it is necessary for me to defend my control of matters in the past nor to explain again my reasons for coming out here into the pack instead of keeping close to shore. You all remember, I am sure, my comments about this a few days ago. You all know our present situation and I am sure you realize it is critical.

"I have selected Sergeant Brainard and Sergeant Rice to join in this conference because I consider them the most intelligent of the enlisted men and I am sure they will represent their wishes. I consider Sergeant Rice's opinion and advice valuable, for he has shown prudent and correct judgment in navigating the ice. I must confess that I myself know nothing of ice navigation and in addition I have the special disadvantage of poor eyesight. It is my intention, in the future, if we get another chance for a run to entrust the ice navigation to Sergeant Rice."

Greely paused for a moment and then continued speaking in a low tone.

"It is now a question of the life of every man of the expedition. No one can value life or have more inducement to live than I myself have. I have a wife and two children to live for. In a situation like this I do not think

I have the right to act alone. I consider it better to have the view of all of you; then I can act to better advantage for our mutual good. I want to point out that, although I am aware of my responsibilities as commanding officer, I assure you I do not regard myself as infallible. I want your council and your assistance. I have pointed out to you before and must do so again the indispensable necessity of hearty and united action and I ask that you support to the utmost any plan which I should adopt. Before I decide on such a plan I want the frankest possible opinion of each of you as to the wisest measures for us to pursue.

"You are all aware that we are drifting slowly south and every opportunity of moving south or southwest has been taken advantage of. It is my opinion that a party with provisions and probably a ship are at Lifeboat Cove on Littleton Island. In our planning, however, I feel that we should not calculate on any provisions other than the two hundred and forty rations which we know are at Payer Harbor."

After this opening statement Greely then looked directly at Kislingbury and said, "Lieutenant Kislingbury, you are the next in seniority and I would like, if you will, that you be the first to give your general views of what you consider best for us to do."

Lieutenant Kislingbury replied promptly, "Lieutenant Greely, for the few days past I have been watching the conditions and actions of the ice. The ice between us and the shore seems to be just a series of floes, one after another, and they all seem to touch each other at some point or other.

"I would construct another sledge," Kislingbury said. "Use that sledge to haul equipment and use the large sledge to haul two boats, one at a time. Each time we haul a boat we can load it with all the stuff it will carry.

Each boat and all our equipment should be moved from one floe to another at the point they touch. We should never start across a floe until both boats, everybody and everything are on the same floe.

"In this way," Lieutenant Kislingbury continued, "we would move from floe to floe in the direction of Cape Sabine. I do not approve waiting any longer for the chance of one day's steaming of the launch which will, of course, have to be abandoned."

Greely asked, "Have you considered, Lieutenant Kislingbury, the weights of everything we have to haul and the number of days' provisions on hand? I might also ask how you plan to cross Buchanan Strait? Do you know that that is a strait and there might be loose ice caused by a current running through to another sea?"

"No, Lieutenant Greely," Kislingbury said, "I have not figured the weights, but from what I have heard I understand we have sixty days' supplies. We can count on twelve days' supplies from the English cache at Cape Sabine and any supplies the ship may have left there if it reached that point. But of this, of course, Lieutenant Greely, you can judge better knowing more of it than I do. My idea would be to keep going right across Buchanan Strait, but if we can't do this we could make for the shore on the north side and possibly work around it or cross it farther in. So far as I have learned, the strait has never been fully explored and it is not a known fact that it is connected with any other water."

"When do you propose to start?" Greely asked.

"Right away. As soon as we can get ready."

Greely then turned to Dr. Pavy. The doctor was thrilled at the opportunity to be telling the commanding officer what to do but did not seem able to reach a conclusion in his own mind about what to recommend. The doctor began by reviewing what other polar parties had done in similar situations. After a long discourse on the experience of others the doctor began to talk about the limitations of their own launch. He talked on and on with the other members of the council uncertain as to what his recommendation was. In truth, the doctor seemed to be making up his mind only as he was hearing himself talk. At last he seemed to decide and concluded with the recommendation that they should start over the ice on the following day hauling one boat and as many supplies as they could carry.

When the doctor concluded, Lieutenant Greely said, "Lieutenant Lockwood, what is your advice?"

Lockwood hesitated and then said slowly, "I am not prepared to say, Lieutenant Greely. I have not thought over the matter and really I have no plan to offer. I am not prepared to say that we should yet give up waiting for the ice to open."

"Then am I to understand," Greely asked, "that you think it better at present to let things remain as they are, to wait for an opening and a chance for another run with the launch?"

Lockwood hesitated again and then replied slowly, "Yes, I think we should wait."

"Sergeant Brainard," Greely asked, "what do you think about our next action?"

"Lieutenant Greely," Sergeant Brainard said, "I think it would be impossible for us to cross the pack with our heavy loads. The ice is still too loose now. I think we should wait and see if the drift will carry us to open water. If it doesn't then we must wait until the ice is solid enough to bear our sledges."

Greely now turned to Sergeant Rice. This must have been a key point in the conference and in the life of the expedition. Lockwood and Greely, of course, were not aware of the conspiracy to depose Greely but Brainard, Pavy, and Kislingbury must have been tense as they waited for Rice's opinion.

If Rice agreed with the conspirators, Greely would find half his council opposed to him. What would he do then? Would he dare oppose his senior officer, his surgeon, and (except, perhaps, for Brainard) his best noncom? And if Greely reversed himself, it might result in the real command of the expedition being exercised, thereafter, by the majority of the council. Dr. Pavy and Kislingbury could hope that they were on the verge of wresting Greely's authority away from him, after all. If Rice sided with them and if with a majority of his advisors against him, Greely still insisted on his own way, his obstinacy could then be reported to the men. The mutiny via medical decree might still be executed. Greely's position and the future of the party could be decided by Rice's words.

All of them gazed at him intently as he gave his reply.

"Lieutenant Greely," Rice said, "I do not think we should move at present. We are gaining something gradually by drift. We have sufficient supplies right now and so long as there is a chance for an opening and we are not losing ground, it will pay us better to wait. If the opening does occur we will make farther advances in a few hours than we would by hauling our boats and equipment from floe to floe for a number of days."

Rice went on to analyze the alternative of dragging their supplies by sledge across the floes.

"Where would we be if we tried to move by sledge over the ice? One boat is all that we would be able to drag to shore. Trying to take two would exhaust all of us. The best we could hope for would be to reach Cape Sabine with one boat. Where would we be then? When it was time to cross Smith Sound for Littleton Island only half of us would be able to get into the one boat. What would happen to the rest of us? It seems to me, Lieutenant, that it would be better for us to wait for the pack to open or until new ice is solidly formed."

Greely had the backing he needed. He could announce his decision with confidence that he would have support for it.

"Thank you, gentlemen," Greely said. "I will let things remain as they are at present. I plan to follow swiftly and persistently any opening that will carry us south or toward land. Any attempt to move over the ice now, I believe, would only be wasted energy. You are all aware that the pack is constantly shifting and lanes might open to us at any time. We will wait no more than five days. If we are carried to the southwest we will make for Cocked Hat Island as soon as the ice becomes strong enough. If the drift carries us to the southeast we will strike for the nearest point on the coast of Greenland—Cairn Point or Littleton Island."

Greely paused. He had given his orders. There was really nothing more to say, but something made him add, "Does anyone have anything further to say?"

Rice responded immediately.

"Yes, sir," he said. "I would like to suggest that we put the canvas sails into some kind of shape for shelter. If we're going to be out here on the ice for some time we are going to need some protection."

There then followed an animated discussion in which they all joined, about the feasibility of making tents from the sails. After it was agreed that Rice's suggestion should be followed, Brainard made another suggestion.

"Lieutenant Greely," Sergeant Brainard said, "following what Lieutenant Kislingbury said about building another sledge. I think that could be done by using the seats out of the launch."

There was quick general agreement that this, too, should be done. Brainard spoke up again.

"Lieutenant Greely, I am certain that the men would cheerfully agree to any reduction in rations if it should be thought advisable now."

Greely turned to Sergeant Rice and said, "What do you think, Sergeant Rice?"

"Well, sir, I am sure that the men will agree. However, it might be that we should first ask the doctor's advice about it."

Greely then turned to the doctor and said, "Well, Dr. Pavy, what do you advise?"

The doctor pursed his lips, thought for a moment, then said, "I think, Lieutenant, that a reduction in the rations would not be positively injurious."

"For the present," Lieutenant Greely said, "I think it will be best to continue on full rations. We have bread, meat, potatoes, and fuel for cooking to last until November 1. We will need to keep our strength up for any emergency." The commanding officer became thoughtful for a moment and then added, "Before we close, gentlemen, I want to say that I have not been indifferent to certain remarks and comments I have overheard which reflect upon me. It is obvious that I cannot enforce matters of discipline at this time, but I want to impress upon you the need for maintaining unity in the command. I hope you will all keep in mind the importance of our working together.

"Thank you for your advice. I will call the council again whenever it seems necessary to me."

The council broke up with the members of it surprised to find that they all felt very much better. The only concrete action that had been decided upon was the building of tents and a sledge. Yet even Kislingbury, whose impatience to move had not been satisfied, felt pleased.

"Well, at least we know what we are going to do," Kislingbury thought. "There is not the uncertainty that there used to be and he is listening to us anyway."

They were adrift on ice in dismal arctic waters but they were still in the United States Army. Private Whisler's enlistment expired on this day, September 4, 1883. He was discharged and re-enlisted. Regulations would be observed with Lieutenant Greely in command even in these extremities.

The following day Greely ordered Sergeant Cross, the engineer, and Sergeant Joseph Elison to begin building two sledges. They would use the seats from the launch, iron bands from the launch boiler, and barrel staves. Shorty Frederick, the assistant engineer, was given the job of devising some shelter from the canvas sails. Frederick, a Second Cavalry man and an experienced plainsman, immediately went to work framing an Indian teepee, using the oars and masts for tent poles. The rest of the party, most of whom had had experience on the frontier, were delighted to see this familiar sight being so incongruously erected on arctic ice.

They continued their drift south for the next several days. A storm the night of September 6–7 moved the floe along faster and closer toward land. The following night the temperature dropped to zero. It was clear to Greely there was no more hope of proceeding by boat. The ice would soon be solid and they would be able to move by sledge. He ordered the work speeded on the sledge building and repairing.

At every opportunity, whenever the sun appeared, Sergeant Israel, their astronomer, would "shoot" their position. Israel's calculations showed that they had made no progress south on September 8. Greely waited one more day and then on Sunday, September 9, he called another meeting of his council.

Once more Kislingbury, Lockwood, Pavy, Brainard, and Rice gathered in the stern of the launch and Lieutenant Greely spoke to them.

"I have called you together," Greely said, "to tell you of my plan and ask you for your opinions and suggestions. I believe it is time now to abandon the launch and one of the boats and make for the shore over the ice, taking along two of our boats."

(Greely did not think it wise to attempt to take two boats but did so only in deference to the comments of Kislingbury at the previous council. One day's experience, he thought, would show the wisdom of abandoning one of the boats they were carrying.)

"We will take all of our provisions," Greely said, "but I am not sure whether we should take the three hundred pounds of stearine [cooking fuel], the shotguns and their ammunition. In addition to the weight of the sledges we have from sixty-five hundred to seven thousand pounds to haul. It is obvious, therefore, that we must travel three times over the same ground. We have more than enough stearine to cook the food now on hand. However, I think we may hope to shoot some game and we will need the stearine to cook such additional supplies as we may be able to secure.

"As soon as we are close enough to land I plan to send an officer and two men on ahead to Brevoort Island. If we learn that there are any boats there, as there should be, we could drop our own boats and make faster time. At present, carrying the boats and all our supplies, I don't expect we will be able to make more than two miles a day. At Cocked Hat Island I intend to drop everything except sleeping bags, cooking gear, and a few days' rations and then we will move as rapidly as possible to Cape Sabine.

"Now," Lieutenant Greely concluded, "I would like each of your opinions about the possibility of any further delay or any modifications of my plan as to what might be abandoned, or any other practical recommendations you might wish to make."

Greely then turned to Lieutenant Kislingbury and asked for his advice.

"Lieutenant Greely, I concur entirely with your plan," Kislingbury said, "and I know of no way that it could be improved upon. I approve of taking everything at present. Should we find we cannot get along carrying all of it, then we can drop such things which are of least value to us. I think one shotgun would be sufficient, but we should take along parts from the other guns in order to replace any broken parts which may occur.

"The other details about how the party should move I think can be arranged when we are ready to move. The number of men necessary for each sled we can determine as we proceed. I think at first the whole thing will be an experiment. We should make it a point for the first few days not to overwork the men, for once a man breaks down he is helpless."

The others gave their agreement and had nothing further to offer except Sergeant Brainard who said, "Lieutenant Greely, I think it would be well if one member of the party could move out to choose the best route for the rest to follow."

Greely agreed that this would be a good idea and gave Brainard that responsibility.

Nagging at Greely's mind was the knowledge that the

relief ship was to remain in Smith Sound near Cape Sabine only until September 15. The whole party could not hope to reach there by that date, only six days away. He first suggested his idea to Brainard who volunteered to accompany Greely on a daring dash across the moving pack directly to Cape Sabine. The two of them could move swiftly and might arrive there in time to catch the relief ship before September 15. There was also a good chance they would drown before they reached land.

The officers objected to the leader's taking such chances. (At least Greely so reports in his diary. Lockwood may have objected but it is difficult to picture the would-be mutineers, Kislingbury and Pavy, offering strong objection.) Greely records that others were willing to volunteer but he would not permit any one else to attempt such a dangerous trip.

In the long struggle across the ice toward land, Greely followed the practice of being the last man off a floe. The last man was always in danger of being left behind if the party was separated by movement of the floes.

After they had made their decision to move they were thwarted for one day by a snowstorm. Greely conferred again with the officers, Brainard, and Rice. They were agreed that the party should move only after the storm abated. Bache Island was only four miles to the west, Cocked Hat Island was only eleven miles to the south. They had reason to hope they would soon be on land again. "And so, that last Sunday evening on the frozen sea," Greely reports, "we offered words of praise to the Almighty, and, with renewed faith in the Divine Providence, with no repinings over past sufferings, but with the determination to do our best and utmost on the morrow, we sought what rest we could in our comfortless bags."

But past sufferings were as nothing compared to what lay ahead.

The snowstorm continued Monday morning and their time was spent in removing all useful articles from the launch and the whaleboat. Records of the expedition's retreat from Lady Franklin Bay were placed in each boat and a signal flag was raised to the mast of the whaleboat.

Greely called the men together and told them that the pendulum used to make observations could be abandoned if that were favored. The men knew, however, that the value of their work during the past two years would be reduced if they were unable to make comparative observations in the days ahead. Although the pendulum weighed one hundred pounds, no one was in favor of abandoning it. Greely could rightfully be proud of the spirit of his men.

The move toward the shore began at 1:45 P.M., Monday, September 10. Sergeant Brainard went on ahead for about one mile to choose a route to the south toward Cocked Hat Island. He then returned to help haul the sledges.

Greely set the example for the other officers by joining in hauling the sledges with the men. The iceboat and about six hundred pounds of supplies and equipment were loaded on the so-called twelve-man sledge (fourteen men were dragging it). There were about seven hundred pounds on the six-man sledge and about four hundred pounds on the four-man sledge. Both of the smaller sledges broke down. Brainard could find no easy route, no level stretch. They were forced to drag their heavy loads through snow a foot deep over rubble ice and around small bergs. They had to make three trips with the big sledge to advance about one and one-quarter miles toward Cocked Hat Island. They made camp about 7:15 P.M.

"Everyone pulled with great energy," Greely wrote in

his diary that evening, "and the heavy work, coming after long inaction, has taxed everyone's strength to the utmost. For myself, I am thoroughly worn out physically, not to mention mental anxiety as to both present and future."

They erected the teepee on the ice floe. Greely, Lieutenant Lockwood, Dr. Pavy, and nine of the men slept in the teepee; Lieutenant Kislingbury with six men slept in the whaleboat; Brainard and six others slept in the iceboat. Since there was more comfort in the boats, Greely had the stronger men sleep with him in the teepee.

Snow fell the following morning and Greely kept the men in their sleeping bags until the weather began to clear. About 8 A.M. they could see Cocked Hat Island in the distance and they started for it. Brainard again went ahead to reconnoiter.

They advanced one mile but three trips were necessary to haul all of their load. After a supper of hot tea and stew, Brainard and Dr. Pavy went on to a large floeberg about two miles ahead to observe. They could see an expanse of new ice, not strong enough to bear the heavy sledges, and much rubble. They returned to report the discouraging news.

Greely again held a conference. He pointed out that spring tides would occur in four days and asked what they recommended. Kislingbury, Pavy, and Brainard favored moving to the edge of the floeberg, which would take two days, and waiting to see what effect the tides had. Lockwood saw some advantage in moving toward the east and sending out men to seek new routes. Rice thought it might be possible to reach the ice to the west. Greely decided in favor of moving the two miles toward the large floeberg to the south.

The next morning, September 12, Greely sent out two parties to reconnoiter. Kislingbury led one to the southwest and Dr. Pavy led one to the southeast. Dr. Pavy and Rice found a good route to the southeast. Before the party started moving, the officers and Rice and Brainard strongly recommended to Greely that the whaleboat be abandoned as it might break down the sledge. He at once concurred. He had not favored taking it along in the beginning but had done so only because Kislingbury had suggested it. The officers and two sergeants were pleased that the commander responded so favorably to their advice. The council members were developing some unity.

The route proved excellent and with the lighter load they were able to make the edge of the floe with the first load in only one hour and twenty minutes. The second load took a little longer but they were able to make the edge of the floe by the end of the day.

The next day they used axes to smooth a path over the rubble ice for the sledges. Because of the weakness of the ice, the loads were necessarily lighter and three trips were necessary for the transfer to the next floe. The ice broke under the large sledge twice. Rice was alert and gave warning, the men responded quickly and no damage was done and nothing lost. Both Dr. Pavy and Bender broke through the new ice but were not wet very much.

Cocked Hat Island was tantalizingly visible and many guesses were made about the distance yet to travel. The optimists said four miles, the pessimists ten miles. Greely recorded his opinion privately as eight miles.

It was September 13. They could count on their rescue ship's remaining at Cape Sabine only two more days.

All optimism was destroyed the next day by a southwest gale. The offshore winds drove the pack off to the northeast. In just three hours they were driven back further than they had traveled in three days. The storm continued all night. The morning of September 15, the day the relief ship might be going south, found them farther north than the point at which they had abandoned the launch. When the storm ended at 4 P.M., Israel's observations showed that they had drifted fifteen miles to the north. Was it possible their rescue ship would wait later then September 15? They could only hope and continue to strive. But their spirit was very low.

Overnight the efforts of five days of struggle were lost. The unpredictable, irresistible Arctic was showing them how weak were the powers of man in this white wilderness.

The following day they continued to drift a little to the northeast. On September 16 the gale was over and the day was clear and warm. The temperature rose to twenty degrees. Greely again conferred with the officers and Brainard and Rice. Dr. Pavy wanted the party to move out to the southwest toward Cape Sabine. Since Cape Sabine was nineteen miles away and the drift of the floe uncertain, Greely and the others favored waiting. Greely sent out reconnaissance parties; Lieutenant Lockwood to the southeast, Sergeant Rice and Eskimo Frederik to the southwest. Lockwood returned to report that the ice was strong and traveling conditions were good.

They were thirty miles from Cairn Point on the Greenland coast and nineteen from Cape Sabine. Greely alone favored making for Cairn Point. They would be in a much better position on the Greenland coast. They could look for help from the Etah Eskimos. They might even be able to make their way down along the coast toward one of the northerly Greenland settlements. "At Cape Sabine," wrote Greely, "our troubles only commence, as few if any of the party believe that we could now cross the straits by boats or sledge." The desperate days ahead were accurately forecast in those few lines in Greely's diary.

Rice and Christiansen returned to report that there was no likelihood of moving toward the south or southwest.

A further complication introduced itself. The floe was revolving. The fickle arctic waters were making a turntable of the vast plate of ice on which the party was encamped. In less than one day the floe turned counterclockwise 180 degress. Brainard commented mildly, "Strange to say, Nature has at last been kind. The change brings us a little nearer our goal."

Fortune favored them twice that day, for Eskimo Frederik succeeded in shooting another seal. This added 125 pounds of meat to their supplies which Brainard estimated now totaled forty days' full rations.

Greely, worried that the men would become too discouraged, ordered Sergeant Israel to report his observations only to the commander. At noon on September 17 Israel was able to report that the floe had reversed its direction of drift and they had made three miles to the west and four miles to the south in one day. Greely thereupon relinquished his plans for striving for the Greenland shore. Although the floe was still slowly revolving, they started out at 1 P.M. to the southeast. Brainard went ahead to select the route. They crossed two floes before they stopped at the end of nine hours. They had progressed only two and one-half miles, yet they counted it a good day. Brainard noted: "After ten hours of the severest physical strain, to lie down in our sleeping bags and stretch our weary limbs, was indeed refreshing. As the bags were spread on the ice with only one thickness of canvas underneath them, our comfort can be well imagined. Even so, this has been the brightest day since leaving Fort Conger. At least, we have not drifted further into the unknown."

On the eighteenth Greely wakened the cooks at 5 A.M.

A feeling of urgency spread. This was a critical day. Greely had directed that everything be abandoned that was not essential. They kept a telescope, a marine glass, rifles, a shotgun, ammunition, records, instruments, food, fuel, and serviceable clothing.

Greely told the men that he was unwilling to risk anyone's life by still carrying the pendulum. It would be kept only if the group was unanimous. It would be dropped whenever they wished. He commented proudly to his diary: "Not only was there no objection to keeping it, but several of the party were outspoken in considering it unmanly to abandon it."

Although they had lightened their load, they still dragged about six thousand pounds on their sledges. It now took only two instead of three trips to move all their supplies and equipment.

The drift of the ice had changed to the south and east. There was a chance that they would float past Cape Sabine through Smith Sound and out into Baffin Bay. If this happened they were undoubtedly lost. All day they struggled desperately toward the shore which once again looked so near.

At noon Israel reported to Greely that he read their position as 78° 50.3' N. Cocked Hat Island was still to the south of them. Greely estimated they were at least six miles from Cape Sabine and four and one-half miles from the nearest land. As they worked toward the shore to the south, the ice they traveled over drifted east. All day long they pushed on, crossing from floe to floe. They would make two trips bringing all their load to the edge of the floe. Then they would put the boat in the water and ferry their load across to the next floe. It took three trips in the boat to get all of the supplies across.

At one point Rice and Greely were pressing ahead of the

party. Crossing a weak place in the ice, Sergeant Rice broke through and fell in the water. Greely pulled him out, told him to strip. Greely stripped too and gave Rice his underwear. The as the rest of the men came up other dry clothes were found for Rice.

Crossing from floe to floe was risky business and all were aware of it. One or two of the men were uneasy about being among the last to cross to a new floe. When they commented on this, Greely rebuked them and pointed out that all of them were taking turns in crossing on the last trip. Greely made a point of being the last man to enter the boat.

At 6:30 P.M. they paused on a large circular floe to have supper. While it was being prepared Greely sent Brainard on ahead. Brainard crossed to the southern edge of the floe and returned quickly with the joyous news. He had seen an open lane of water running from the edge of the floe directly to land which seemed about three miles away. He had scanned the coast with marine glasses but saw no flag, cairn, or other evidence that would suggest the relief party had been there. But it was land and the way was open.

They were all tired beyond feeling but they knew the crisis they had reached. A little more effort could end their torture. They rose and once more dragged their sledges toward the southern edge of the floe. By 9 P.M. they had completed their labor. It was September 18 and they no longer had the light all of the time. It was getting dark. They dared not risk crossing the open water with moving floes in it. It was extremely doubtful that they would have had the strength for any further labor that day. They had no strength for erecting their teepee or providing themselves any protection other than unrolling their sleeping bags on the rough ice. They had expended every ounce of energy in their thirteen hours of labor—

in sledge-dragging, loading and ferrying the boats, loading and dragging the sledges again. They had crossed five floes. But they had reached the edge of the last one. In the morning they could cross open water to the shore.

They slept while the Arctic committed another roaring, cruel jest.

The storm broke from the southwest about midnight. It raged with a strength and a fury that permitted little activity. No breakfast was made that morning. Greely ordered pemmican and water to be served to the men in their sleeping bags. At noon Sergeant Israel was unable to take a latitude observation. They all knew, however, that again the Arctic had broken their hopes and destroyed the results of their long efforts. Once more they had been blown out into the middle of Kane Sea. Brainard recorded his dismay: "We are farther north and east than ever before, perhaps twenty miles from land. To cross the floes over this distance seems a hopeless undertaking when we can average only about a mile and a quarter per day. And now we have been shown what child's play the wind can make of our struggles. How can we put our heart and strength into hauling the sledges!"

They were forced to spend the day in their sleeping bags while the storm raged about them. Snow drifted into the bags. Waves blown up by the wind splashed over the floe and soaked them. There was nothing to do but lie there, as Brainard wrote, "listening to the roar of the waves and meditating over our helplessness."

Lieutenant Greely, however, would not concede their helplessness. They would not surrender to the Arctic. At 5 P.M. Israel was able to get bearings. They were twelve to fourteen miles east of Cape Sabine, seven miles west of Cairn Point on the Greenland shore, about on a line running due north of Cape Alexander. The storm ended at 6 P.M. and Greely immediately called a conference of the officers and Brainard and Rice.

All, except Greely, thought there was a chance of reaching some point on the west coast even if they drifted below Cape Sabine. Greely pointed out that it was almost impossible to believe they could travel twelve miles west while the current was carrying them nine miles south. In the past three days they had been able to travel only four miles west while they drifted twelve miles south. That is, they went two thirds of one mile west for each mile they went south. He returned to his hope of reaching Greenland, pointing out that they need travel only seven miles east while drifting twenty-two miles south; only two miles east in thirty-one miles of southing to reach Littleton Island; and only one and one-half miles east in thirty-five miles southing to make Cape Alexander. Greely urged that they drop everything but two thousand pounds, carrying only their records and twenty days' rations, and start across the moving ice for Greenland. They would be able to carry everything in one load and would be able to ferry in only two loads. They would be able to travel twice as fast as they had been traveling. Greenland, he emphasized, was the only place where they could be certain of relief. They had been within four miles of Cape Sabine and had seen clearly that there was no party there.

He was unable to persuade them. Even the daring Lockwood favored a delay until the floe settled down. All advised waiting.

"I am sorry that I seem to be alone in my opinion about what is best to do," Greely said. "But the time has come for action and I must decide what action to take. Tomorrow at noon, unless conditions prevent moving, I will give the necessary orders to carry out my plan. Substantially it is this. We will take the twelve-man sledge, twenty days' provisions, and move toward Greenland.

"Lieutenant Lockwood, you and Sergeant Rice, after breakfast, will go out and select the most favorable route.

The next morning, September 20, was cloudy and foggy, winds were blowing from the north, the temperature was low, and occasionally snow fell. They could see nothing and did not dare move. But Greely attempted to brighten the day by ordering some of their remaining coffee to be served at breakfast in honor of Sergeant Jewell's birthday.

In the afternoon Eskimo Frederik shot a large bladder-nose seal. It was almost eight and a half feet long and weighed about 650 pounds. This was a substantial addition to their dwindling food supply. The Eskimos were delighted, for this seal was very rare in Greenland waters. Eskimo Fred was rewarded with a special ration of rum and was highly praised by Greely. The happy hunter was delighted and went off whistling, blowing across the top of an empty cartridge shell.

The bad weather continued for the next several days and prevented any movement of the party toward either shore. The snow continued to fall and melt, soaking the sleeping bags and clothing. Since the abandoning of the whaleboat, Rice's group was sleeping on the ice. Greely invited them to come into the teepee. They refused. It would have been little improvement and would have crowded the teepee. Instead, they constructed an ice house to protect themselves from the wind and drifting snow. The Eskimos continued to hunt and Jens succeeded in killing three harbor seals. Schneider busied himself with adding canvas tops to the leather boots. The footgear was disintegrating under the heavy wear in ice and slush.

In the next few days the drift carried them west again toward Cocked Hat Island. The weather continued bad and some of the men came down with diarrhea. Dr. Pavy suspected it was caused by the seal meat, so the sick were put on a diet of corned beef. On September 23 they were midway between Cape Sabine and Cairn Point, about nine miles from land in either direction. The weather was cold and stormy. The waiting, the inaction, made the men more miserable and Greely tried to revive them by a small issue of rum.

On the twenty-fourth Greely sent Brainard and Schneider out to the west on the urging of Dr. Pavy, who thought they could move in that direction. They returned to say it was impossible to risk their heavy loads over that ice. Pavy was outraged and berated Schneider so strongly that Greely stepped in and made him stop.

Greely knew, as the doctor knew, that they now had to make it to Cape Sabine somehow. They were being carried away from Greenland and being carried south toward the vast expanse of Baffin Bay. If they drifted south of Cape Sabine and were carried into the open sea, they would all perish. Greely sent out Lockwood, Brainard, and seven men in the little iceboat to make further reconnaissance. They went off to the west and the southwest, pushing their boat through slush and rubble ice. They could find no floe capable of supporting the loaded sledges. Movement in any direction was too dangerous for the party to attempt.

The weather grew worse on the twenty-fifth, driving the pack about them in furious motion. The grinding and the roaring of the floes as they broke against one another added to the fearfulness of the scene. Ice blocks piled high along the edges of the floes as they met in loud collision. At 1 P.M. the floe on which they were camped was pressured between two larger ones. The pressure increased and the floe cracked. The entire party was then adrift on the small floe (about two or three acres wide and thirty to forty feet thick) broken away from the main section. The wind increased and drove them on south.

They were drifting past Cape Sabine. What would happen to them now?

The storm continued its fury during the next day, the twenty-sixth, and continued to drive them south. Greely sent first Eskimo Frederik and later Rice and Schneider to see if an attempt could be made for the shore. The sea was so rough and the pack moving with such turbulence that those sent to investigate were barely able to get back. The troubles of the party were complicated by Lockwood, Kislingbury, and five others being afflicted with diarrhea.

They were in a position so precarious that even the most desperate measures could hardly be less dangerous than remaining where they were. A large floe was pressing down on their little floe from the north. Several times it opened cracks in the smaller floe. Despite the gale, the risky passage over the rubble ice between the two floes, and the uncertain movement of the whole white turbulent world about them, Greely ordered the men to prepare for crossing to the larger floe crowding down on them. They moved with hardly a moment to spare.

Greely, two days later, described the events vividly: "Just as the whaleboat party quitted their snowhouse, one of these repeated shocks, of unusual violence, split our floe again, opening a wide crack, which soon swallowed up a portion of the abandoned house. Even as we rapidly rolled up the teepee, a narrow crack formed under our feet. Fortunately, at that time an immense floe to the northward was setting, with tremendous pressure, against our own floe, from which it was separated by some fifty feet of small rubble ice, that was held together simply by the pressure. The slightest movement of either floe would open this rubble so that the sea would swallow up any one on it. It was a hazardous passage, not to be thought of under other circumstances, but in our desperation it afforded the only possible means of escape. With wonderful celerity, boat, sledge and provisions were rushed across the chasm; the articles of least value being left till the last. Even as the last man passed over the rubble the floes moved, and one man just escaped dropping through as the lessening pressure opened again the pack."

They were on the new floe but in such condition as to make further effort seem the remotest impossibility. They had been drifting on ice for a full month. They had been wet repeatedly in zero or near zero weather. They had undergone the most strenuous exertions dragging their supplies or ferrying them from floe to floe. They had little to eat. Half of them were suffering from diarrhea. Twice they had been within a few miles of land and had been blown out to sea to start their struggles anew. Now a northwest wind was cutting through them at a speed of about fifty miles an hour. The snow whirled about them and filtered into their clothes.

They staggered to some little shelter behind small hills of blue ice. The teepee was erected. Rice's group, without their icehouse to creep into, sought shelter under a small sail set up behind a little berg.

The storm roared on as though the Arctic were furious that this audacious little band would still struggle after all the setbacks the frozen north had dealt them. A supper was prepared under the teepee the evening of September 26 in which Rice's group joined. They returned to their sleeping bags and did not venture out for the next two days. Hunger and a wet sleeping bag were preferable to fighting the vicious gale on the way to and from the teepee. It was not possible to cook breakfast on the twenty-seventh, so Greely had a little frozen pemmican distributed and some rum. After the snow which had filled the teepee was shoveled out, they were able to cook supper. But the little fire for the cooking raised the temperature so high in the teepee that everything seemed to melt. Bags and clothing were wet through once again. They had reached a new depth of misery.

The next day, September 28, the storm began to lose its fury. The hapless group noted with pleasure that their floe seemed to have ceased its southerly drift. Greely sent Rice to observe conditions toward the west. He returned to say the sea had subsided and it would be possible to move to the west if the boat carried small loads. Greely hastily had the men moving their possessions toward the western edge of the floe and set Rice and others busy ferrying to the next floe. The sea was rough and the wind was still strong but they managed to get everything across to the next floe in four trips. They were able to move swiftly across that floe to the one beyond, carrying everything but the boat in one load. They were stopped by weak, new ice and darkness. They went to sleep conscious that they had been this close to land before and a gale had thrown them far out to sea while they slept.

The Arctic relented. Perhaps the Arctic was tired opposing men who would not cease striving for their goal.

Greely wakened the cooks and Brainard at 4:30 A.M., set the cooks busy preparing breakfast, and sent Brainard out to find a route to land that seemed less than one mile away.

Brainard returned at 7 A.M. to report that land was almost four miles away but the route was favorable. They started moving immediately and soon came to open water. They ferried across the narrow strip of water, loading and unloading, sledged ahead again and reached another open lane of water. Once more they turned to the wearying task of loading and unloading. But now they knew they were on ice that held fast to shore. With Lockwood in charge, the first group moved out ahead. Following his usual practice, Greely was with the last boat to ferry across to the fast ice.

At 5:20 P.M. Lieutenant Lockwood and his group stepped on land. It was September 29. For thirty-three days they had been trapped in the ice and tossed back and forth across Kane Sea like bagatelles. Now they were on land again.

Their joy was marred by two circumstances. First, they were far south of Cape Sabine where they were to find supplies and, hopefully, meet their rescue ship. Second, Sergeant Cross once more demonstrated his irresponsibility. He had been with the first party to reach land. Because of a frostbitten foot he was left with the first supplies landed while others went back for the rest. Cross then availed himself of the fuel alcohol to celebrate and when the others returned he was quite drunk.

Their troubles were clearly not over and the unity of effort that Greely called for would not be easily attained.

They completed the landing of their supplies and equipment at 6 P.M., thoroughly exhausted. Greely described the place, which he named Eskimo Point, as "nothing but immense boulders of granitic rock, piled one upon another." Since August 9 they had been striving to make their way south. Now, on September 29, after almost seven weeks of hardship, they had reached this bleak, unpromising spot. Had their rescue ship sailed two weeks ago on September 15? Was a rescue party waiting across the channel on Littleton Island? Or were they to wait out the winter on this forbidding, rocky point of land? Brainard wrote: "Several ravens and a brace of ducks were observed flying about us during the march. The former are birds of ill-omen and many remarks were heard from the superstitious."

It was a coast where evil forebodings were easily fostered. Such forebodings were soon fulfilled.

CHAPTER FOUR

THE FAILURE OF THE "PROTEUS"

On the afternoon of July 22, 1883, First Lieutenant Ernest A. Garlington, commanding the relief party for the Lady Franklin Bay Expedition, went ashore at Cape Sabine. (Two hundred sixty miles farther north, Lieutenant Greely was preparing to travel south to Cape Sabine.) Garlington went ashore with some of his men to inspect the caches, make magnetic and other observations, and to leave a record of his progress.

Garlington's party was going north on the *Proteus* commanded by Capt. Richard Pike, the same vessel and the same captain who had taken Greely north two years earlier. The *Proteus* had been chartered by the Army. Thus, while Pike was captain of the ship, he was under Garlington's command.

There had been some sentiment in Washington to give this mission to the Navy. The Army had sent a relief party north in 1882 which failed to reach Lady Franklin Bay. The 1882 party aboard the *Neptune* was commanded by William M. Beebe, Jr., a private soldier in general service. Beebe's qualifications for such unusual responsibility seem to have been that he was private secretary to the Chief Signal Officer, General Hazen, and had served as an officer on Hazen's staff during the Civil War.

The *Neptune* did not leave St. John's until July 8, 1882, arriving at Disko on July 17, and then went north without stopping at Upernivik. The ship arrived at Littleton Island on July 29 after about one week of struggling through the ice-packed waters of Melville Bay. Beebe found his vessel stopped about a half-hour after passing Littleton Island. He was faced with a solid wall of ice from twelve to twenty feet high stretching all the way across Smith Sound. He spent the next forty days steaming back and forth trying to find a way through the pack. During this time Beebe and his men went ashore at Cape Sabine and examined the cache made by Nares in 1875. He found the cache damaged, so it was rebuilt. Later he established a cache of his own at another point on Cape Sabine and a second cache on Littleton Island. After repeated futile efforts to push his ship north, and seeing the brief arctic summer disappearing, Beebe, on September 5 turned the *Neptune* to the south. This first expedition sent to reach Lieutenant Greely and his party returned to St. John's on September 24, 1882.

The failure of the *Neptune* to reach Lady Franklin Bay made it vitally important that the relief effort of 1883 should succeed. General Hazen advised against turning responsibility over to the Navy. However, he requested that a Navy ship escort the *Proteus* "to bring back information, render assistance, and take such other steps as might be necessary in case of unforeseen emergencies." But General Hazen did not make this request until the middle of May 1883. Only four weeks remained to prepare the U.S.S. *Yantic*. This was not a ship for arctic navigation and specific orders were given that she was not to enter the ice pack. Later, at Garlington's request, U.S. Navy Lieutenant J. C. Colwell was assigned to him aboard the *Proteus* as a naval aide.

Garlington's experience did not at all prepare him to lead what was really a naval expedition to the Arctic. After graduating from West Point in 1876, he had been assigned to the famous Seventh Cavalry in Dakota Territory and served there capably. When the announcement was made of a relief party to bring home the Lady Franklin Bay Expedition, Garlington volunteered.

Ernest A. Garlington comes down to us over the years as a not very attractive personality. An intelligent, even a brilliant garrison officer, he quickly incurred the intense dislike of some of the fourteen soldiers who were to serve under him on this arctic voyage. Garlington was too young to have been tested in the crucible of the Civil War. There were other ways, such as Indian fighting, for an American soldier to prove his professional skill in the 1880s. Garlington was thoroughly familiar with techniques of Indian fighting. He had had no arctic or sea experience. A few hours after landing at Cape Sabine, Garlington's ability as a leader was put to a severe test.

Before leaving St. John's, Garlington and Commander Frank Wildes, captain of the *Yantic*, agreed on their plans and wrote down their agreement.

MEMORANDUM OF AGREEMENT BETWEEN LIEUT. GARLING-
TON AND COMMANDER WILDES

Yantic to proceed to sea with the *Proteus*, and remain in company as long as possible. *Yantic* will proceed to Disko under sail, and will leave letters for Lieutenant Garlington at Disko and Upernivik.

Cairns enclosing bottles or tins will be left at Cape York, S.E. Cary Island or Hakluyt Island, Pandora Harbor, and Littleton Island. *Yantic* will remain in Pandora Harbor not later than August 25th, Disko not later than September 20th.

Lieutenant Garlington to leave letters in Disko and Upernivik, and records on Southeast Cary Island, or Hakluyt Island, Littleton Island, and Pandora Harbor if entered.

Proteus to endeavor to communicate with *Yantic* at Pandora Harbor before August 25th.

Should *Proteus* be lost, push a boat or party south to *Yantic*.

Pandora Harbor will be headquarters, but before departure *Yantic* will run up to Littleton Island.

The present-day reader, conscious of the everyday use of the radio for instantaneous communication with ships at sea, may be bemused by this primitive method. But the technique of communicating by leaving notes in cairns was well established in arctic exploration. The method agreed on by Garlington and Wildes would have been sufficient to overcome the misadventures in the days ahead. But the agreement was not followed.

The *Proteus*, a faster ship, had steamed away from the *Yantic* immediately after they left St. John's. Garlington's orders called for him to move north as rapidly as possible. The ships met again at Disko, but the *Proteus* sailed while the *Yantic* was having her boilers repaired and was taking on coal. The *Proteus* made good progress across Melville Bay and reached Littleton Island about 10 A.M., July 22. The ice pack blocked any further progress north, so Garlington ordered that the *Proteus* go over to Cape Sabine.

It is seldom that the man in the rear echelon can fully understand the needs and circumstances of the men who are up front. The sense of urgency carried by the man on the line, who lives with the knowledge that death or disaster can be avoided only by constant vigilance and striving, decreases almost geometrically with the distance from the line of conflict. There are some men, usually those who have had experience on the line, who can anticipate the needs of the men they are supporting, who can guess the several possible courses of the struggle and take precautions. Garlington was not one of these.

Greely's last letter to the War Department made it very

specific that if the relief ship did not arrive in 1883 he would retreat southward to Cape Sabine. In those few hours he spent on shore at Sabine, Garlington could have devoted a few minutes' thought to the possible events of the next several weeks. His orders called for him to push north as fast as possible to Greely and his men at Lady Franklin Bay. Garlington well knew that the *Proteus* might not be able to make it. He also knew that the *Proteus* might be lost. What, then, would be the situation? Not only the Greely party but the men on board the *Proteus* might be retreating to Cape Sabine.

A little reflection would have suggested proper precautions, adequate plannning. There were ample supplies on board the *Proteus*. There were four units of provisions, 250 rations each, prepared at Disko to be cached along the way.

But Garlington did not reflect. He did not plan for possible misadventure. As the men were making magnetic and other observations, he saw lanes of water opening through the ice to the north. Without pausing to make any caches, he hastened his men on board and ordered the ship to head north. The *Proteus* moved away from Cape Sabine at 8 P.M. and picked its way through loose ice.

The *Proteus* made about twenty miles northward when it was blocked by ice. Captain Pike tried ramming the ice. He forced the ship forward about three hundred yards. Then the ramming was halted and new leads through the ice were sought. At 5 A.M. Captain Pike succeeded in working his ship into some open water. But facing the ship now was the solid ice pack. There was clearly no chance of breaking through this barrier.

The *Proteus* was turned around and headed to the south.

Ellesmere Island and Greenland form a narrow corridor from the Arctic Ocean to Baffin Bay. The great masses of ice formed to the north are pulled back and forth by the force of the tide. When the tide changes, it brings bergs charging with terrible momentum against other ice masses. Should the *Proteus* get caught in such a crash it would be destroyed. During the day Captain Pike tried to move his ship farther south and into a safer position. About three o'clock the ship was making its way through a crack in the surface ice. Open water was only hour hundred yards away. The ice began to close as the ship was being turned.

If the turn had been completed the *Proteus* would have lain with her bow facing into the ice. Quite probably the ship would then have been in no serious danger. But the ice closed in and held the ship fast as it was lying east and west. The pressure of the ice locked the ship fast and no movement was possible. The *Proteus* was a strong ship but the arctic ice was unrelenting. The pressure quickly grew to a tremendous force.

The ice which trapped the *Proteus* about three o'clock was almost seven feet thick. About four-thirty the starboard rail was broken down. The very threatening nature of the nip was obvious from the first and Garlington and his men were working to get the stores up on deck. It was not long before the side of the ship gave way. The ice pushed its way in below decks and water rushed into the hold.

As long as the ice maintained its pressure the ship would not go down. With a unified command the consequences might have been different. There was time for abandoning ship in good order. But good order in such a crisis is almost entirely dependent on the commander's control of his men. Garlington had control over only fifteen men, and, except for Colwell, these men had had neither arctic nor sea experience. Captain Pike was in command of the ship's crew, a crew that had been recruited hurriedly in St. John's. The ingredients were plainly not there for swift, unified action at a critical time.

Garlington concentrated his efforts on trying to get the stores from the deck to the ice. But this was done with haste and poor control. About one third of the stores thrown from the deck fell too close to the ship and sank into the water. Colwell devoted his attention to getting the whaleboats and dinghy free of the ship. Without these boats the entire party might well have been lost. Captain Pike seemed unable to maintain control over all of the ship's crew. These men, after first securing their personal baggage, turned to looting the ship's supplies.

The captain's efforts to stop the looting and to bring the men under control were met with jeers. The men of the crew declared that their pay stopped when the ship sank; therefore they were no longer under the captain's command.

The tide turned about seven-fifteen that evening, the pressure of the ice was released, and the *Proteus*, with most of the supplies for the Lady Franklin Bay Expedition, went to the bottom.

All of the ship's crew and the relief expedition were now on the ice. Some of the supplies had been saved, the two whaleboats, the dinghy, and the three ship's boats. Lieutenant Colwell, with some of the soldiers and some of the crew, loaded one of the whaleboats with about five hundred rations and made for Cape Sabine about four miles to the west. Garlington took command of the second whaleboat and Captain Pike took the three ship's boats.

Colwell unloaded his boat at Cape Sabine and hastened back to the floe. Garlington then attempted to make for the shore with his boatload of men. The ice was heavy and close. Garlington had had no experience as a sailor and only two of the soldiers in his boat knew how to row. They couldn't make their way through the ice and had to return to the floe.

Colwell then led the way to Cape Sabine in his whaleboat with the other boats following. Captain Pike loaded supplies in his ship's boats and so could not bring off the floe all of the ship's crew. This caused loud outcries among those left on the ice. The captain told them to shut up, he'd be back for them. There were muttered threats and Colwell heard one of the crew declare that they should sieze a boat and push south. Let the captain find out how he could get along without them. This attitude won immediate general assent from the crew left on the floe.

Colwell skillfully led the caravan of boats through the threatening ice to the shore. Both Garlington and Colwell then made another attempt to return to the men and supplies left on the floe. The soldier, Garlington, did not succeed and returned to shore. The sailor, Colwell, reached the floe. After loading his whaleboat with the crewmen he found little room for the supplies still on the ice. However, one of the sergeants with some of the soldiers managed to take a boat out to the floe. They brought in more of the supplies and the dinghy.

All lives had been saved but the ship and most of the supplies had been lost.

The situation was bad—but not hopeless. In fact, it had been anticipated that just this situation might occur. In the agreement between Garlington and Captain Wildes of the *Yantic* it was expressly stated: "Should the *Proteus* be lost, push a boat or party south to the *Yantic*." Colwell now made this very suggestion. He volunteered to take a boat with a few supplies and the best boat handlers and race south to find the *Yantic*.

Garlington refused Colwell's offer. He had become convinced that the *Yantic* would not be able to get past the ice to Melville Bay. The *Yantic*, he concluded, would not come up to Cape Sabine or Littleton Island, nor would it be able to reach Pandora Harbor. Garlington decided upon full retreat.

Two caches were left at Cape Sabine by Garlington. One cache included about five hundred rations of bread, canned goods, tea, sleeping bags, and other supplies. This cache was made hastily and was not marked by a flag or otherwise. Garlington left a cache of clothing protected only by rubber blankets.

In a message left in a cairn for Greely should he come to Cape Sabine, Garlington told the story of the wreck of the *Proteus* and described the supplies cached in the area.

The retreat then began. Garlington made certain that he was well supplied for the retreat. The boats were loaded as fully as possible with food and supplies. Additional food and supplies were taken in tow in the dinghy. In reply to later criticism that other or larger caches might have been left at Cape Sabine for Greely's party, Garlington explained that he was providing for Greely's rescue by insuring a successful retreat. The only hope for Greely's party, after the sinking of the *Proteus*, lay in obtaining another ship to bring north adequate supplies. This was his intention, Garlington declared, in making a rapid retreat.

The logical course for the retreat to follow was the line of communication that had been established in the memorandum of agreement between Wildes and Garlington. In reverse order, the points of communication were Littleton Island, Pandora Harbor, Hakluyt or the Southeast Cary Island, and Cape York. By touching at each of these points Garlington could expect to meet the *Yantic* as it tried to make its way north. If the ship passed the boats while they were at sea, messages left by Garlington's party at each point would give the *Yantic* the story. The *Yantic* could then reverse its course and quickly catch up with the boats.

However, the line of communication was not strictly followed. The retreating boats stopped at Littleton Island and Pandora Harbor, leaving messages at both places. They then went on to Northumberland Island. Fog and storms had delayed the retreat, so that it was July 30 when the boats prepared to leave for the Cary Islands. A storm on July 31 forced them into land seven miles north of Cape Parry. They were delayed here for two days. The next port of call for the boats should have been Hakluyt or the Southeast Cary Island. Colwell advised Garlington that it would be dangerous for the heavily laden boats. He suggested that he, Colwell, take a small crew of good boat handlers and a light boat and make the run to the island. Again Garlington decided against separating his party. He decided instead to head for Saunders Island and later Cape York.

Thus Garlington was skipping one of the post offices, Cary Islands, and stopping at Saunders Island before going on to the last post office on his retreat route, Cape York.

The *Yantic*, coming north, left Upernivik at noon on July 31. At 1 P.M. on August 1 she was off Cape York. However, the ice extended fifteen miles offshore. Captain Wildes decided against attempting to break his way through the ice into shore. The *Yantic* skipped Cape York and pushed on to the next post office, the Southeast Cary Island, arriving there at 9:30 A.M., August 2. If Garlington had taken his boats there, or had agreed to let Colwell take a boat there, the meeting with the *Yantic* would have been accomplished that day.

But Garlington was on his way south now and the *Yantic* was on its way north. There was no news of the retreat on the Southeast Cary Island and no news about the *Yantic* on Cape York.

Garlington remained at Cape York until August 16. Meanwhile, the *Yantic* went up to Littleton Island and on the afternoon of August 3 discovered the record left by Garlington. It was here that Captain Wildes first learned of the sinking of the *Proteus* and of Garlington's retreat. Wildes then logically decided to catch up with Garlington by touching at each one of the post offices on the way south. He returned to Pandora Harbor and learned from the message left by Garlington that he was on his way south and would call at Cary Island and Cape York. He hoped to meet some vessel—"U.S.S. *Yantic* or the Swedish steamer *Sofia,* which should be about Cape York."

Wildes then went south again in pursuit of Garlington and his party. He reached the Cary Islands on August 4 at midnight. There was no record of any visit by Garlington and the record left by Wildes two days earlier had not been touched. Wildes was puzzled but concluded that somehow he had passed the boats on the way down from Pandora Harbor. He decided to go over the area more carefully.

The next two days were spent in searching between the Cary Islands and Cape Parry. On the evening of August 6 on Northumberland Island a search party from the *Yantic* found evidence of a camp about one week old. There was no message left there but Wildes concluded that Garlington and his boats had gone on to the south. The *Yantic* touched again at the Cary Islands and then went on toward the mainland.

On August 9, the day Greely and his men were leaving

Lady Franklin Bay, Captain Wildes was approaching the mainland near Cape Dudley Digges. He found ice extending far offshore. Cape York was forty miles farther south and it was there that Garlington had said he was headed. Garlington arrived at Cape York on August 10. But Captain Wildes at Cape Dudley Digges, like Garlington at Cape Sabine, was governed by prudence. He found the ice growing heavy in almost every direction and he was running short of coal. He later reported: ". . . the imprudence of remaining in this vicinity became sufficiently obvious, and I bore up for Upernivik, which was reached on August 12th."

The *Yantic* waited at Upernivik for ten days. By August 22 Captain Wildes was persuaded that the end of the summer was at hand and it was too great a risk to his ship to remain any longer. Taking on fifty tons of coal at the Kudlisoet coal cliffs, he went on to Disko, arriving there on August 28. By this time the Greely party had advanced as far south as Cape Hawks and was now beset.

Twelve days earlier, on August 16, Garlington had at last consented to let Colwell push on ahead to try to catch the *Yantic*. Colwell and six men headed straight across Melville Bay toward Upernivik. The remainder of the shipwrecked party took the longer course around the shore of the bay.

Colwell's little party in its lone boat ran into trouble almost from the start. The next seven days were spent in trying desperately to keep afloat despite furious gales, heavy snow, and awesome icebergs crashing about on all sides. Three of the crew became seasick. All of them were hungry, thoroughly soaked, and exhausted most of the time. There was little chance to prepare anything to eat and they were reduced to nibbling on wet hardtack.

On a few occasions they tied up to a flat berg and heated food and tea on an alcohol burner. Once they were able to stop at a rocky island for a few hours' sleep ashore. On the nineteenth the fury of the weather abated but Colwell still faced the hazard of fog, icebergs, and lump ice. They used the sail when they could and at other times used their oars. On the evening of August 22, Colwell estimated that they were near Upernivik but they were encased by fog. At 2 A.M., August 23, they saw the northern shore of Upernivik. They rounded the island and at 5 A.M. they landed.

Colwell's journey has been described as "among the best work done by arctic explorers. For perseverance, good judgment, and courage in the officer who accomplished it almost singlehanded, it could not well be outdone." In all the dismal story of the 1883 relief expedition, in contrast to the timidity and incompetence of Wildes and Garlington, Colwell shines forth as a man of courage, ability, and determination.

Colwell's arrival at Upernivik, however, did not complete his labors. He was just one day late. The day before, the *Yantic* had left to go south to Disko. Colwell waited at Upernivik only long enough to give himself and his crew about eight hours' sleep. He would not consider any further delay. He had to catch the *Yantic* and bring her back north.

The Governor of Upernivik persuaded him to use his heavy, open launch rather than the light whaleboat. And at 3 P.M., August 23, only ten hours after arriving in Upernivik, Colwell and his little crew were on their way again. The exhausting seven-day journey from Cape York to Upernivik had covered almost six hundred miles. They still had 230 miles to go to Disko.

His crew was exhausted but time was short. The arctic

summer was almost over. Colwell could not be sure how long the *Yantic* would stay at Disko. Colwell urged his men on. They had to catch the *Yantic*.

It took another seven and a half days to reach Disko. Most of the time was spent in rowing. It was exhausting work, for the launch was considerably heavier than the whaleboat. But, finally, on August 31 Colwell and his men reached Disko and found the *Yantic*.

That evening the *Yantic* started north once more and reached Upernivik three days later. Garlington and the remainder of the party had arrived there on August 24, the day after Colwell left to find the *Yantic*.

Six weeks after the sinking of the *Proteus* the rescue expedition was at last aboard the *Yantic*, the supporting vessel. It was September 2.

The Greely expedition was beset in the ice of Kane Sea, struggling to push on to Cape Sabine or Littleton Island. Wildes and Garlington, if they assumed Greely was obeying his orders, might well imagine out of their own recent experience, the trials being faced by the Lady Franklin Bay Expedition. Wildes and Garlington now had to face the question of "What is to be done for Greely?"

CHAPTER FIVE

ESKIMO POINT TO CAPE SABINE

At Eskimo Point, Lieutenant Greely wasted no time in preparing his party for the future. It was the end of September, shelter had to be provided, food had to be obtained. Some of the men were sent hunting. Corporal Salor and Eskimo Fred were sent north to the shore of Rosse Bay. If a vessel had visited the area and had not been able to reach Cape Sabine, a cache might have been made near Rosse Bay.

Salor and Eskimo Fred were not successful. The shore ice had not yet formed and they were unable to travel along the shore to Rosse Bay. What were they to do? They had to reach Cape Sabine but they couldn't even get as far as Rosse Bay.

The energetic Sergeant Rice had a suggestion.

"Lieutenant Greely," Rice said, "you know, I think we might be able to reach Sabine if we sent a couple of men overland across the glacier."

"Across the glacier, Sergeant?" Greely exclaimed. "That would be a very difficult journey."

"Yes, there might be some obstacles," Rice admitted, "but we could travel light. Jens and I could do it, taking only a large one-man sleeping bag. We could both crowd into it. And we wouldn't have to take a sled, just the supplies we could carry on our backs. Food for about four days. That would be enough for us to reach Cape Sabine. Then for the return trip we would have food from the English cache at the cape."

Greely gazed at the beginnings of the two stone houses the party was now working on. He looked at their small pile of supplies. There was no question that somehow someone would have to reach Cape Sabine. They could wait, of course, until the shore ice had formed, but then the winter would be more advanced and the hours of daylight would be more limited. Rice's plan was daring but, as Greely reflected, it was probably the safer course to follow. The future of the party would be more secure if the supplies at Cape Sabine could be obtained and it was possible, even probable, that there was news for them at the cape.

Greely turned to Rice. "All right, Sergeant, I think your plan is certainly worth trying. Tell Jens that you will leave tomorrow morning. I will prepare messages for you to carry to leave in the cache on Brevoort Island."

"Thank you, Major," Rice exclaimed as he turned away to tell Jens the news of their journey.

Greely smiled and shook his head. Rice was thanking him for the opportunity to risk his life for the sake of the rest of the party. "Thank you, Major," Rice had said. From time to time some of the men had made complimentary use of Greely's Civil War rank in addressing the commanding officer. Usually they used it when they felt particularly pleased with their commander. He had not heard anyone address him as major since they had left Fort Conger. He found himself pleased that Rice had used that title in thanking him.

Rice and Jens left the next morning, October 1, at eight-forty. Ellis and Whisler helped on the first leg of the journey by carrying their packs as far as Rosse Bay. The two helpers returned to Eskimo Point and reported to Greely that the gale which had blown up that morning was very strong at Rosse Bay. They also carried a message from Rice: "Don't worry about me if I'm not back until October

9th. The journey should take about four days each way."

The brief message told so much under the circumstances. At Eskimo Point the gale was so vicious that the men stayed in their sleeping bags most of the day. But Rice and his little partner, Jens, were struggling north through the storm in hope of finding food, supplies, and news for those waiting behind.

Sergeant Long, the expedition's good hunter, came close to getting a walrus for them. He shot it in a water pool but the walrus sank just as Long was reaching for him with a pole. It was a disappointment but it was also encouraging. If they were able to get a couple of walruses they would be able to survive the winter.

Greely pondered their future course. If only they had a second boat. With another boat the full party could be carried with reasonable safety. All their instruments, records, and other materiel could be cached there at Eskimo Point. They could then go south following the coast of Ellesmere Island to Clarence Head. If the Cary Islands were blocked by ice it was only another seventy miles to North Devon.

However, they had but one boat. It was best, Greely thought, to finish building the permanent stone huts at Eskimo Point and keep the hunters out searching to add to their food supply while they waited the return of Rice and Jens.

They gave no consideration to crossing Smith Sound to Littleton Island. They knew from experience they could average only two miles a day across the moving ice pack. The channel was, at the narrowest point, twenty-five miles wide. Smith Sound had a southerly current of four to eight miles a day. For every two miles they worked toward the east and Littleton Island they would be carried from four to eight miles to the south. They could not hope to overcome the strong current, the tide that rose and fell twelve feet turning the pack in every direction, the pack that consisted of a few floebergs and lots of rubble ice and slush, the frequent heavy storms, and the continued appearance of new ice that would block the movement of a boat but would not support a sledge or a man.

No, they could not make it to Littleton Island until Smith Sound was frozen. They could not attempt to travel to the south. They would have to stay where they were. If they could get some walrus or bear meat they should be able to survive the winter.

The days were growing shorter and soon the continual arctic night would be upon them. On October 1 the sun was so low that the astronomer, Sergeant Israel, could not take a reading.

Greely had to make a decision about the food. They had thirty-five days' supply at the daily rate the food was then being issued; ten ounces of bread, one pound of meat, and two ounces of potatoes. This was just about one-half the standard arctic ration.

Greely realized that in any decision he made about distribution of the food he would need the wholehearted support of his men. Perhaps the conflict with Lieutenant Kislingbury, perhaps the grousing of Connell, Cross, and others was having its effect. Perhaps the successful use of the council during the later days of the retreat had persuaded the commanding officer that he could let others advise him about his decisions without relinquishing his responsibility as leader of the expedition. He knew full well that under present circumstances he could not expect unquestioning obedience to his orders about food. His decision would need the support of the rest of the party.

Greely decided to consult not only his council but everyone in the party. He started with Kislingbury.

"Lieutenant Kislingbury, I want to ask your advice

about our food supply. We have on hand rations for thirty-five days, not counting those that might be found at Cape Sabine. How long do you believe this supply should be made to last?" Greely asked.

"Lieutenant Greely," Kislingbury replied, "I would say that while we are working on the huts we should maintain the present ration. After we have finished the work I think the ration might be reduced, perhaps cut in half. It is my feeling the more we can delay our crossing to Littleton Island the stronger the ice will be and the better chance we will have."

"Thank you, Lieutenant," Greely said. "Those are my views on the matter, but I feel that this is a decision that we should all share in. I will also consult Lockwood, Dr. Pavy, and the men as well."

Except for Dr. Pavy the opinions of the rest of the party were similar to the advice given by Kislingbury. All felt that the food should be made to go as far as possible.

Dr. Pavy would not agree. We may wonder why Greely expected the doctor would do otherwise. He probably wanted to get along with the doctor and thought that the doctor would want to get along with him. Greely also wanted the doctor's support. He wanted to be a democratic leader now, but he was embarrassed by the doctor's attitude. The doctor didn't want to commit himself to any reduction of rations. This was quite proper as a medical opinion. It certainly was not going to do them any good physically to get along with less to eat. What kind of opinion did Greely expect? The doctor's opinion was based on medical considerations (and no doubt a general inclination to disagree with the commanding officer). Greely had to base his order on broader considerations. The reduction in rations would certainly reduce their strength, perhaps dangerously, but it would keep the party alive longer. Everyone recognized this and was in favor of it.

Greely announced that the rations would be reduced. Their daily issue would consist of six ounces of bread, two and one-half ounces of potatoes, twelve ounces of pemmican, bacon, corned beef or one pound of seal meat, and one ounce of extract of beef. There would be a further reduction when they went into winter quarters and were not expending energy as they were now.

He counted on improving their supply by getting the 140 pounds of meat from the English cache at Cape Isabella. And surely there must have been some supplies left for them by their own government at Cape Sabine. They would know when Rice and Jens returned.

At Eskimo Point work continued on building the stone huts for winter quarters. The work on reduced rations was producing its effects on the climate of the party. Griping increased. Lieutenant Lockwood was offended by disrespectful remarks made by Sergeant Elison. Lockwood reported him to Greely, who dressed down Elison in front of the rest of the men. Greely blamed Elison's conduct on the bad example set by Lieutenant Kislingbury. "This indiscretion, on the part of one of my best men," Greely wrote, "illustrates forcibly the demoralizing influence of the improper criticisms already made by his superiors."

It was getting colder. By October 4 the temperature was down to six degrees. They were still working hard building their huts and their resistance to the cold was low.

Lockwood wrote in his diary: "This is a miserable existence, only preferable to death. Get little sleep day or night, on account of hard sleeping bag and cold."

On October 6 the equipment that would be given to the groups in each of the three huts was divided into three piles. Greely, to avoid any basis for complaint, ruled that his group would have last choice. First choice between the other two groups was decided by drawing lots.

Greely had given the duty of hunting to Kislingbury, Long, and the two Eskimos. Others would fill in only when necessary. The hunters kept busy every day but with little success. On October 6 the whole party was brightened when Eskimo Frederik brought in a seal.

Cooking a meal, however, was less a pleasure than a painful task. They were using stearine for fuel (to save their alcohol) and the fumes burned their eyes and lungs. This discomfort added to their generally miserable condition. Greely wrote: "The huts have been built of heavy stones, which, with bare hands, we have been obliged to dig from the snow and ice, and carry in our arms to the site. My hands are bruised, bleeding, and swollen, joints stiff and sore, clothing badly torn, hand- and foot-gear full of holes, and my back so lame I cannot stand erect. . . . All the officers have worked with the same assiduity and constancy, except Lieutenant Kislingbury, the hunter, who also labors zealously at times when not hunting."

On October 7 Greely noted that it was his wife's birthday and wrote of his worry about her and his children should he not survive.

In reflective moments Greely might worry about his wife and daughters but more immediately he was concerned about Rice and Jens. Where were they? He sent Ellis and Whisler out to the top of the glacier to look for them. They were not in sight.

Long and Eskimo Frederik continued hunting but their principal game was found out on the ice. One day they shot a walrus (food for weeks) but it slid into the water. The next day Eskimo Fred was able to shoot two seals but each of them sank before he could paddle out to them in his kayak. It was heartbreaking to have this food, which was life itself, escape them.

Rice was not back on the eighth and the concern of the party grew. The day was devoted to collecting moss which was used to seal the edges of the roofs of the huts and to provide a covering for the rocky floors.

"Don't worry if I'm not back until the ninth," Rice had said. He was not back that morning and Greely went up to the glacier to look for him. When he returned, Lieutenant Kislingbury went out to look without success.

At last, in the distance the two figures were seen approaching. There seemed to be an urgency in their stride and all in the party felt they were bringing news of some kind. As they came closer the feeling grew to certainty, for it was seen that Rice and Jens were wearing new army boots and other equipment. They hurried in somewhat breathlessly and Rice quickly told them that he brought news—good news and bad news.

The *Proteus* had been sunk, crushed in the ice off Cape Sabine. But there were about 1,300 rations cached at or near the cape. Lieutenant Garlington, who was in command, left a message saying that he was going south after a navy ship, the *Yantic* or a Swedish steamer.

And, Rice reported, a wonderful coincidence. The whaleboat that they had abandoned when they were out on the floe had drifted ashore in Payer Harbor. It was there now and it was undamaged. The entire party was keyed up as Garlington's message was read aloud by Kislingbury.

UNITED STATES RELIEF EXPEDITION
CAPE SABINE, JULY 24, 1883

The steamer Proteus was nipped midway between this point and Cape Albert, on the afternoon of the 23d instant, while attempting to reach Lady Franklin Bay. She stood the enormous pressure nobly for a time, but had to finally succumb to this measureless force. The time from her being "beset" to going down was so short that few provisions were saved. A depot was landed from the floe at a point about three miles from the point of Cape Sabine as you turn into Buchanan Strait. There were five hundred rations of bread, sleeping bags, tea, and a lot of canned goods; no time to classify. This cache is about thirty feet from the water line, and twelve feet above it, on the west side of a little cove under a steep cliff. Rapidly closing ice prevented its being marked by a flag-staff or otherwise; have not been able to land there since. A cache of two hundred and fifty rations in same vicinity, left by the expedition of 1881; visited by me and found in good condition, except boat broken by bears. There is a cache of clothing on point of Cape Sabine, opposite Brevoort Island, in the "jamb" of the rock, covered with rubber blankets. The English depot on the small island near Brevoort Island in damaged condition; not visited by me. Cache on Littleton Island; boat at Cape Isabella. All saved from the Proteus. The U.S. steamer Yantic is on her way to Littleton Island, with orders not to enter the ice. A Swedish steamer will try to reach Cape York this month. I will endeavor to communicate with these vessels at once, and everything within the power of man will be done to rescue the brave men at Fort Conger from their perilous position.

It is not within my power to express one tithe of my sorrow and regret at this fatal blow to my efforts to reach Lieutenant Greely.

I will leave for the eastern shore just as soon as possible, and endeavor to open communication.

E. A. GARLINGTON

First Lieutenant, Second Cavalry, A.S.O., Commanding

In addition to what was stated in the message, there was much that was implied. Greely found most meaningful the promise that "everything within the power of man" would be done to rescue his party. He might have discounted some of that promise if he had given equal weight to Garlington's expression of regret about "this fatal blow" to his efforts to reach Greely.

Greely had a variety of factors to consider. There were now four boats available to them. The two they had brought ashore at Eskimo Point, the now recovered whaleboat at Payer Harbor, and the boat reported by Garlington at Cape Isabella. The sun was very low and only a week or so of daylight was left to them. They had the means to attempt to travel south and perhaps strike for the Cary Islands. But it would be a very dangerous voyage, fighting the ice and racing the arctic night. They had now a substantial increase in their food supply at Cape Sabine, additional clothing, and the assurances of Lieutenant Garlington that another rescue attempt would be made.

Greely did not ponder long. Rice, in making his remarkable journey to Sabine and back, had discovered a strait running between Rosse Bay and Buchanan Strait. Finding it impossible to go along the edge of Rosse Bay to Cape Sabine, Rice had turned to the northwest and made his way to the northern shore of Cape Sabine along what Greely named Rice Strait. They now had a route to move their sledges to Cape Sabine.

Greely estimated the supplies at Cape Sabine would weigh almost twelve thousand pounds. It would not be possible for them to move the supplies to Eskimo Point. The hunting was probably better at Eskimo Point. Their stone huts, built with such arduous labor, were here. But at Cape Sabine there were food, clothing, and a good chance of a rescue ship's finding them. It was October 9. The decision could not be delayed. They would pack their sledges and move to Cape Sabine.

A NEW RESCUE EXPEDITION?

Lieutenant Garlington, after the sinking of the *Proteus,* ordered a swift retreat. His haste, he later explained, was motivated by a desire to make new arrangements for the rescue of Greely and his men. Their hasty retreat did not end when Garlington had his men and the crew of the *Proteus* on board the *Yantic* at Upernivik. The *Yantic* immediately steamed away from the Arctic and was back in St. John's eleven days later, September 13. It was the day after Greely and his men had abandoned their launch and whaleboat to start hauling their sledges across the ice floes toward Cape Sabine. On arrival at St. John's, Garlington telegraphed Washington, D.C.:

St. John's, N.F.
September 13, 1883

To Chief Signal Officer, U.S.A., Washington:

It is my painful duty to report total failure of the expedition. The Proteus was crushed in pack in latitude 78.52, longitude 74.25 and sunk on the afternoon of the 23rd of July. My party and crew of ship all saved. Made my way across Smith Sound and along eastern shore to Cape York, thence across Melville Bay to Upernivik, arriving there on 24th Aug. The Yantic reached Upernivik 2d Sept. and left same day, bringing entire party here. All well.

E. A. Garlington

This message was most noteworthy for what it did not say. We can imagine the officers in the Signal Office in

Washington puzzling over each line to determine what had been done for Greely and his party. (Unfortunately, for Greely and his men, the most ardent supporter of the Lady Franklin Bay Expedition, Gen. William Hazen, Chief Signal Officer, was then on a trip to army installations out in the Territory of Washington.)

After receiving and studying Garlington's telegram, the Signal Office immediately wired St. John's asking what supplies had been left for Greely and if anything more could be done. The next day Garlington replied:

> No stores landed before sinking of ship. About five hundred rations from those saved, cached at Cape Sabine; also large cache of clothing. By the time suitable vessels could be procured, filled, provisions, etc., it would be too late in season to accomplish anything this year.

Too late to accomplish anything. Why, then, did the *Yantic* rush back to St. John's? The *Yantic* had been at Upernivik on September 2, only five or six days from Littleton Island or Cape Sabine. In Garlington's memo of agreement with Commander Wildes it had been stated that the *Yantic* would run up to Littleton Island about August 25. Could an attempt not have been made one week later? Twenty-five men were depending on the supplies that Garlington had failed to provide at Cape Sabine or Littleton Island. But the *Yantic* hastened back to St. John's. Panic, it seems, was still in command of the relief expedition at Upernivik.

Dissatisfied with Garlington's reply, Secretary of War Robert Todd Lincoln ordered that another wire be sent asking Garlington if a new expedition could be started immediately and what its chances for success would be. Garlington replied that the chances were "extremely problematical; chances against its success, owing to dark nights now begun in those regions, making ice navigation extremely critical work." After citing the difficulties, he concluded:

> However, there is a bare chance of success, and if my recommendations are approved, I am ready to make the effort. My plan is to buy a suitable sealer, take the crew from volunteers from crews of *Yantic* and *Powhatan,* now in this harbor, paying them extra compensation. Lieutenant J. C. Colwell to command the ship; two Ensigns and one Engineer to be taken from those who may volunteer from same ship; also employ competent ice-pilot here.

Secretary of the Navy Chandler made a similar inquiry of Commander Wildes, captain of the *Yantic.* Wildes replied that another expedition using a foreign ship and a foreign crew would only mean "fresh disaster." He declared that the *Proteus* had been handled "very unskillfully" (an astonishingly conclusive judgment to be made by one who was hundreds of miles away at the time of the crisis). The crew's behavior at the time of the wreck was shameful, Wildes stated. He advised that the next ship sent must be "American-manned, and officered by Navy, and thoroughly equipped." This year, however, he thought nothing could be done because Melville Bay would be blocked by ice before October 1. A ship could not winter at Upernivik and it was not possible to sledge north from that point.

No one could accuse these counselors, Wildes and Garlington, of lacking caution.

There were those, however, who were not so timid. General Hazen, obviously frustrated to be at the other end of the country at this critical time, sent wire after wire to Washington trying to stimulate a new expedition.

Still another recommendation was telegraphed to Washington by one whose voice could not be regarded lightly, Chief Engineer Melville, hero of the *Jeannette* expedition. This man who had piloted an open boat across stormy arctic seas to the Lena delta, who had so remarkably kept himself and his little crew alive after the *Jeannette* was crushed in the ice, was one who could speak with authority. He wired Washington recommending that the *Yantic* be sent out again immediately to go as far north as possible. A sledge party could then be put ashore to go overland to Littleton Island. Melville volunteered to lead the sledge party.

Public awareness was growing of the desperate situation that would face Greely and his men. The government had failed to provide supplies in 1882 and had failed again this year. Twenty-five men were very probably at Cape Sabine. Questions were arising for which the Administration had no adequate answers.

Why was the *Neptune* in 1882 instructed to bring her supplies back to St. John's if she failed to reach Lady Franklin Bay? Why were the supplies not cached at Littleton Island and at Cape Sabine where they might have done Greely some good? What good were the supplies in a warehouse in St. John's?

Public indignation was heightened by the announcement of the Signal Office that Garlington had been ordered to land the house and supplies for the winter at Littleton Island *on his way north*. Clearly, if Garlington had done so, the Greely expedition on arriving at Littleton Island would not be in desperate straits. If Garlington had landed his house and supplies at Littleton Island on the way north his relief party need have retreated only that far. They could then have remained there in accordance with Greely's instructions "to keep their telescopes on Cape Sabine and the land to the northward." The announcement of the Signal Office, which gave the public the impression that Garlington had been given such instructions and had disobeyed them, was made probably because the Chief Signal Officer was not in Washington and Lieut. Louis V. Caziarc was in charge of the office.

Caziarc had written a memorandum recommending that the house and stores be landed on the way north. A copy of this memo, unsigned and undated, was included in the envelope of instructions given to Garlington. Noting conflicting points between the unsigned enclosure and instructions signed by the Chief Signal Officer, Garlington questioned General Hazen. Hazen told Garlington that the unsigned memo was not a part of his orders. (This exchange was not written down and was only brought out months after the *Proteus* sinking by a court of inquiry.)

Immediately upon learning of the *Proteus*'s sinking, Washington was stirring. The Secretary of War held conferences. The Secretary of the Navy held conferences. Then, both Secretaries held joint conferences with their principal staff officers and with some arctic experts. However, the most significant indicator of official Washington opinion was the reported attitude of some congressmen that they would in the future have little inclination to vote money for any more arctic expeditions.

News dispatches reporting on the conferences with arctic experts gave pessimistic views about an immediate attempt to rescue Greely and his men. The dominant attitude seemed to be that such an attempt would only lead to "fresh disaster."

In contrast, a news report from St. John's stated that the whalers could not understand why a ship was not sent out immediately for Greely's rescue. Many whaling ships had sailed in late September. If there was risk involved, no doubt it was discounted by men who earned their livelihood facing the risks of arctic navigation. There were men up there who needed help. The obvious thing to do was to try to help them as long as there was a reasonable chance.

In Washington, however, there were men who survived by not taking chances. From the first, War Secretary Lincoln had shown little enthusiasm for arctic exploration. His attitude had only intensified with the failure of the two attempts to reach Greely. In contrast, the interest of Navy Secretary Chandler had grown. He was more and more convinced that this was a job, not for the Army, but for the Navy. His ambitions were restrained by President Chester Arthur who had advised Chandler not to give any encouragement to these reckless would-be volunteers offering to rush off into the Arctic after Greely. This was not something to be decided hastily.

(The President then went off on a trip to Newport. He lunched at the summer residence of Mr. and Mrs. Vincent Astor. The lunch, reports said, "was simple but served in splendid style.")

But neither the President nor Secretary Lincoln was to be allowed a vacation from the problem of Greely's rescue. The Inter-Department Committee had reached the conclusion those two desired, that no further rescue attempt should be made in 1883. But this retreat from the question of "What is to be done?" was not accepted by Mrs. Adolphus W. Greely.

During the time that Greely was preparing himself for the expedition, Mrs. Greely studied with him. She was thoroughly informed about conditions in Ellesmere Island and Greenland and was familiar with her husband's orders and plans. When it became clear that a rescue expedition was not an immediate likelihood, Henrietta Greely began to mobilize her forces to get action in Washington.

After Greely had embarked for the Arctic, his wife had

The Lady Franklin Bay Expedition members. This photograph was taken by Rice before the departure. He may have taken this exposure by means of a spring device which gave him time to move from the camera to his seat at the extreme right. *(The National Archives)*

The head of Dr. Octave Pavy (rear, third from right) was pasted in sometime later. Dr. Pavy was in Greenland at the time this photograph was taken.

Front row—(left to right) Connell, Brainard, Lt. Kislingbury, Lt. Greely, Lt. Lockwood, Israel, Jewell, and Rice.

Rear row—(left to right) Whisler, Ellis, Bender, Cross, Frederick, Linn, Biederbick, Henry, Long, Ralston, Salor, Dr. Pavy, Gardiner, and Elison.

Three years' supplies being unloaded from the *Proteus* at Fort Conger, Discovery Harbor, August 1881. The structure at the right is a game stand where game is stored by hanging. (*The National Archives*)

Fort Conger. The wooden, prefabricated barrack provided good shelter for the expedition and the Greely party endured their first Arctic winter without severe hardship. Rice took this photo in March 1882, shortly after the sun returned. (*The National Archives*)

Lt. Greely's corner in the officers' room at Fort Conger. A rocking chair adds a curious, homey touch. August 1882. (*The National Archives*)

(Left to right) Eskimo Jens, Lt. Lockwood, and Sergeant Brainard about to leave Fort Conger, April 1882. It was on this trip that they attained the "Farthest North." The Stars and Stripes attached to the sled Sergeant Brainard was to plant atop a peak at their "Farthest," 83 degrees, 24 minutes north, 40 degrees, 46 minutes west. (*The National Archives*)

Sledge parties leaving Fort Conger to provide advance support for Lockwood's push for the "Farthest North." April 1882. (Left to right) Lt. Greely, Whisler, Brainard, Ralston, Frederick, Henry, Lt. Lockwood (at least, this is the identification listed in Archives records. The figure bears more resemblance to Dr. Pavy), Linn, Ellison, Biederbick, Salor, and Connell. (*The National Archives*)

Private Schneider training pup-team to work as sled dogs. These pups were all born at Fort Conger. Schneider has them hitched to a sled loaded with blocks of ice and seems to be giving the pups a serious lecture. The dogs paid attention and Schneider's training program proved successful. (*The National Archives*)

Eskimo Jens and Dr. Pavy skinning a seal at Fort Conger. (*The National Archives*)

Scene on the ice off Cape Sabine after the sinking of the *Proteus*, 7:15 P.M., July 23, 1883. Two figures scramble across the broken ice away from the spot where the ship has just gone down. Note the two boats on the ice in right background. *(The National Archives)*

Rice labeled this frozen seascape "A Discouraging Outlook." It is a view of the ice in Robeson Channel, June 1882. *(The National Archives)*

"Hard Road to Travel" was Rice's caption for this view of the ice seen from Cape Murchison. *(The National Archives)*

taken their two daughters to San Diego to wait out the time in her father's home. Now, when her husband's fate was being decided in Washington, she was at the other end of the country. She discussed her problem with an old family friend, Douglas Gunn, San Diego newspaper editor.

"You don't have to go to Washington, Henrietta. We can get the Washington newspapers and every newspaper in the nation working for us."

Mrs. Greely had lived in Washington for a short time after her marriage. She knew what it was like. She would be lost among so many others seeking official action or legislation.

"You have friends in Washington," said Gunn. "Let them work there for you. And I will work from here to arouse every newspaper in the country to demand that your husband and his men be rescued."

One of Mrs. Greely's closest friends in Washington was Mrs. William Hazen, wife of the Chief Signal Officer. Because of her husband's official position, Mrs. Hazen had to exercise her influence discreetly. But she had many friends in the national government and her father was a newspaper owner.

With this initial dedicated support, Mrs. Greely's crusade began.

It was soon determined by Mrs. Hazen that Navy Secretary Chandler was in favor of another relief attempt. Mrs. Greely and her allies decided, therefore, to campaign for giving the Navy the responsibility for the next rescue expedition.

In the Congress support was initially sought of the representatives and senators from Massachusetts, Greely's native state. Soon other support came forth, notably Senator Eugene Hale of Maine.

As pressure mounted during October, the Administration began to respond. On October 31 President Arthur called a court of inquiry on the sinking of the *Proteus*. It was clear from the beginning that all the inquiry could achieve would be the placing of blame.

Mrs. Greely was not concerned so much about finding fault as she was about urging corrective action.

The initial reluctance of the President and War Secretary Lincoln to send another rescue expedition in the fall of 1883 was sufficient to kill any prospects of any such effort. Even if the most optimistic attitude were accepted, there were only a few weeks after Garlington's return when such an expedition could have been sent out. It may well have been that the American public thought it wrong, indeed, shameful, that men in the service of their country should be left to face arctic cold, starvation, and death because the government did not live up to its agreement. It took a while, however, for the public attitude to develop and to manifest itself.

The development might have been hastened had there been leadership in Washington to stimulate public opinion in favor of prompt and vigorous action. But President Arthur was cautious. (He held that office only by the accident of assassination. Such accession to power does not usually produce a vigorous executive.) The President's chief adviser on the problem, Secretary Lincoln, was not merely cautious but antagonistic to arctic exploration generally, and to another rescue expedition in particular. His attitude was probably correctly reflected in a remark attributed to him in that October of 1883. "I do not see any use," Lincoln was reported to have said, "in throwing away any more money on dead men."

We can imagine how callous and brutal this remark must have seemed to Henrietta Greely and others who had a husband, brother, or a son lost up there in that white wasteland. But this brutal remark served to fortify Mrs. Greely's determination to move the government to action. If the executive branch was indifferent to its responsibility, she could appeal to the Congress and the people. The voice of the people and the people's representatives could not be ignored in the United States of America. Mrs. Greely and her allies turned to the public, to their senators and representatives, with increased energy to make certain that the Congress which convened in December would take action for the rescue of the Lady Franklin Bay Expedition.

CHAPTER SEVEN

PREPARING FOR WINTER

Greely's decision on October 9 to move the entire party to Cape Sabine involved much more work than merely dragging their sledges over the glacier, through Rice Strait and around the northern shore of Bedford Pim Island. That trip in itself, over the route discovered by Rice, was a distance of more than twenty-five miles. Since it was necessary to make a second trip to carry all of their supplies and equipment, the actual distance they would have to travel would be about seventy-five miles.

After arriving at Cape Sabine they would once more have to go through the exhausting labor of building some kind of shelter for the winter. They would also have to send out parties to collect the supplies cached at the various points near Cape Sabine.

There were four caches in the Cape Sabine area. Garlington had left two, one on the point of the cape and the other three miles away on the northern shore. There was a cache (made by the Beebe expedition in the *Neptune* in 1882) near the point of the cape. A fourth cache (made by the Nares expedition of 1875) was on Stalknecht Island, a few miles offshore from Cape Sabine.

After Greely announced that they were to prepare to move to Cape Sabine, the irrepressible Rice came to him with another suggestion.

"Lieutenant Greely, there's another trip I'd like to make."

"What is that, Sergeant?" Greely asked.

"I'd like to take Eskimo Fred and go down to Cape Isabella. You know, it's possible that the *Yantic* left supplies there for us. The ice is heavy around here and she may not have been able to come this far north. It's worth looking. Eskimo Fred and I could make the trip in a few days while the rest of the party is moving to Cape Sabine."

"Eskimo Fred rather than Jens this time?" Greely asked.

"Jens is a little tired from the trip to Sabine," Rice replied.

Greely looked down at the ground to hide his smile. "So Jens is a little tired," he thought. "What about Rice? Doesn't Rice also get tired?" He looked at Rice again.

"Sergeant, it will be a dangerous and a very trying journey. But it is possible, as you say, that the *Yantic* may have been able to reach Cape Isabella. You will be able to check the cache made there by Nares, too. Tell Eskimo Fred to be ready to leave with you tomorrow."

Rice smiled. "Thank you, Major."

Greely knew that Rice was proposing a trip even more difficult than his previous one. It was only about fifteen miles from Eskimo Point to Cape Isabella. But by the time of Rice's return the party would have moved to Cape Sabine. Rice would have a thirty-mile round trip from Eskimo Point to Isabella plus the twenty-five miles to Cape Sabine, a total of fifty-five miles. Was it worth it? There was a slim chance that additional supplies might have been left for them. And Greely knew he could depend on Rice. The lieutenant gave his approval. Rice and Eskimo Fred would leave the next morning, October 11, for Cape Isabella. The rest of the party would begin the transfer to Cape Sabine.

At five-thirty the next morning Rice and Eskimo Fred set out for Cape Isabella. Lieutenant Lockwood started with the first group for Cape Sabine dragging the sledge.

The temperature was down to four degrees below zero. Greely went along with Lockwood's group helping to pull the sledge for the first two miles. Some of the party remained to prepare the rest of the supplies and equipment for carrying. Then, carrying what they could, they followed to catch up with the first group. Cross and Bender were left with the supplies remaining in camp.

Bender was not an alert guard and Cross was apparently as cunning as a confirmed alcoholic can be. When those on the march returned to camp, they found that Cross had managed to steal some of the alcohol again and get drunk.

Greely was appalled and the men were furious. This was not merely irresponsibility. It was treachery. Alcohol was food. Alcohol was fuel. Taking alcohol was taking away days of survival for them.

"What," Greely asked his diary, "can be done with such a man?" Some of the rest of the party had offered an answer when they discovered what Cross had done. He should be shot, they said. They saw it in very simple terms. It was his life or theirs. But this kind of talk was quickly squelched. Despite all their differences, the party had survived and was still working together. Brainard wrote: ". . . no one wants to bring disgrace to the expedition at this late date."

The next morning they started off again with the remaining supplies and equipment, leaving behind the iceboat and oars. They traveled from 8:15 A.M. until two-thirty in the afternoon. The temperature was now down to eight below and there were but few hours of daylight. Six hours was about all the travel time available to them. They were able to make about one mile an hour. The exhausting work, the low temperature, and the limited rations made them all very weak. At the end of the day's travel Greely was barely able to stand and it was obvious that the rest of the party were in about the same condition.

Lieutenant Kislingbury and Dr. Pavy told Greely they did not believe the men could keep going. The rations should be increased. They suggested the English sledge ration, about forty-two ounces of solid food. Greely recognized the real need for an increase in rations but he was also conscious of their limited supply. He agreed to increase their daily ration to twenty-seven and one-half ounces, including one pound of meat. He also decided to provide an issue of rum at the end of each day's work as long as they had such strenuous labor.

The next day, October 13, Kislingbury and Pavy, apparently encouraged by Greely's partial acceptance of their advice on rations, tried to persuade him to drop everything that could not be hauled in one load. The men were too tired to carry everything, they contended, and the material dropped could be brought over to the cape later on. This suggestion Greely would not accept. They would carry all of their records, instruments, and provisions until they had everything where the caches were located. The commanding officer was concerned about their survival but he was also concerned about the survival of the work they had accomplished.

Traveling conditions were good that day and they made five miles in two trips, camping at the beginning of Rice Strait after crossing Rosse Bay. In all, they covered fifteen miles—hauling five miles, unloading, returning for the second load, and traveling the route again. They worked eight hours, beginning before and ending after daylight.

They faced a new arctic danger as they were crossing Rosse Bay. The bay was clearly very deep, for there were bergs rising out of the ice as high as twenty feet above them. As they were making their way around one of these bergs, a massive submerged part of it, breaking away from the bottom of the berg, rose swiftly and exploded through the ice in front of them. There was a great roar as chunks of ice flew through the air about them. They were all startled and for a moment immobilized. Fortunately no one was injured and the excitement served to relieve the monotony of their labor.

The following day they were able to reach the northern end of Rice Strait. It was another exhausting day with many chances taken in hauling their heavy sledge over new ice. Gardiner, still suffering with his bad finger, was relieved of the work of hauling and went ahead to test the ice in front of the sledge party. The consciousness of the danger added to their burden. The weakness of all of them grew more apparent. At the end of this day Greely announced that since they now had everything on the island where the caches were located, the material which could not be hauled in one load would be cached there. It was a considerable relief.

The next morning, unable to restrain himself, the commanding officer with Gardiner and Jens, went on ahead to find and examine the caches. They moved ahead quickly and in two hours reached the first of Garlington's caches. There was bitter disappointment for them in the discovery that instead of the 500 rations of meat reported in Garlington's message, there were only about a hundred. It was but the first disappointment of the day.

Greely, Gardiner, and Jens spent a few hours exploring the surrounding area. They found the cache made by the *Neptune* expedition but it was covered by snow. Since they had no shovels with them they could not inspect it. Greely then determined that the best place to establish their winter quarters was near the small lake close to the first Garlington cache. It was flat ground and the lake would provide them with fresh water.

Lockwood and the rest of the party came on later in the day. They had been delayed about two hours. The sledge runner had split. They had had to unload the sledge and repair the runner before going on.

Then, surprisingly, a little later Rice and Eskimo Fred returned. They had made the journey to Cape Isabella but had found only the 144 pounds of English meat. Since Rice and Eskimo Fred had no sledge, they did not bring the meat back with them. They were unable to find the whaleboat reported by Garlington. And there were no other caches. Apparently the *Yantic* had not come up that far. In his own mind Greely now questioned whether there was even a cache on Littleton Island as the Garlington message had stated.

It was a disappointing day. They had finally reached Cape Sabine, the object of all of their labors of the past ten weeks. And what had they found? Their relief ship was out on the bottom of Smith Sound. The supplies left for them were pitifully small. It seemed unlikely that they could expect another relief ship that fall. And, as yet, they had no shelter for the bitter, dark winter that would be upon them in a few days.

The commanding officer would not let them rest. There was work to be done if they were to survive the winter. The temperature was now below zero most of the time. Storms were becoming frequent. The strong winds and biting snow made any movement difficult in their weakened condition. But in the next several days Greely kept the men working steadily, building the one stone hut that would house the entire party.

The hut Greely planned measured twenty-five feet by eighteen. The stone walls were two feet thick and three feet high. Five poles were laid across the top of the walls and the whaleboat was placed upside down on the poles to form the center of their roof. Canvas was laid across the top to complete the roof. A small entranceway was left at one end with a door four feet by three, covered with a sheet of canvas. Adjoining the entranceway they built a storehouse for their supplies out of snow blocks. They also built a covering of snow blocks for the roof and all around the walls of the hut. In a short time, they knew, storms would cover their hut with drifts of snow. This would add insulation to keep in the tiny heat they would be able to provide with their limited fuel.

They fastened the barometer and an Eskimo lamp to posts which they set up in the middle to support the center of the whaleboat. They brought in what sand they could gather to cover the rocky ground that was their floor. The little stove was placed in the center. The area under the boat was the only space where it was possible for a man to raise himself on his knees. In no place was the roof high enough for a man to stand. It was a poor shelter but it was the best that could be done because of the scarcity of rocks and their limited materials.

By October 19 they had completed enough of the work on the hut so that they could move into it. The following day they were hit by a blast of wind and snow. The temperature dropped to thirteen degrees below zero. They were thankful to be able to escape the cruel weather in the shelter provided by the uncomfortable hut. Greely wrote that they were "so huddled and crowded together that the confinement is almost intolerable." Despite their condition, the cold, their exhaustion, and their hunger, the men seemed to "retain their spirits wonderfully." Greely reminded the men that they would soon have to decide what amount they would permit themselves as a daily ration. He left the question "undecided until the English cache reported damaged by Lieutenant Garlington is visited by us. God only knows what we shall do if it is spoiled, this hut will be our grave; but until the worst comes we shall never cease to hope for the best."

The storm ended the next day, October 21, and Greely immediately set the men to collecting the supplies from the various caches. Lockwood and most of the men were sent after the material that had been cached at Rice Strait as they had made their way over from Eskimo Point. They took a tent and camp equipment.

Long and the two Eskimos would camp at Rice Strait and continue hunting as long as there was any daylight. Long had suffered with some chest troubles throughout their stay in the Arctic. But he was a very skillful hunter and had great endurance. Greely was pleased when Long volunteered.

Greely went with a few men to pick up the cache made by Beebe which was only about one mile from the hut. There was as yet no ice foot along the coast, however, and they had a very difficult journey through wet snow and ice. Several of them, including Greely, found on their return that they had frozen their feet.

The dependable Rice was sent with three others to the cache on the point of Cape Sabine to bring back as much clothing as they could on their backs. While collecting the clothing (which had been much strewn about by a curious bear) Rice noticed a page of newspaper which had been used in the packing. The name Henry Clay caught his eye. It was an article by their friend who had left them at Fort Conger because of Dr. Pavy's antagonism. This discovery inspired Rice and the others to collect each scrap of newspaper (many pages were wet and torn) to be carried back to camp. There they were dried and later provided much information and entertainment for men who had received no news of the rest of the world in more than two years.

It was from one of these scraps of newspaper that they learned President Garfield had died. The news had a special impact on the commanding officer who could recall his last meeting with the President before leaving with the expedition. At a small reception in the East Room of the White House, the President had discussed with Greely his trip to the Arctic.

"Under your leadership, Lieutenant," Garfield had said, "I am confident that the work will be a success. The honor of our nation will be maintained in this scientific contest with other civilized countries."

At that time it had been Greely who was facing danger and risking his life. But in a few weeks Garfield had taken the assassin's bullet in his back. Now, from a scrap of newspaper which had been wrapped around a lemon, Greely learned the President had died.

Rice had noticed on returning from the point of Cape Sabine that ice was forming along the shore. He advised Greely that it might be possible to reach the cache on Stalknecht Island with a sledge over the new ice. Accordingly, Greely sent Lockwood and eleven men the following morning with the sledge to bring back as much of the English cache as they could. With the determination and singlemindedness that was typical of Greely's attitude toward the objectives of his expedition, he directed Lockwood to take their records and the pendulum and place them in a cairn. Meticulously, he specified that the cairn be erected in as prominent a place as possible on the south side of Payer Harbor. If a relief ship visited any place on the western side of Smith Sound, it would most likely go first to Payer Harbor. He and his men might all be dead of starvation by that time, but their work would have been saved. "I am determined," Greely declared, "that our work shall not perish with us."

Lockwood and his group reached Payer Harbor and the young officer looked for a prominent place to locate the cairn. He saw that the best place was on Stalknecht Island, just where the Nares expedition had made the cache he was sent to take up. The island was at the mouth of the harbor near the south shore. Sensing that this cache would be a signal to their rescue ship (or a memorial monument if the ship arrived too late), Lockwood constructed a great pile of stones on a promontory on the seaward side of the little island. He put their records in the sextant box and built up the stones around it. He placed the pendulum in the center of the stones so that its arm rose up above the top of the pile like a giant finger pointing at the sky. If a relief ship came to Payer Harbor that cairn would be seen.

The return trip from Payer Harbor with the English cache proved to be more than the weakened men could achieve. They were able to drag the full load as far as the point of Cape Sabine and then their strength was depleted. Their difficulties were increased as Lockwood and Pavy each injured a foot in traveling over pointed ice.

The physical state of the men was dramatically illustrated two days later when the supplies were brought in from Stalknecht Island and Cape Sabine. The sledge had broken and the day was spent in working on the roof and in checking the supplies. It was found that some of the dog biscuits were "thoroughly rotten and covered with a green mold." When Greely directed Brainard, who was acting as supply sergeant, to throw away the molded biscuits, some of the men asked that it be given them. Greely said he would not dare let them eat "that mass of corruption

. . . the injury from eating such food must be far more certain than any possible benefit could be." In accordance with Greely's orders, "the slimy, moldy substance was thrown away." However, when the lieutenant was not aware of it, some of the men went after it and every bit of the rotten dog biscuits was eaten.

By the end of October all of the four caches in the Cape Sabine area had been brought into the hut. The whaleboat which had drifted ashore in Payer Harbor had been broken up and brought in for fuel.

On October 26 Greely noted: "Our last day of sunlight for a hundred and ten long days, and how to pass this coming Arctic night is a question I cannot answer." He asked the men for their opinions about their rations for the winter months. He proposed that beginning November first their diet would be reduced to six ounces of bread, four ounces of meat, and four ounces of vegetables. This would extend their present supplies until March 1, leaving enough for ten days' rations at twenty ounces a day. In those ten days they would cross Smith Sound, which should by then have frozen, by sledge to Littleton Island.

He consulted the men with ease now. He was keenly aware these decisions were matters of life and death for them. The men knew it, too, and were desperately eager to share in the decisions. Greely found letting the men discuss these decisions did not at all reduce his status as commanding officer.

Greely's proposal stirred vigorous discussion. The principal objector was Dr. Pavy. They could not possibly keep alive on such a reduced ration, he insisted. They ran a great risk of so reducing their strength that scurvy or other disease would set in and they would find it impossible to recover. Lockwood and others objected to the doctor's views. In the view of most of the party it was better to stretch the supplies as long as they could. They favored putting the ration at the lowest limit. If it were found necessary the ration could be increased.

They did have hope that their hunters, Long and the two Eskimos, might be able to add to their food supply. Christiansen had killed one seal which provided them about seventy-five pounds of meat. A seal added a few days' supply of meat but what they really needed was a walrus or a bear. Such a killing would give them real assurance of getting through the long arctic night.

They were already afflicted with sickness and injury. Schneider and Connell were ill. Gardiner was still undergoing severe pain from the felon on his hand. Greely and Henry were hampered by frozen feet. And little Israel was, in Greely's words, "suffering excessively from our unaccustomed privations, but he refrains from any utterances in the nature of complaints."

There was one more cache of food that had not yet been brought in to the hut. At Cape Isabella there was the 144 pounds of beef left by the Nares expedition, the cache that had been found by Rice and Jens. Rice again volunteered to go after it. Greely agreed and decided that Rice would lead a sledge party including Frederick, Linn, and Elison. It was a long journey, eighty miles round trip. But 144 pounds of meat would add one ounce a day to each man's ration—and that one ounce might mean the difference between life and death for many of them.

The sledge party, facing almost continual darkness for their trip since the arctic night had begun the week before, set out on November 2. They took a light sledge, a four-man sleeping bag, a tent fly, rifle, cooking lamp, and a pot. They carried a daily food supply of eight ounces of meat and eight ounces of bread per man. For cooking they had five ounces of alcohol. They were, Brainard wrote, "equipped with the best we could offer, for every member of the party has denied himself some article of clothing which will add to their warmth and comfort." It was in such an effort that the unity Greely so desired flourished. All of them knew the hardships that Rice and his companions were undertaking to bring them a little more food. Each of them seemed happy to join in the mutual sacrifice so that the welfare of all might be promoted.

On November 3, the day after Rice's party left, Long came in from Rice Strait to report that he had killed a harbor seal which probably weighed about one hundred fifty pounds. This was joyous news and seemed a good omen for the sledge party on its way to Isabella. The joy of the party was dampened, however, because of an injury Lieutenant Kislingbury had suffered. While helping to pull the sledge to bring in the last of the supplies he had ruptured himself. It proved to be very painful. While being examined by Dr. Pavy, he twice fainted. At first it seemed so serious that the doctor said the injury might be fatal. However, in a couple of days this fear was dispelled as Kislingbury improved.

Bender, using the sheet-iron which had sheathed the whaleboat, devised a small stove. For fuel they had the wood from the boat and the barrels in which the food was cached. To make the most of this wood, they cut it into splinters.

Ralston, Schneider, Bender, and Brainard added to the food supply by each killing a fox. Greely decided that the foxes would be issued as extra rations, according to the following schedule: one during the first week in November, the second for the last week in February, the third fox for the second week in November, the next fox killed for the third week in February, and so on. This schedule gave them some immediate reward and something to look forward to.

They were much bothered by the smoke from the cooking. But Bender, their ingenious mechanic, was equal to the challenge. From several tomato cans, he fashioned a chimney which he fitted up through a hole cut in the bottom of the whaleboat on the roof. Time after time Bender's mechanical skill and imagination averted a crisis for them.

On November 4 Brainard reported to Greely that he suspected that someone had stolen some food from the storehouse. Their urinal tub was kept in the little corridor which adjoined the storeroom. It would not be difficult for a thief to get at the supplies while the rest were sleeping.

Work had started on a storehouse separated from the hut and now Greely directed that this be completed as soon as possible. They would be able to construct a frame and a door, and fortunately they had on hand a lock and key.

Long returned to Rice Strait with supplies to last him and the two Eskimos for a few more days. They were having a difficult time out there. They had only the minimum fuel to cook their food; none, of course, to heat their little tent. The temperature had dropped severely to twenty-five degrees below zero. A few days later Long sent Eskimo Fred back to the hut with the news that the hunters would have to return and requested a sledge party to help bring in their equipment. For Greely this was depressing but not unexpected news. It added to his worries about Rice's party. How were they making out on their long trip to Cape Isabella in this unendurable cold?

Lockwood, with Dr. Pavy, Brainard, and five others went to help Long and the Eskimos bring in their material.

When they all returned, Greely ordered that they be given an issue of a half gill of rum each. Because Brainard, who was on the journey, was exhausted, Schneider was designated to distribute the rum. Schneider helped the others and helped himself. The drink Schneider gave himself must have been generous. It made him visibly drunk. He was found outside in the storehouse. Greely could not be sure whether Schneider had stolen any food but stealing the rum was as serious a crime. He gave Schneider a furious bawling out and then ordered that no one would enter the storehouse except the issuing sergeant.

The next day Lieutenant Lockwood discovered a can of milk that had been hidden by someone. It had been opened but it was still full. Apparently the thief had had to hide it immediately after opening it to avoid being caught. The marks on the can showed that it had been opened with a knife blade broken in a distinctive manner. It was soon determined that such a knife was owned by Private Henry. Henry declared that he had loaned the knife to Schneider. So once again Schneider was under suspicion.

Greely was sorely disturbed by these incidents. If stealing continued there could be no hope of discipline or restraint. They would become a pack preying on each other. The food would go to the strongest or quickest. The stealing might even lead to killing. They would all be dead in a few weeks. Their only hope of survival was in working together.

Greely would have been more seriously disturbed if he had known that in Henry the party had a killer in its midst. Private Charles Buck Henry was the last to join the expedition before it left the States. He was accepted by Greely almost at the last moment after a vacancy occurred in the roster. Henry applied from Greely's old outfit, the Fifth

Cavalry at Fort Sydney, Nebraska. He was the only volunteer from that outfit and was recommended by the commanding officer. Neither the commander of the Fifth Cavalry nor Greely knew that Henry had served in the Army previously under his true name of Charles Henry Buck. In the early 1870s he was with the Seventh Cavalry on the frontier. (His troop was near the scene of the Custer massacre.) Buck's most noteworthy achievement as a soldier was the forgery of his commanding officer's signature on an order for whisky from the Post trader. His reward was two years in the penitentiary. He escaped and sometime later became involved in a gambling fight in Deadwood, Dakota Territory. In the fight he killed a Chinese and escaped capture. Then, curiously, he re-enlisted in the Army, signing up with the Fifth Cavalry as Charles Buck Henry. So, unknowingly, Greely accepted as the final member of his party a forger, deserter, and killer.

At midnight, November 10, Greely was awakened by the sounds of footsteps approaching the hut.

"Who's there?" Greely called out.

A moment later in stumbled Sergeant Rice. He was breathing very heavily and was obviously almost worn out. He rested on the ground for a few seconds before he spoke. Then between frozen lips, he gasped, "Elison is dying in Rosse Bay."

The whole party was soon ablaze with excitement and questions. Everyone wanted to volunteer to go to the rescue. Greely ordered that Brainard and Eskimo Fred would start out first with brandy and food. They would be followed by a sledge party of Lieutenant Lockwood, Dr. Pavy, and the four strongest men, Jewell, Ellis, Schneider, and Jens.

Rice reported that Elison was in a terrible, pitiable

state, that he would probably be dead before the rescuers could reach him. It had taken Rice sixteen hours to travel the twenty-five miles. He didn't think Frederick and Linn would be able to keep him alive. The three of them were huddled in a frozen sleeping bag.

One of the men who had gone after food for them was in danger. There was no question of what course was to be followed now. They had to do their best to help him.

In a temperature of twenty-eight degrees below zero, Brainard and Eskimo Fred set out through the arctic night to go to the rescue of a dying man twenty-five miles away.

CHAPTER EIGHT

THE PRESIDENT ACTS

The government was to blame. What was to be done? During the months of October and November 1883, public clamor increased for the rescue of the Greely party. President Chester Arthur became more certain that action would have to be taken. It seemed most likely that the action should be taken by the Navy.

It had been clear all along that Secretary of War Lincoln had no enthusiasm for and little interest in arctic exploration. The President, of course, was probably not certain that Lincoln had made the remark about not wasting money on dead men, but there was no question that the sense of the remark accurately reflected Secretary Lincoln's attitude. In contrast, Secretary of the Navy Chandler was ready and willing to undertake another attempt for the rescue of Greely.

Any executive with a modicum of sense will turn, when he wants a job done, to a man who wants to do that job. President Arthur turned to Secretary Chandler to take the responsibility for the new attempt to rescue the Greely expedition.

It is probable that the President, having in mind the questionable conduct of Garlington and Wildes, told Chandler to find a commander for the rescue expedition who would have the determination and courage necessary to do the job. Secretary Chandler, searching the list of likely naval officers for this task called in Commander Winfield Scott Schley.

Commander Schley, in December 1883 was forty-four years old. Four years had passed since he had held a command. Most of that time he had spent as lighthouse inspector for the Second Naval District with headquarters in Boston. Those were happy years for the commander's family. They were able to establish a home in Brookline, to make new friends, and to live a settled existence, unusual for them. But the protracted shore duty must have raised some question in the mind of a career naval officer. In his fourth year of shore duty, Commander Schley might have begun to wonder a little if the Navy believed him capable of any greater responsibility. He knew he had performed creditably as commanding officer of the *Essex* on a three-year tour that had included cruises to Vera Cruz, the Congo River, and various stations in the South Atlantic. Returning home in 1879, he had welcomed an opportunity to be a family man once more. He had spent all too little time with his wife and children, but they were a navy family and had learned to adjust to it. It was good for a man to be with his family, it was good to be home, but four years of being a land-based sailor was a long time. Schley must have welcomed the call to report to the Secretary of the Navy early in December.

In the privacy of his office Navy Secretary Chandler told Commander Schley of the President's decision for a naval expedition to rescue Greely. It was an ironic situation. An audience with the Navy Secretary suggested an administrative or diplomatic assignment rather than a sea command. Schley could recall discussing the Greely expedition with some fellow naval officers at the Charlestown Navy Yard back in 1881 at the time the expedition set forth. There was some ill-informed talk, Schley recalled, about the purposes of the expedition. Schley's own comment was that regardless of what the purpose of the expedition might be he was sure that at some time some poor naval officer would be put in command of an expedition to rescue the soldiers. Now the casual jest was coming true with ironic twists.

Schley was ready and willing to accept the command, but it seemed to him a futile effort. There was no reason to expect that this third mission would succeed where two others had failed. Even if he did break through the massive ice pack and reach the point where Greely was supposed to be encamped, what could he hope to achieve except to bring home for burial the bodies of men who even now were probably dead?

"Of course, Commander," the Secretary said considerately, "if there is any personal reason in the way of your accepting this assignment it will in no way reflect upon your record, nor prejudice action on a future request you may have for preferred duty."

"On the contrary, Mr. Secretary," Schley replied emphatically, "no officer could refuse such duty and retain his self-respect. If it is necessary to volunteer for this mission, I wish to volunteer. If it is necessary to be ordered, I ask to be ordered. I would be honored to have the opportunity to command this mission."

With such a response the Secretary must have known he had the right man for the job. Schley's record was remarkable. He had probably spent almost as much of his adult life at sea as ashore. Two cruises to Europe before graduation from Annapolis in 1859, a trip to Japan immediately afterward, service under fire—and distinguished service—during the Civil War, combat leader of a successful raid against a fort in that distant hermit kingdom of Korea. There was hardly a place in the world this man had not sailed to—Mexico, Africa, Brazil, the South Atlantic, even the fringe of the Antarctic. He had been everywhere except the Arctic. Well, now he was going there and he should get through if anyone could.

A short man of vigorous bearing, Schley's face reflected years of experience at sea and in command. The stern eyes, the straight nose, the firm mouth framed in a full mustache, and a short beard (in the fashion of the time)— all gave his face an appearance of sternness and firm character. He was clearly a man accustomed to command.

He was secure enough in himself to suggest courteously two conditions to his acceptance of this mission.

"Mr. Secretary," he said, "since the commander of this expedition will be responsible to the nation as well as to the Navy, I would wish to make my own selection of the officers who will serve with me."

The Secretary replied, "Of course, Commander."

"There is a second request I would like to make, Mr. Secretary. Wives and families of even experienced Navy men are inclined to worry a good deal about assignments they regard as hazardous. The period of anxiety for our families will be reduced if we can keep this secret as long as possible."

"That is perfectly understandable," said the Secretary. "We shall try to do so. I would see no need to announce the appointments until after Congress has taken the necessary action."

Thus, two major decisions had been made: the expedition would be a naval one and a commander had been chosen. Now it would be necessary to get the Army to agree to turn the mission over to the Navy, and then win the approval of Congress for financing another rescue mission.

The President proceeded by first naming a board "to consider an expedition to be sent for the relief of Lieutenant Greely and his party." The board was appointed on

December 17 and consisted of Brigadier General William B. Hazen, Chief Signal Officer, U.S. Army; Captain James A. Greer, U.S. Navy; Lieutenant Commander B. H. McCalla, U.S. Navy; and Captain George W. Davis, Fourteenth Infantry, U.S. Army. Two army officers and two navy officers. The sides were evenly balanced. It seems beyond question, however, that the board must have been familiar with the President's wishes to place the command of the new expedition under the Navy.

The board met on December 20 and the next day recommended that immediate steps be taken to buy two powerful steam whaling ships. These two ships and a naval ship to serve as tender, the board advised, should immediately be prepared for arctic service.

Three plans were presented to the board when it first met. One by Lieutenant Garlington, another by Lieutenant Commander McCalla, and a third by Captain Davis.

Garlington volunteered to lead an expedition of two ships which would proceed to Cape York, Pandora Harbor, Littleton Island, and Cape Sabine.

McCalla's plan suggested a naval expedition of two whaling ships with a naval vessel for tender. He advised that a base be established at Littleton Island before the first ship pushed on to explore Smith Sound and the area toward Lady Franklin Bay. The second ship would remain in the vicinity of Littleton Island with the tender which would serve as a second reserve ship.

Captain Davis's plan called for a whaling ship and a naval tender. Both ships would be manned by navy crews but each would carry a detachment from the Army of two officers, a doctor, and ten enlisted men.

The board later received suggestions and advice from various officers who had had arctic experience. In addition to Lieutenant Garlington and Lieutenant Caldwell, the board heard from Dr. Bessels and Captain Tyson, who had served on the *Polaris* expedition; George Kennon, who had lived for several years in northeastern Siberia; Chief Engineer Melville and Lieutenant Danenhower, survivors of the *Jeannette* expedition; the board also received advice from British explorers, Sir George Nares, Captain Albert Markham, and Major Feilden.

While the board was meeting and discussing these plans and advice, Congress was convening and awaiting a recommendation for action.

In addition to weighing the advice, the board was engaged with the problem of compromising the interest of the Army with the wishes of the President for a Navy expedition. It was clear that General Hazen was reluctant to give up all Army participation in the rescue. He felt a special responsibility for the Greely expedition which was not shared by his civilian superior, Secretary of War Lincoln.

The board, after almost one month's study, was in agreement on almost all points except the matter of Army participation in the project. On January 17 (probably after some prodding from the President) the board submitted a preliminary statement of its recommendations. The expedition should be under the command of the Navy and should proceed as far north as early as possible. No vessel had passed Cape York earlier than June 1. Therefore, it was recommended that the expedition should depart from New York not later than May 1 and arrive at Upernivik by May 20. To meet this schedule it would be necessary to obtain the vessels very soon. The President sent these recommendations to the Congress the day he received them and urged that the Congress act promptly.

The detailed report of the board was submitted a few days later. It was recommended that two vessels be prepared for a cruise of two years, each vessel would carry supplies for its own crew and for that of the other ship as well as for the Greely party. These ships should be whaling or sealing ships of about five hundred to six hundred tons. They should be brought to a navy yard and prepared for service in the Arctic.

Because of the possibility of the ships' wintering in the Arctic, it was recommended that the crews be kept to a minimum, each ship to carry no more than thirty-four men. Detailed recommendations were made for special equipment, clothing, and supplies.

Now, if the Congress would act, the plan could be put into operation. Mrs. Greely and others working for a rescue expedition turned hopefully to their friends in the legislature.

CHAPTER NINE

THE RESCUE OF ELISON

On November 7, after five days of hard traveling, the sledge party of Rice, Frederick, Linn, and Elison had reached the summit of Cape Isabella. The difficult traveling not only exhausted them but made them very thirsty, and to relieve that great thirst, Linn and Elison began eating snow.

All of the men had been repeatedly warned against eating snow to relieve thirst. The danger of frostbite as a result of reducing the body temperature had been impressed on them time and time again. The danger was especially great in temperatures as low as the twenty degrees below zero then being endured by the sledge party.

The four men were able to drag the sledge no closer than two miles from the summit of Cape Isabella. They left the sledge and took carrying bags to climb to the cache at the top. Rice, Frederick, Linn, and Elison spent seven hours on November 7 working their way to the summit of Cape Isabella. Clambering over the rocks and ice, they wondered how the British expedition had been able to carry the heavy supplies up the hill to make the cache. The view from the summit was later described by Frederick:

> The sky was clear, the moon bright, and to the southward we saw open water as far as the eye could reach. Waves, with white caps, came rolling in to the very cape itself. Even at this season a vessel could have navigated without difficulty. Could we have embarked at this point,

I have no doubt that we would have all reached our homes in safety.

They loaded the cans of meat in their carrying bags, slung them on their backs, and began the descent. On the way down the others noticed that Elison was not moving as quickly as he once had and he was not as talkative. They discovered that his face and hands were partially frozen. This was not the first time Elison had suffered from such trouble during the trip. Now, however, it seemed especially difficult to restore the circulation. When he recovered, they proceeded down the hillside to the sledge.

The descent was almost as difficult as the ascent. The climb up had taken seven hours and it took almost as long for them to make their way down. When they had started, Rice had expected they would reach the top and return to the sledge in a few hours. That few hours stretched out to fourteen and in that time the only nourishment they had was a cup of tea.

On reaching the sledge they found that Elison's hands were again frozen and so were his feet. They all climbed into the sleeping bag to get some rest and to help restore circulation to Elison's limbs. Frederick took one of Elison's hands and placed it between his thighs. Rice took the other hand and did the same. They were using their own body warmth to restore life to Elison's limbs.

After their sleep and a breakfast of hot tea and a few ounces of bread and meat, they felt stronger. They started to drag the sledge toward Eskimo Point but ran into deep, soft snow and rough ice.

Elison soon began showing once more signs of suffering from the frost. Frederick tried to help him along by putting his arm around him and, eventually, almost carrying him. But Elison's legs became very stiff and he seemed unable to control them. Soon his nose also started to freeze and turn white. The rest of his face turned a livid blue.

Although a pair of sleeping stockings had been placed over his fur mittens Elison's hands soon were without feeling and the tips of his fingers began to turn chalk white. The whiteness sped up over his hands and began to move up to his wrist.

They plodded along trying to keep moving but soon Elison was walking as though he were on stilts. His feet seemed to be frozen solid and the frost was reaching up over his ankles. They stopped and forced themselves into the sleeping bag again with one man on each side of Elison in an attempt to thaw him out. They placed his hands on their bare breasts and wrapped every piece of clothing available around his feet.

His eyes which had been staring vacantly were now completely closed. His speech was incoherent, and fluid was oozing out of his nose and eyes. He lost control of his bladder. His urine wet the sleeping bag and his companions. After a few hours' rest they pushed on again the morning of November 9 toward Eskimo Point, eight miles to the north. They had to leave behind the meat and such equipment as they could spare. The three of them were too weak to haul the sledge and guide Elison. They marked the location of the meat by upending a rifle in the snow.

They struggled on, pulling the sledge, with Elison staggering along blindly behind them. As Rice, Frederick, and Linn trudged ahead, they would often look back and find Elison wandering off in another direction or leaning in bewilderment against an iceberg.

It would have been impossible for them to pull the sledge with Elison on it, nor could they guide him and pull the sledge too. They found they had to resort to tying Elison by a lead rope to the end of the sledge. So Elison was partially led and partially dragged on toward Eskimo Point.

At their old camp they broke up the English iceboat they had left there when they moved to Cape Sabine. With wood from the boat they made a fire and were able to thaw out Elison. Once more they started on their way back toward the hut which was still twenty-five miles away from them. They had gone no farther than one mile when they saw that Elison was frozen as badly as before. He was staggering along unseeing. Again they tried the expedient of tying him to the end of the sledge. Elison could now hardly move his feet and was in dreadful pain.

"Let me alone," he would plead. "Let me alone so I can lie down and die."

Now a north wind began to blow and soon developed into a strong gale. Sergeant Rice halted them. He motioned them to walk back to Elison where they formed a small half-circle around him. They had to turn their backs to the wind so they could talk.

"Listen," Rice said, "we just don't have the strength to get Joe and the sledge back to the hut. Shorty," Rice said to Frederick, "you and Dave will stay here with Joe in the sleeping bag. You can thaw him out as we did before. While you are doing that, I will go on to the hut for help."

"Do you think you should try alone, George?" Frederick asked.

"I'll be all right," Rice replied. "You'll need Dave here with you to take care of Joe."

Once more the frozen sleeping bag was opened and Frederick and Linn struggled into it with their frozen partner between them.

With only a bit of frozen meat to eat on the way, Rice started on the long journey through the darkness for help. As he stumbled along the strait which had been named for him, Rice found that he was traveling over new ice which was barely able to carry his weight. Time after time he heard the ice crack beneath his feet and he expected any moment to fall through into the cold, dark water below. Tortured by hunger, thirst, and exhaustion, Rice plodded ahead through the darkness. His desperate situation made him reckless and it seemed to matter little to him whether he lived or died. He fought on as the north wind howled down through Rice Strait biting into his face. Time after time he had to turn his back to the wind and hold a hand against his face to thaw out his nose.

As he turned into Buchanan Strait hours later, the moon came out and provided some light for his footsteps. However, he was now traveling not over new ice but trying to pick his way through ice filled with hummocks. He stumbled repeatedly, bruising his legs, or arms, or body. He plunged on through the darkness, his mind closed to feeling. Finally, at midnight, he reached the hut with barely enough strength to crawl inside. With just a few moments to catch his breath, he gasped out his message, "Elison is dying in Rosse Bay."

Excitement grew as Rice filled in the details of their terrible trip. It was some time before Greely could get control of the situation and issue orders for the rescue of Elison.

Brainard and Eskimo Fred started out as the advance party carrying food and brandy. They, too, had trouble trying to find their way through the hummocks of ice. Brainard found some comic relief from the tension as he listened to Eskimo Fred cursing the ice with words he never knew before he had started out with the expedition. It took the two men twelve hours to make their way back to Eskimo Point and the pitiful three frozen into the sleeping bag. Brainard found that Linn and Frederick had been able to improve Elison's condition somewhat, but in thawing out Elison they had suffered greatly themselves and their faces and limbs were partially frozen.

The gale was still blowing and the temperature was still about twenty below zero. Brainard found it difficult to build a fire. He was either burning or freezing his fingers. Eventually, he was able to heat a meat stew and make some hot drinks for the suffering trio.

Linn and Frederick were both considerably weakened by the night's ordeal. Elison had cried with pain continually and had urinated frequently. Apparently the strain had affected Linn's mind. He had begun to talk incoherently and had tried to crawl out of the sleeping bag. It was with great difficulty that Frederick was able to restrain him.

The sleeping bag was so completely frozen that Brainard was unable to get the three out of it. He spoon-fed them as they remained in the bag. While feeding them, he tried to reassure Elison. The poor fellow was a pitiable sight, his frozen face was almost inhuman. He was obviously in great pain and in a weak low voice he pleaded with Brainard, "Please kill me, will you?" Brainard again tried to cheer the frozen man who shook his head and asked again to be killed; helping him would only mean that the others would also die.

The hot food and drink improved the condition of the frozen men but Linn and Frederick told Brainard they were not sure they had the strength to stand. Brainard had to abandon his plan to carry Elison on the sledge toward the relief party which was following him. After giving the three such additional comfort as they could, Brainard and Eskimo Fred prepared to make their way back toward Lieutenant Lockwood and the sledge party to lend a hand in the drag ropes. As he turned away, Brainard saw a fox walk straight to the sleeping bag as though he wanted to crawl in with the other occupants. Brainard dived at the fox and tried to hit him with an ax, but he missed and the fox got away.

The storm blowing from the north continued as Brainard and Eskimo Fred made their way toward the relief group. They were almost to the beginning of Rice Strait when they saw the sledge party approaching. All were exhausted, after fighting their way through the cold for more than twelve hours. They made camp and rested.

At four-thirty the cook prepared their meager breakfast, and at six o'clock Brainard started out ahead of the rest to return to Elison, Linn, and Frederick.

Brainard found them shivering with the cold and still helplessly frozen in the bag. He set about preparing breakfast for them but was unable to light the alcohol lamp. Using a few pieces of the boat they had carried with them, Brainard began a wood fire. Once more he was alternately burning and freezing his fingers. Eventually, however, he was able to serve them some hot meat stew which again materially improved their condition.

Sometime later the sledge party arrived and the sleeping bag was chopped open. They placed Elison in a single dog-skin bag and then wrapped him in a large piece of canvas.

Linn and Frederick, after moving about and stretching their legs, started out ahead of the sledge party to return to Camp Clay. After loading Elison and the other equipment on the sledge, the Lockwood group started out on the return at 9:30 A.M.

It was 5 P.M. before they reached the northern end of Rice Strait. All day long they had pulled the sledge facing into the north wind which ripped into their faces. It was a great relief to pause for a few hours, erect a tent for shelter, and make some hot tea. All of them devoted some time talking to Elison and trying to restore his spirits. The tea and the comradeship worked wonders and Elison was almost cheerful again.

At ten minutes after eight they started off again on the last leg of their journey. Recalling the trip later, Brainard wrote:

> As we entered Buchanan Strait, the wind died away and the moon rose and shed soft light over the barren ice fields, making the night one of the most attractive that I have ever known. The ice bound coast with the chaotic masses of pulverized bergs at its borders, and the weird sense of desolation spreading about us on every side were never so apparent as now. A feeling of awe seemed to take possession of the party and we moved forward slowly and in silence with our half-conscious burden.

They reached the hut at 2:10 A.M., November 13. Linn and Frederick had arrived nine hours earlier and had told the part of the story they knew. The sledge party bringing in Elison was given a joyous welcome.

The temperature was 34.5 degrees below zero.

CHAPTER TEN

DEBATE IN WASHINGTON

Lieutenant Greely was facing a situation "of great peril," President Chester Arthur told Congress on January 17, 1884. The President was transmitting to Congress the recommendations of the Secretaries of War and Navy and was asking for congressional action without delay.

In this kind of situation Congress frequently feels frustrated or irritated. The President, even though he may have delayed his decision for months, can pose as the national leader pointing the way. Congress, in sharp contrast, often appears as a group of would-be leaders, each pointing in a different direction. The President may demand specific action on a specific issue. But congressmen see his demand against the background of the whole presidential program.

If the President's party does not have a majority in Congress, the demands of partisanship may intensify the natural division between executive and legislative powers.

In January 1884 all of these factors were present, plus one additional complication. The Congress was under divided control. The Senate was controlled by the Republicans, the House by Democrats. President Arthur was Republican, but a "Stalwart" Republican. He had been nominated as Vice-President with Garfield merely to mollify his faction. A number of Republican senators shared the amazement of the man who exclaimed upon Garfield's assassination, "Chet Arthur, President of the United States. Good God!"

There were many reasons, therefore, for a protracted struggle between the President and the Congress on what to do for the Greely expedition.

In the House the President's message was referred to the Committee on Appropriations. In the Senate, however, the message was referred to the Committee on Naval Affairs. It is probable that Senator Eugene Hale, Maine Republican, who was on both the Committee on Appropriations and the Committee on Naval Affairs for the Senate, felt that the latter committee would be more sympathetic to the recommendations for Greely's rescue.

One week later a proposal for Greely's rescue was submitted to the House of Representatives by the Committee on Appropriations. The proposed resolution would authorize the President to purchase not more than three ships and to make all other necessary expenditures to "dispatch an expedition to the Coast of Greenland, Smith Sound, or Lady Franklin Bay, for the purpose of relieving and bringing home Lieutenant A. W. Greely and party." The President was also required to submit to Congress the following year a detailed account of the expenditures made for this purpose. Congressman Samuel J. Randall, Pennsylvania Democrat, chairman of the Appropriations Committee, described the proposed action as "in obedience to humanity, to the agreement made with Lieutenant Greely."

There was a short debate about the resolution. One question was raised. "Was the President free to buy ships already in existence or, if he chose, to have ships especially constructed for the rescue expedition?" Mr. Randall replied that he believed the words "purchase of not exceeding three vessels" meant that the President could buy vessels already built or vessels to be built.

Another question was raised. Did the proposal put any

limit on the funds the President might spend? Mr. Randall replied that the Committee on Appropriations thought it best to make an exception "to the general rule and not make any limitation as to the amount appropriated." It was best to leave this matter to the discretion of the President and trust that the funds would be used in accordance with the best economy.

James H. Budd, California Democrat, asked "if it would not be well to prescribe what kind of sailor shall have charge of this expedition." He believed DeLong was lost in the *Jeannette* expedition because "a drawing room sailor was in charge of it." Mr. Budd favored "old, weather-beaten seamen who understand their business." Again Mr. Randall replied that he thought the Congress could trust the President of the United States to make a wise decision. The Democratic congressman saw the need for swift action. He was not afraid to give the Republican President extraordinary but necessary authority to take such action.

With no further question or objection, the resolution was passed. It remained now only for the Senate to pass the appropriation and for the President to approve.

The next day the resolution was received by the Senate and referred to the Committee on Naval Affairs. The proposal was reported to the Senate the following day, January 24, by Senator Hale.

Senator Hale began by saying that he regretted it had not been referred to the Committee on Appropriations. However, the Committee on Naval Affairs had studied the question that morning and had discussed it with the Secretary of War and the Secretary of the Navy. Immediate action was necessary "if any expedition is to be sent out to relieve the men who have been there in northern cold and darkness for two years." Referring it to the Committee on Appropriations now, Senator Hale warned, would involve delay which might defeat the purposes of the expedition.

One senator rose to say he saw no reason why the resolution should be referred to the Committee on Appropriations. Every member of the Senate was "perfectly familiar with the situation of Lieutenant Greely and his party."

The presiding officer interrupted the debate to explain that he had referred the resolution to the Committee on Naval Affairs because "the chief point in the measure was not so much the appropriation of money, which was, of course, necessary, as the methods to be provided for sending out an expedition."

Senator John J. Ingalls, Kansas Republican, asked if there was an amount specified in the resolution. Senator Hale replied that there was not a specific amount. "It cannot be told precisely how these vessels shall be fitted, where they shall be obtained." The question was one that could be safely left for the President to decide, he said. Pressing the point, Ingalls asked if Senator Hale could state what the probable expense would be.

Senator Hale could not so state, but reminded the Senate that this was the last expedition that could be sent. "Unless Lieutenant Greely and his party are found this summer, they will doubtless pass away and we shall never hear more of them."

Senator George G. Vest, Missouri Democrat, said he could not hear Senator Hale clearly—did he say this was the last expedition to be sent to the North Pole or the last to be sent to rescue Greely?

Senator Hale said this was the last opportunity to rescue Lieutenant Greely and his party. He believed that neither the War nor the Navy Department had any inclination to send any more such expeditions.

Nature guarded "the mysterious region" around the North Pole "with the most zealous solicitude," Senator Ingalls said. "Expedition after expedition has followed into that dangerous and tempting region with simply one result, and that is an absolute failure to discover any of the mysteries that are alleged there to exist, and with a loss of life that is appalling to contemplate."

Senator Ingalls was not willing to commit Congress "to the declaration that any amount of money that may be thought necessary shall be spent by the executive officer of that Department without limitation upon an errand that is understood in advance to be fruitless and hopeless." Congress should declare that such expeditions as Greely's should cease. Anyone desiring to penetrate the northern regions should do so at his own peril and expense. Humanity did not require the Congress "to send men from the Navy or to permit volunteers to be allowed to go there year after year to know that the only result will be disaster and death."

How did they know, Senator Ingalls asked, that there would not be a new request next year for another rescue expedition to find this rescue expedition?

Senator Hale replied at length describing the wonderful story of the Greely expedition and the failure of subsequent ships to supply or relieve Greely's party. Until it was established, as far as possible, that the effort was hopeless, he was in favor of attempting rescue; but the question raised by Senator Ingalls was one for the future. The problem now was a question of doing something for Greely's party.

Senator Hale pointed out that the kind of ships recommended by the Secretary of the Navy were rare. There were only a few such ships in the world. They varied in value from $75,000 to $140,000 each.

Senator William P. Frye, also a Maine Republican, disagreed with Senator Hale's contention that there was no time to build the ships. There was a shipyard in Maine which could build all three ships in sixty days, he declared.

Senator Ingalls then moved to put a limitation of $1,000,000 in the proposed resolution. Senator Hale said that amount was very much larger than the cost anticipated by the Secretary of the Navy or the Secretary of War.

Senator Francis M. Cockrell, Missouri Democrat, then moved to make the limitation $100,000. Senator Hale objected that the amount would be "utterly inadequate." Senator Cockrell retorted: "If $100,000 will not do I should like the Senator to give us some idea as to whether $150,000 will do or $200,000. Let us know something about what we are appropriating." Senator Hale replied that the cost might run close to a half-million dollars.

Senator Cockrell moved to make the limitation $500,000. The debate continued for some time over the amount of money estimated for the expedition and whether a limitation should be included in the resolution. Senator Omar D. Conger, Michigan Republican, who had been so instrumental in promoting the Greely expedition, reminded the Senate that this project had originated in Congress, that the United States was not alone in sending out such an expedition but had co-operated with other governments. He pointed out that the world would not permit the Greely party to be forgotten. "This government may fail to send a suitable expedition for their relief," Senator Conger said, "but there are other governments that will send an expedition if we do fail, and fail to send a sufficient one, to the dishonor and disgrace of this Republic."

The presiding officer then put the question to the Senate on limiting the appropriation to $500,000.

The Senate divided equally—ayes, 22; noes, 22. The presiding officer declared the motion lost and then put the question on limiting the appropriation as proposed by Mr. Ingalls to $1,000,000. This motion failed—ayes, 8; noes, 26.

Still another attempt was made to insert a limitation in the resolution, an amendment was offered limiting the amount to $700,000, but this too was lost—ayes, 18; noes, 28.

Senator Hale might have felt at this point that the resolution was going to be passed by the Senate without amendment and the President would soon have the proposal before him for signature. However, Senator Eli Saulsbury, Delaware Democrat, rose to insist that the expedition should be composed only of volunteers. He did not believe than any man should be ordered to take part in this dangerous expedition. Senator Hale offered no objection. Without debate, the Senate promptly approved the amendment and then passed the resolution as amended.

The following day the Senate amendment to the resolution was considered by the House of Representatives. Congressman Randall told the House that he was "advised that it may embarrass the officials of the government in the management of the expedition." He moved that the House should not concur with the Senate amendment. The Randall motion was adopted by the House.

The following day the failure of the House to concur was reported to the Senate. It then became necessary to appoint a conference committee to meet with a conference committee of the House. Five days passed before the conference committees of each House were able to report on their discussions. On January 30 the committee recommended to the Senate that the proposal be adopted without the amendment requiring that the expedition be composed of volunteers.

Objections were immediately made to the recommendation. Senator John Sherman, Ohio Republican, declared that it was "wrong and unjust to place it in the power of anyone to order an officer of the Navy to go on an expedition that is certainly outside the line of his duties."

Senator Saulsbury, who had introduced the amendment, also voiced his objection. He had no doubt that there were officers and men who would gladly volunteer for the duty. But he was unwilling to give the Secretary of the Navy power "to punish any officer of the Navy by assigning him to a duty which he was unwilling to perform, when others would have been glad and willing to take the position." He did not know that the Secretary would have any such feeling but he was not willing to give him such power.

Pleading with the Senate to adopt the resolution as originally presented and to recede from this amendment, Senator Hale presented the views of the Secretary of the Navy. Secretary Chandler wrote:

> This is not to be a scientific exploring expedition, but one to rescue men who were deliberately sent out by the government with promise of reenforcement or rescue, and are now perhaps starving or freezing.
>
> Without the limitation, volunteers can be accepted if it is desirable but if none offer by the time the expedition is ready, are the ships not to move? If there are naval officers better qualified to go than any who may volunteer, shall the lives of the explorers, old and new, be trusted to the inferior men? In my judgment, Congress,

while giving the President for the relief of Greely the money of the government without limit, should also give him all its powers.

The officers of the Navy do not, I believe, desire to be protected by statute from orders on any honorable service, however perilous.

Senator Hale argued at length in support of the views of Secretary Chandler. He did not deny that the relief mission was a dangerous one. Any officer who declined to serve on such a mission, Senator Hale declared, should not remain in the Navy. If the Senate adopted the idea of permitting an officer to decline dangerous service the country would never have a Navy that would do it honor. "No such spirit as that," Senator Hale stated, "would ever have given to the American Navy its Paul Joneses, its Decaturs, its Farraguts and the two Porters."

Senator Ingalls then rose to object with heavy sarcasm to the recommendation that the Senate recede from its amendment. The Senate was to be congratulated, he said, in having committees which were so courageous, so persistent. The amendment had been adopted by the Senate without a single objection and now the conference committee returned to tell the Senate that the House "insisted squarely that they would not consent to any amendment whatever to the bill that they had passed and sent to us."

Senator Ingalls thought that sometimes the Senate might insist. "It would be a refreshing novelty; for if there has been an important amendment adopted by the Senate to any bill coming over from the House making appropriations for the last two years that has not been abandoned, I do not recall it." He thought it was time for the Senate to show a little of that courage "which the Senator from Maine tells us has been exhibited by the Navy in their efforts in incur the dangers and perils and hazards of the deep." The report of the conference committee should not be agreed to, he said. The insistence of the House on its views was an affront to the Senate.

Senator Hale replied that he did not think that Senator Ingalls, "by one of those characteristic attacks of his on a subject matter that is passing along satisfactorily, is going to inflame the Senate into believing that we are at the point of surrendering our rights and the prerogatives of this body to the other branch." There would be times when the Senate would insist and the House would yield. There would be other times where the House would insist and the Senate would yield. The amendment had been adopted in a hurry without full consideration. He saw no danger to the prerogatives of the Senate.

The Chair interrupted to announce that the hour had arrived for the Senate to proceed to the House of Representatives for the funeral of the late Representative Mackey. Once more action on rescue for the Greely expedition was put off.

The conference committee report was taken up again by the Senate the next day, January 31. The debate raged back and forth along the lines it had followed the day before. Opponents of the conference report argued against relinquishing the rights of the Senate to the House or to the executive department. Much oratory poured forth about the devotion to duty of the officers of the Navy, their courage and their willingness to accept dangerous service. Previous disasters were recalled and the tragedy of the *Jeannette* expedition was discussed. It was clear that the Senate was closely divided. Eventually ayes and nays were called for. To accept the conference report there were 25 ayes and 27 nays. Twenty-four senators were absent. The report was rejected. For a moment it might have seemed the rescue proposal was dead. But a determined senator was still fighting.

The presiding officer was about to pass over to the next item of business when Senator Hale interrupted and asked for another conference on the amendment proposed by the Senate. This motion brought forth new debate on whether the Senate should insist upon a limitation to the appropriation for the expedition. Senator John R. McPherson, New Jersey Democrat, declared that it would be better to let the joint resolution be considered lost and that a new measure with a limit on the appropriation be passed. This action could be taken in one hour and no objection would be raised if the limitation were included in the measure. Congress should not hand the Secretary of the Navy a blank check. Senator McPherson said, "I wish here distinctly to state without any reservation whatsoever that the Secretary of the Navy does not seem to comprehend that all the people have not implicit confidence in him or his methods." Senator William B. Allison, Iowa Republican, reminded Senator McPherson that the resolution came to the Senate, not from the Secretary of the Navy, but from the House of Representatives and that the House was controlled by Senator McPherson's [Democratic] party. Senator McPherson replied that he was not bound by the action of the House. He held a commission from the people of New Jersey to "guard the Treasury against invasions like this."

A discussion then ensued about the parliamentary situation if the Senate should refuse to appoint another conference committee. Senator McPherson asserted his belief that the joint resolution would then be dead. Others declared that the resolution would not be dead.

Senator Sherman pointed out that the House membership had never had an opportunity to vote by yeas and nays upon the amendment suggested by the Senate. He knew that Senator McPherson did not intend it but "in parliamentary law it is a discourteous proceeding" to refuse a conference. Senator Sherman said he objected to receding from the Senate's amendment on grounds different from those held by Senator McPherson. Service on this expedition, he felt, was not "within the legitimate line of duty of an officer of the Navy and, therefore, if we desire it to be done it should be done by volunteers as a matter of professional duty or as a matter of pride or to gain a reputation."

Senator McPherson said promptly that he had no intention of being discourteous to the House of Representatives but he was anxious to take some action to place a limitation on the money to be expended for the expedition. He would agree to another conference committee. At the proper time he would again attempt to put a limitation on the appropriation.

The motion for another conference committee was adopted by the Senate unanimously.

Another conference and more delay.

Senator Hale, pressing for action, arranged a meeting of the conference committee within the next few days. However, the House committee still refused to accept the Senate amendment. On February 8, Senator Hale submitted to the Senate a report that the conference committee was unable to agree. He asked unanimous consent to have the report considered immediately by the Senate. There was no objection. We can be sure that Senator Hale had been busy conferring with the Secretary of the Navy and with his fellow senators who had been raising objections.

Senator Hale warned that if nothing further were done

the proposal to rescue Greely would fail. The Senate had insisted upon its amendment, Senator Hale reminded his colleagues, because of their belief that the Secretary of the Navy should not be given the power to force officers or men to sail on this dangerous voyage. Time had provided a means of meeting the Senate objection, he said. The Secretary of the Navy had advised that he planned to get around the difficulty by providing that the crew be volunteers. Secretary Chandler also had stated that there would be no difficulty in getting superior officers to volunteer for this mission.

Under such circumstances, Senator Hale said, he thought the House might well have accepted the Senate's amendment. However, the House conference members insisted that the President should be given all necessary powers to carry out the execution of the mission. Therefore, Senator Hale asked the Senate (since the purposes of its amendment had been achieved) to recede from insisting upon formal adoption of the amendment. He begged the Senate not to let the matter "hang suspended, because every day adds certainly to the danger of this expedition being another failure. There is no time to spare. Each twenty-four hours is important. . . ."

It was a curious situation. The Democratic House had expressed its confidence in a Republican President. Senator Hale was pleading with a Republican Senate to do the same.

The presiding officer pointed out to Senator Hale that the question was "not regularly before the Senate"; all that the Senate had before it was a report of the conference committee that it had failed to agree.

Senator Hale replied that he had very little "knowledge of the parliamentary rules applicable in this body. It seems to me that in the emergency—that the Senate has voted and has agreed to consider the bill so that it is now before the Senate—we may very well and very reasonably waive any point as to the action of the House."

The presiding officer again stated that the bill was not formally in the possession of the Senate. True, the document was attached to the conference report and was actually on the desk of the presiding officer. Nevertheless, it was his opinion that the proposal was "in the parliamentary possession of the House of Representatives."

Senator Ingalls rose to support the Chair. Since the bill was in the parliamentary possession of the House of Representatives, it could not properly be made the subject of a motion in the Senate. The proper procedure for Senator Hale to follow, he said, was to ask an expression of the Senate as to whether it would recede from its amendment. If the Senate would so recede, then Senator Hale should ask for another committee of conference so that the Senate could so instruct the House as to its new position. The bill then could be properly transmitted to the Senate and placed before that body for action.

Senator Ingalls said he had heard much talk of the emergency nature of this action and the need for unlimited discretion to be given to the Secretary of the Navy and the President. He had read in the papers in the past two days that the Secretary of the Navy had already purchased a British ship and that the command of the expedition had been offered to one or two officers. Perhaps there was an emergency, Senator Ingalls said, of a different kind.

"If the action of Congress is not necessary at all; if fleets are to be purchased and expeditions organized while measures are undetermined, then it is a matter for consideration whether there is not, as the Senator from Maine said, an emergency that we should take into consideration," Senator Ingalls declared.

Senator Hale replied that the Secretaries of War and of Navy had "personally taken the responsibility" of obtaining the necessary ships, "but I can inform the Senator from Kansas and the body that the government has not been committed." Neither the Secretary of War nor the Secretary of the Navy proposed to commit the government without due authority. There were few ships in the world fitted for dangerous arctic navigation. Such ships were already being prepared to begin their annual voyages. If arrangements were not made to purchase the ships, they might sail before Congress had completed its action and the government was able to buy them.

Senator Hale and other supporters of the resolution were becoming restless and irritated by the repeated obstructions they were meeting. Doubtless, to them, the parliamentary objections made by opponents of the bill seemed merely dilatory. Men's lives were at stake and some senators appeared to be indifferent to the emergency nature of the measure before the Senate. Whether or not the House had taken the proper action, Senator Hale declared, the bill was in the Senate "and it seems to me that there ought to be a way by which the Senate can agree to take some action upon it, so that it may be known what its attitude is." Senator Hale appealed to the conscience of the objecting senators by declaring, "If Lieutenant Greely is to be left to perish with his followers, I hope they may die in a parliamentary manner."

The remark must have stung some of those who were objecting, but Senator Ingalls was impervious. He continued his protest that the Senate was being forced to relinquish its prerogatives, that the Secretary of the Navy was dominating the legislative body, that Congress was not performing its proper function but was delegating its authority to the executive branch.

At last the presiding officer expressed his view that "the regular thing to do would be to return the bill to the House of Representatives with the statement that the Senate is unable regularly to consider the matter which is pending between the two Houses until the House shall have acted again on the amendment of the Senate." After the House had restated its disagreement, the bill could then properly be transmitted to the Senate for action. Senator Hale expressed his concern about getting involved in too many technicalities but declared that he wanted to do the proper thing so that action could be taken.

Senator Ingalls then became involved with the Chair about the parliamentary situation. He pointed out that the Senate had a conference committee report. The Chair replied, "But the report, unhappily, is only a report that there is no agreement." It was still a report, Senator Ingalls insisted, and that was the end of it in a parliamentary sense. The Chair responded that it was "the end of it until the House again acts on the amendment of the Senate. The want of action there is what makes the difficulty."

This kind of parliamentary debate went on for some time longer, but eventually the Senate agreed to the suggestion of the presiding officer that the measure be returned to the House with a message that the Senate could not act until the House had voted on the proposal again.

A few days later, on February 11, the House swiftly and without objection reaffirmed its disagreement to the amendment of the Senate. The message was received by the Senate the same day and Senator Hale moved for immediate consideration.

Once more the Senate went over ground that it had covered several times before. The question of volunteers, of a limit on the appropriation, of the prerogatives of the

Senate, of the unwarranted action of the executive branch, the unyielding attitude of the House of Representatives— all these were once more put forth by opponents of the measure.

At one point the debate took off on a tangent. A Democratic senator, anticipating future disagreement between the two chambers on another measure, challenged Senator Hale. Would he display the same "cordial yielding, humble attitude" toward the Revenue Reform Tariff Bill that the Senate could expect from the House? Wisely ignoring the bait, Senator Hale pleaded for a vote on the measure before the Senate.

Senator Saulsbury argued that the Senate should not recede from its amendment. He was in favor of relieving the Greely party if it could be done. The two Houses of Congress would bring in a proper bill if it were possible. "A bill has come to us," Senator Saulsbury said, "without a single limitation upon the power of the Secretary of the Navy to enter the vaults of the Treasury of the United States and take *ad libitum* any amount of money that he may see proper while we are here in session charged with the duty of appropriating money."

Senator M. C. Butler, South Carolina Democrat, objected that the Secretary of the Navy had no such power. The President was given entire control. Here was a Democratic senator defending the Republican administration against the challenge of another Democratic senator.

"Oh, let the Senator from South Carolina talk if he will about the President of the United States," Senator Saulsbury exploded. "Does he not act through the heads of departments, does he not act through the Secretary of the Navy? The Senator certainly tried to perpetrate a joke upon the Senate when he made that suggestion."

"No," Senator Butler declared. "I assure, my friend, I

did not try to perpetrate a joke. I am in dead earnest."

At last it seemed the Senate had expended all its energy. The proponents had made their case for the bill. The opponents had presented their objections. It was now time for a decision on the rescue of the Greely expedition. The presiding officer called for the vote. The roll was called and the result announced—ayes, 29; nays, 22; absent, 25.

The motion to recede from the amendment was, therefore, adopted. Congress had reached agreement on the proposal for the rescue of Lieutenant Greely and his men.

It had been a strenuous time for Senator Hale and others who were working for this action—strenuous and tense. There were so many places and so many ways this resolution could have been blocked or lost.

The proposal for the Greely rescue expedition was an extraordinary measure. There was validity to the charge that it gave "a blank check" to the Secretary of the Navy, but Congress recognized that it was an extraordinary situation. There was an especially hazardous job to be done. The public was demanding that the job be done. Secretary Chandler wanted to do the job. Therefore, Congress voted him, via the President, the authority to spend the money necessary to do the job.

It had taken three conference committees, and we can only guess how many informal private conferences, to arrange for agreement on the measure. Partisan differences and other obstacles were overcome. By its usual standards, Congress had acted in swift fashion.

It had taken the executive branch more than four months—from September 13 to January 17—to decide on a recommended course of action. Congress had made its decision in twenty-two days.

The American people are often impatient with their

seemingly slow-acting Congress. There was soul-searing sarcasm in Senator Hale's acid comment that he hoped Lieutenant Greely and his men would "die in a parliamentary manner." But legislators in both parties and in both Houses were aware of the need for action and were sensitive to public sentiment. Mrs. Greely and her friends had done an effective job. Congressional leaders knew it was not necessary to violate the rules of procedure. When a majority of Congress is determined to take action, Congress can act speedily.

The rescue proposal had been received by Congress on January 17. It was passed on February 11. The next week the President signed the bill.

Now the expedition could be organized and the ships go north.

CHAPTER ELEVEN

THE LONG DARK WEEKS AND
THE FIRST DEATH

The trip to Isabella proved to the Greely party that there would be no extended trips made during the coming dark weeks. They were facing their third winter in the Arctic. They were long experienced in arctic travel, but they no longer had the strength which was theirs during the first two years.

The men who had made the rescue trip to Isabella were almost without strength for days following. Their condition, Henry recorded, "was indeed pitiful to see." On their return he wrote: "The men sank exhausted upon their damp bags and laid like logs for a considerable length of time; nor were any of them fit or able to stir about for the next week." One exception was Sergeant Brainard who two days later resumed his regular duty as commissary sergeant, and on the following day, November 15, worked with a few of the other men strengthening the walls of the commissary storehouse with snow blocks.

The work was made necessary by a new danger which threatened their security. Brainard had discovered that someone had broken into the commissary the night before.

Elison was slowly showing some signs of improvement. When he had been first brought into the hut it was discovered that his feet and legs were badly frozen almost to the knees. His hands, wrists, and nose were also so badly frozen that they appeared, in Biederbick's words, "like a piece of ice."

Elison was placed on a mattress covered with a sheep-skin sleeping bag which had been cut open. Three woolen blankets were placed over the frozen man. Dr. Pavy and Biederbick set about to thaw his frozen limbs. They used pieces of cloth soaked in cold water and gradually raised the water to warmer temperature. Biederbick was at Elison's side changing the cloths periodically for the first twenty-one hours until the limbs were completely thawed. Then Dr. Pavy and Biederbick took turns doing twelve-hour tours of duty caring for their patient.

During the first few days of this treatment Elison suffered severe pain in his hands and feet. The treatment seemed effective, however, and Dr. Pavy was soon able to report to Lieutenant Greely that it was barely possible that amputation would not be necessary.

The commanding officer was one of those whose physical condition was so weakened that he was able to do little if any outside work. But, indeed, there was little outside work to be done. Greely was concerned about the spirit of the party "during the weary time now upon us." Most of the men now were remaining almost continually in their sleeping bags.

In an effort to maintain the morale of the party, Greely decided "to give, daily, a lecture, of from one to two hours in length, upon the physical geography and the resources of the United States in general; followed later by similar talks on each state and territory in particular." Greely's talks were later supplemented by those of others in the party who discussed personal experiences or geography of places with which they were familiar. In the evening there were readings from the few books that were brought from Fort Conger and from the *Army Register* left in the cache by Lieutenant Garlington.

The manner of their days was described by Brainard in his diary on November 21:

> The routine of life in this wretched hut is as follows: the cooks are called at six a.m., breakfast is usually ready at seven and eaten sitting up in our sleeping bags. This over and while the cooks are cleaning up, conversation becomes general. Favorite subjects are cookery and the good dishes which we remember to have partaken of in the past.
>
> Between nine and eleven Lieutenant Greeley discourses on the geography of the United States. I then go out and issue provisions to the cooks for the following day. One of the others goes to the lake to cut a hole through the ice and provide water for cooking. It is also this man's duty to empty the large urinal tub kept in the alley.
>
> At two-thirty the cooks light their fire for dinner, and about four o'clock the meal is served. We then sit up and converse on all sorts of subjects till six, when the readings begin. We usually retire between eight and nine o'clock.

An especially good meal, Brainard wrote, was "stewed sealskins and fox intestines, thickened with moldy dog biscuit. Nothing in our cuisine department is ever wasted, not even the cleanings of fox intestines."

Of the rotten dog biscuit which was used to thicken their stews, Brainard said: "The meanest cur in the streets would have refused it, but to us it is life."

In his diary on November 21 Brainard also recorded the invalid list:

Lieutenant Kislingbury, rupture, is now convalescent.
Henry, toe frostbitten very bad.
Elison, extremities frozen, lower limbs to knees, condition
    critical.
Gardiner, felon on forefinger, improving slowly.
Linn, rheumatism, and system broken down from recent
    exposure; his mind also affected.

Biederbick, felon on forefinger, condition doubtful.
Salor, lame back, but able to go out occasionally.
Connell, very weak from reduced diet.
Cross, frosted foot is improving.
Bender complains frequently of soreness in his chest and
lame joints.

Despite the arctic night, Long and Eskimo Fred were out almost every day hunting. Several times a week a fox would be brought in, always giving great joy to the party, for that night the fox's intestines would be added to the stew. All agreed that this added greatly to the flavor. When Long was not hunting with Eskimo Fred, he served as cook. Greely had divided his command into two messes. Long cooked for one and Shorty Frederick cooked for the other. The trials of the cooks were sympathetically described by Brainard:

The poor cooks retired early this evening, both ill from constant inhaling of smoke from the damp burning wood. While the meals are being prepared, the hut is filled with a dense smoke which nearly suffocates us. All except the cooks can protect themselves by crawling down in their sleeping bags, but they are obliged to stand over the fire blowing it continually and thus suffer such misery and discomfort as can scarcely be appreciated by others. . . . We are all more or less unreasonable, and I only wonder that we are not all insane. All, including myself, are sullen, and at times very surly. If we are not mad, it should be a matter of surprise. I wonder if we will survive the horrors of this ice-prison.

Greely was well aware of the psychological as well as the physical dangers that his men faced. He knew of the Spitzbergen party lost in the Arctic during the dark winter which had perished, although well supplied with food, because of severe psychological depression brought on by the isolation and darkness. For diversion and mental stimulation he had planned the lectures and the reading. The routine of their daily menu would be broken on Sundays by a hardtack pudding (a "son of a gun"), a mixture of hard bread, raisins, canned milk, and seal blubber. This pudding, strangely enough, was regarded not only as "most delicious" but, perhaps more important, quite filling. Brainard reported: "All during the entire week, we look forward to this satisfying dish with pleasant expectations." Greely also provided that holidays and birthdays would be observed to the limit of their meager supplies.

The commanding officer was continually plagued by the problem of deciding the minimum of food which would provide their daily diet and still keep them alive. Elison's tragic experience added to the problem. Dr. Pavy urged a very large increase in the ration provided to Elison. The commanding officer had to weigh the special need of the injured man against the continuing need of the rest of the party. Greely compromised by ordering an increase for Elison of four ounces of bread and four ounces of meat; thus Elison was getting eight ounces of meat and ten ounces of bread daily. However, to provide this it was necessary, Greely decided, to reduce the rations for the rest of them slightly. Henceforth, each man would receive daily four ounces of meat and six ounces of bread. Greely took some satisfaction in noting that no one said anything in opposition to this decision. There seemed to be general recognition that Elison had suffered for all of them, that his helpless condition was a result of an act of self-sacrifice; therefore, all of them were willing to deny themselves a little for Elison's benefit.

For Thanksgiving, Greely provided an extra issue of rations. The cooks were given six pounds of rice, five pounds of raisins, two pounds each of extract of coffee and chocolate, and two pounds of milk. A double ration of coffee for breakfast served to start the day off well for all. The main meal of the day was a fox stew with bacon followed by rice pudding, chocolate, and seven ounces of hard bread. Shorty Frederick, with an issue of twenty-five gills of rum and twelve lemons, in Greely's words, "under skillful manipulation, gave us the most delicious punch we had ever tasted."

The whole effect of the day seemed to be one of spiritual and psychological uplift. Greely felt that the Psalms made a deeper impression than ever before. In the evening, following the punch, the time was devoted to songs and stories which kept them all entertained until midnight. They went to sleep that night happier and with more hope than they had known for many weeks. In short, the observation of Thanksgiving Day was a thorough success.

The exhilaration of Thanksgiving Day was followed by a period of dullness. A snowstorm blew up and added to the discomfort of the group huddled in the hut. A drip from the roof, snow drifting in, and the temperature falling—all served to lower their spirits. The storm increased in violence and continued through December 2. The snow continued blowing into their hut until there were eight inches in the passageway and on the bottoms of the sleeping bags. They worked for hours clearing the snow from the hut. Then the cooks attempted to prepare their meal. The heat from the cooking lamps melted snow remaining in the hut and the cooks were wet from melted snow on the floor and from the ceiling.

The violent wind had also tossed the ice around in Smith Sound. Open water could be seen as far north as Cape Albert. Their hopes of crossing to Littleton Island by sledge over the frozen sound were diminished because of the storm.

The crankiness of all of them was typified by Bender's complaint that he had not been treated fairly in the distribution of bed clothing. Most of them were irritated, feeling that Bender had already received more than others. Greely answered the complaint by giving Bender one of the blankets from his own sleeping bag. This served to annoy Jewell and Israel who shared the sleeping bag with the commanding officer. Bender was also given part of another blanket and a buffalo overcoat which had been found in the wrecked cache.

A more serious problem was discovered on the night of December 4. Greely, lying awake stewing over their situation, heard bread being taken from Elison's bread can. He was certain the thief was Dr. Pavy. He was shocked that the doctor could stoop to stealing from his helpless patient, but he was uncertain of what course to take. Accusing the doctor would only bring forth a denial and bitter argument. The doctor's services were essential to the survival of all of them. Greely restricted himself to informing Lockwood and Brainard of the doctor's thievery.

The dark days went on. They were settling into a regularity, indeed a monotony, that was changed only by advancing weakness and increasing difficulties. Greely continued his daily lectures, now going over the states one by one, each day lecturing on a new state. The evening readings were designed to provide variety in readers and subject matter. Gardiner would read a chapter or two from the Bible. Jewell would read a chapter of Pickwick, and Greely, characteristically, would read selections from the *Army Register*. Sergeant Rice cheered them all one evening with a vivid description of a year he had spent on a tropical island in the Gulf of Mexico. Another diversion for them was provided by Lieutenant Lockwood. He asked each man to describe his favorite menu. Lockwood copied each of the menus in shorthand. Then the menus were written out and each man given a copy. They agreed if they were able to escape from the Arctic that each of them, on his next birthday, would follow the menu he had dictated to Lockwood.

Their spirits were raised by the continuing success of the hunters in getting foxes. Long went out almost every day and several times a week returned with a fox. Occasionally Brainard, also, went out. Early in December their luck was especially good when Long and Brainard shot five foxes in four days. On December 8 Brainard was able to confide to his diary with both pride and modesty, "Tonight I killed two blue foxes at the same time. Rather good for darkness and indifferent marksmanship."

Greely's optimism was increased by a report of Dr. Pavy that Elison's feet would not be lost, although part of one hand would be. Elison was rather cheerful, talking frequently and, since his face had healed, he was even able to smoke occasionally. The doctor's optimism, however, was not shared by Hospital Steward Biederbick. His inspection of Elison showed a clear line of demarkation just above the ankle, on the left hand, at the base of the fingers, and on the right hand below the second joint of the fingers. Biederbick told Lockwood privately that Elison would lose both feet and part of his hands at the line of demarkation.

The miserable condition under which the party was living began to be reflected more frequently in their daily behavior. On one occasion Gardiner spoke privately to Greely to say that he objected to having to pass food to Sergeant Rice. Gardiner knew the cooks were fair, but when the plate passed through his hands he could not help sensing the weight and later comparing it with the weight of the plate of food given to him. He knew this was petty, he told Greely, "but I just can't help it." The only excuse Gardiner could offer was their miserable starving condition. Greely could understand Gardiner's feeling and, in fact, had avoided handling another man's plate for the very same reason.

In the absence of exercise it was difficult for the men to maintain a healthy mental attitude. They had little inclination to leave the comparative warmth of the hut for the cold gale that they so frequently met when they left their shelter. One daily duty, emptying the urinal tub and bringing water for the cooks, was rotated among the men. Other outside duties were most frequently performed by Sergeant Brainard, repairing the vestibule or the storehouse when damaged by storm, bringing in the food from the storehouse, chopping open the water hole when it was frozen over. One day Sergeant Brainard worked for four hours repairing the vestibule. Near the end of that time, he was overcome by dizziness and started to faint. He fell against the sledge and held onto it until he had recovered.

When Brainard came back in the hut, Greely spoke to him.

"Sergeant Brainard, come here, please."

Brainard crawled down the narrow center passageway, past the feet of the men on either side, to Greely's sleeping bag. Brainard stretched out alongside the lieutenant while Greely said softly, "Sergeant, I am obliged to remind you that I have ordered you to do no other work than the issuing of our food. You have been repeatedly overworking yourself and I insist that you must not do it."

"But, Lieutenant," Brainard whispered, "what is to be done? Look at them." He pointed to the row of figures stretched out in their sleeping bags with the flaps pulled down over their heads. "No one has much energy for the work and it must be done."

After a long moment, Greely said, "Yes, Sergeant." And Brainard crawled away to his own sleeping bag.

Greely was silenced. Each one, he thought, does the best he can. He could not criticize the apathy of the men when he himself felt too weak to do any of the hard physical labor.

On December 17, Brainard wrote:

> I cleared the snow from the vestibule this morning. No one was willing to assist except Rice. He is always ready to do as much for others as for himself. Long and Frederick are cooks for the two messes and, of course, are never allowed to perform any of the outside work. Unless some of the men exhibit more ambition, they will never be able to save their lives when we attempt to cross Smith Sound. I am very weak, but cannot refrain from working as long as I am able to move about.

Two days later Brainard recorded that when he asked for volunteers for odd jobs no one responded "except Rice, Salor, and occasionally Schneider. Cross saws and prepares wood for the cooks. We will need more energy than this in the party if we are to save ourselves."

The water hole was thickly frozen over and no one would volunteer to help the man who had the duty of hauling water that day. Greely himself went out to assist. He found himself so weak that his "work amounted to nothing except its stimulating and encouraging effects." The ever-dependable Brainard went to the assistance of his commanding officer and succeeded in breaking through the ice and getting water.

Because of the atmosphere in the crowded hut and his

growing weakness, Lockwood felt "an apathy and cloudiness impossible to shake off." He always found it difficult to decide how much hard bread to save for breakfast the next day, "hunger tonight fights hunger tomorrow morning." He wrote plaintively:

> I always eat my bread regretfully. If I eat it before tea, I regret that I did not keep it; and if I wait until tea comes, and then eat it, I drink my tea hastily and do not get the satisfaction I otherwise would. What a miserable life, when a few crumbs of bread weigh so on one's mind! It seems to be so with all the rest, all sorts of expedients are tried to cheat one's stomach, but with about the same result.

If they worried about their difficulties, they needed only to look at Elison and realize how lucky they were. Late in December, Brainard described Elison's feet as "black, shrunken and lifeless. His ankles are a horrible sight. The flesh has sloughed away, leaving the bones devoid of covering. He suffers much, but is very patient and bears his trouble with fortitude."

For Sergeant Brainard, December 21 was a double event. It was the day when the sun was farthest from them and began its journey back. It was also his twenty-seventh birthday. The arctic night was at its deepest but Brainard's spirits were given a lift by his commanding officer.

Greely, giving Brainard the half gill of rum extra to mark the day as was the custom, said, "Sergeant, I wish that we might be able to do more to help you celebrate properly. You have done extraordinary work for us this winter."

"Well, Lieutenant," Brainard said, "everyone is trying to do his best."

"I know," Greely said, "but your great endurance, your

good temper, your fairness in dealing out our food—these things, Sergeant, have been invaluable. I want you to know how deeply I appreciate your efforts."

As if to earn the tribute anew, Brainard went hunting a little later and shot at a blue fox. The fox escaped, although he was hit. Brainard, following the blood on the snow with a lantern, discovered the fox dead 250 yards away. He returned triumphant with the animal. The entrails would go into that night's stew, in accordance with Greely's rule, and the hunter would be given the heart and the liver. Greely added to the joy of all by announcing that this fox would be added to the allowance for Christmas dinner.

Everyone's spirits seemed to be picking up with the knowledge that the sun was now on its return journey to them. Lockwood wrote:

> The top of the hill, the most glorious day of the dreary journey to this valley of cold and hunger, has at last come, and now nearly gone. Thank God, now the glorious sun commences to return, and every day gets lighter and brings him nearer. It is an augury that we shall yet pull through all right. By a great effort I was able to save an ounce of bread and two ounces of butter for Christmas. I shall make a vigorous effort to abstain from eating it before then, and have put it in charge of Biederbick as an additional safeguard.

They struggled to hold onto their strength and strained to hang onto their sanity. Not everyone helped in that effort. A couple of days before Christmas, Whisler was showing strong evidence of the effects of the harsh conditions. Brainard noted: "Whisler has been particularly disagreeable today and not at all choice in his language toward his companions." At the slightest excuse, apparently, Whisler was inviting someone to come outside and fight. The invitations were ignored and possibly many of them felt as Brainard did: "Under the circumstances, he is not to blame for what he said."

The weather for Christmas Day was clear and calm but the temperature was down to thirty-five degrees below zero. Spirits, however, were rising among the little band in the stone hut on Cape Sabine. Once again Lieutenant Greely had provided for extra food to be issued to provide a holiday banquet. It was generally agreed at the beginning of the day that all would maintain a cheerful and congenial attitude; no one would do or say anything to spoil the happiness of the holiday. For Lieutenant Kislingbury it was a double holiday, for Christmas was his birthday. He was thirty-six years old.

The breakfast Christmas morning was a thin pea soup made with seal blubber and preserved potatoes. Later in the morning there was a serving of cloudberries, and at one-thirty Long and Frederick, the two cooks, began to prepare the Christmas feast. The main item on the menu was to be a stew made of seal blubber, preserved potatoes, bread, and pickled onions. This was to be followed by a rice pudding made with rice, raisins, seal blubber, and condensed milk. Finally, there was chocolate, followed by Frederick's special punch made of rum and lemon.

The determination to make this a perfect holiday spread throughout the group. Good feeling prevailed and there was much reminiscing of other holidays at home. Memories of happier occasions and more elaborate Christmas dinners were exchanged freely. Good will grew and blossomed. In Greely's words, "a general desire was expressed to heal over any old wounds or uncharitable feeling."

The entertainment for the evening began with a rereading of the records left by Lieutenant Garlington. The promise of rescue contained in those records had a special impact on Brainard. He went out and repaired the broken flagstaff which had been erected on the nearby peak over-looking the water. He returned to predict that Lieutenant Garlington would arrive to rescue them during the full moon in January. His optimistic prediction was supported by Dr. Pavy, Lieutenant Kislingbury, and some of the others. Such optimism, Greely noted privately, "I cannot participate in, but am reluctant to discourage." Garlington's records were followed by the reading of Henry Clay's letter which so accurately predicted their circumstances.

Next, each one was required to sing a song or tell a story. The music was varied. There were French, German, and English songs. Even the two Eskimos, Jens and Frederik, contributed, Brainard said, "their peculiar, sweet melodies and Danish songs."

Lieutenant Lockwood contributed a reading of the birth-day bills of fare which each of them had dictated to him the previous month.

The cup of comradeship overflowed. Cheers were called for, for Elison who had suffered so much, for the cooks who had provided them with this feast, for their com-manding officer, and for the respected and beloved Ser-geant Rice who would make the attempt to reach Little-ton Island early in February.

Writing glowingly of the events of the day in his diary, Brainard commented: "Much praise is due Lieutenant Greely for all the entertainment he manages to provide for us. The diversions keep us hopeful."

Lockwood, too, reported the happy occasion. Rereading his notes the following day he found them "very imper-fect," so he recorded more of the details to underline the pleasure that all had experienced on Christmas Day. Lock-wood was able to make the unusual report that "several of us ate too much yesterday." The Christmas celebration had filled them all with thoughts of home and the following day there was much discussion of home and family. Speaking of his enjoyable family reunions, Lockwood said, brought tears to his eyes. He spoke also of his sister and told his comrades "of Mary Murray, whose many virtues I eulogized highly."

The good will and the high spirits of the party were dissipated a couple of days later over a discussion about cooking with blubber instead of alcohol. The commanding officer felt that the use of blubber would extend their alcohol supply although it would, of course, reduce their food supply. Lockwood felt that blubber was more important as food than fuel. Greely and Lockwood, according to Brainard, had "a very disagreeable discussion." Brainard took this as a sign of Lockwood's "weakening" condition.

Sergeant Cross also showed signs of weakness and frequently was unable to attend to the duty of sawing wood.

Continued low temperatures added to their troubles by freezing the water hole with a heavy coating of ice. The work of cutting through the ice to get water exhausted those who had that duty.

The New Year was welcomed in with no other ceremony than that of the commanding officer's wishing them all a Happy New Year. On New Year's Day there was an issue of cloudberries and each man received an extra gill of rum and a quarter of a lemon. The temperature was down to thirty-two degrees below zero.

The frozen parts of Elison's limbs had so deteriorated that some of his fingers and his right foot were almost falling off. On January 2 Dr. Pavy removed the right foot simply by cutting a fragment of the remaining skin. Elison was not even aware that he had lost a foot. The following day Dr. Pavy removed one of Elison's fingers in a similar manner.

In the next week Brainard twice had to report to Greely that someone had stolen food from the storehouse. The first time a hole had been cut in the canvas roof and a piece of bacon had been stolen. Three days later Brainard discovered that one of the bread barrels had been broken with an ax and several pounds of bread were missing. Brainard told Greely he suspected who the man was but had no proof of it. When the theft became known, several of the men announced that they would give an ounce of bread from their own ration each day if the thief would cease stealing. The thief, of course, did not accept the offer.

Greely noted that Brainard was showing signs of weakness. He knew that the sergeant was working too hard, but that was Brainard's disposition. Greely was coming to depend more and more on Brainard. The commanding officer spoke to the sergeant and suggested that Brainard should receive an extra ounce of bread daily because of his extra duties. Brainard refused but told Greely that he would let the commanding officer know whenever he felt such an increase was necessary for the continuation of his extra duties.

Dr. Pavy was concerned about Cross's condition. He told Greely that Cross should not spend all his time in the sleeping bag but should get some exercise. The doctor also reported that Cross, Schneider, Linn, and Ellis all showed signs of scurvy. Lieutenant Lockwood was further weakened by diarrhea.

In the next several days Cross's scurvy became more marked. He also showed signs of mental weakness.

Still another problem was added to their difficulties. It was discovered that the water they were drawing from the lake was becoming salty. Apparently there was a direct flow of sea water into the lake. The loss of this source of fresh water meant that their precious fuel would have to be used to melt snow and ice. To extend their alcohol and blubber, they resorted to burning tar rope and boot soles. This provided them with heat, but also produced much smoke to irritate their eyes and add to their discomfort.

On January 16 Cross's weakness had so advanced that he was unable to walk. The following day, however, he seemed better and was able to go outside and split some wood for exercise.

About two o'clock the next morning Jewell awakened Greely with the news that Cross was in trouble. Greely lit the lamp and discovered that Cross was unconscious and had tried to crawl out of his sleeping bag. Dr. Pavy examined Cross and advised that some brandy and soup be given him immediately. With some difficulty they were able to get Cross to take this nutrition although he was not entirely conscious.

Cross hung on to the middle of the morning, never regaining consciousness. At 2 P.M., January 18, he died.

It was almost two and one-half years since this group had first faced the dangers of the Arctic. They had survived through cold, storm, and all the dangers of arctic exploration. Now, at last, the Arctic took the life of one of them. Inevitably they wondered how many more would be claimed before the sun returned, and rescuers were able to reach them.

Dr. Pavy, speaking in French, told Lieutenant Greely that Cross's death was due to scurvy, but to spare the feelings of the rest of the party the doctor described the cause as "a dropsical effusion of the heart" due to "insufficient nutrition." The euphemism was employed to avoid the word they all feared—"starvation."

Biederbick and Brainard prepared Cross's body for burial the next day by wrapping it in a large gunny sack.

In the dark, crowded hut Lieutenant Greely read the Episcopal burial service while the men were still in their sleeping bags. At noon, Lieutenant Kislingbury and six of the men dragged Cross's body on the sledge, covered by an American flag, to the top of a little hill at the end of the lake. Greely walked along behind the sledge. Because of the extreme cold and the scarcity of footgear, the funeral procession was limited to eight. A poor effort was made to dig a grave but the men were unable to make it deeper than fifteen inches. The usual volley for a military funeral was omitted. The ammunition could not be spared. Brainard described the scene:

> One cannot conceive of anything more unearthly— more weird and solemn—than this ghostly procession of emaciated men moving slowly and silently away from their wretched ice-prison in the uncertain light of the Arctic night, having in their midst a dead comrade about to be laid away forever in the frozen ground. It was a scene that I can never forget.

Brainard concluded his diary entry for that day with the cryptic comment that the bread ration had been increased to seven and one-half ounces. Here was the cold, bitter statistic of their existence. One mouth was gone, a little more food for the rest of them.

CHAPTER TWELVE

PROCURING THE SHIPS

When the President and Congress fight, the people of the United States sometimes despair, forgetting that this is the kind of democracy we have chosen for ourselves. Separation of powers or a division of authority almost inevitably means conflict. This conflict can, it is true, sometimes result in stalemate. At other times it may produce a restraint on executive action, a restraint that serves to keep the Executive from running too far ahead of popular will. Or the Executive, wisely using his position as national leader, may act so vigorously as to compel Congress to follow along with him.

The Executive is most frequently tempted to act in such a vigorous fashion when he is convinced of the need for avoiding delay and fully persuaded that he has the support of the substantial majority of the people. Such was the situation in the winter of 1883–84 in Washington. President Chester Arthur was at last convinced that the American people expected vigorous action for the rescue of the Greely expedition. The President knew Congress would have to act, but the President and Navy Secretary Chandler could not wait for Congress to debate, make up its mind, and finally take action. Ships had to be procured for the rescue expedition. Whaling or sealing ships were necessary for ice navigation. Ships of the United States Navy were not built for such work. Only the whaling and sealing ships of Dundee, Scotland, and St. John's, Newfoundland, were adequately prepared to face the ice of Baffin Bay and waters farther north.

The Dundee ships sailed at the end of January for St. John's. There they took on some additional crew and left for a sealing cruise along the coast of Labrador. In May they moved over to the waters off Cape Farewell, at the southern tip of Greenland. In June they moved up the Greenland coast and continued over to the west of Baffin Bay to Lancaster Sound.

Thus, once the President had made up his mind that a new expedition would be sent after the Greely party in the spring of 1884, he had to take action immediately to secure the ships for that attempt. In December questions were telegraphed to the United States consuls at St. John's and Dundee about the possibility of buying whaling vessels.

Such vessels were built of wood because of its greater elasticity. The ship's hull was thus better able to absorb pressure of ice. Ironwood sheathing covered the hull to protect it against jagged edges of the ice floes. A two-bladed screw propeller was fitted to the ship so that it could be raised in case of the vessel's being trapped in the ice. The bow of the ship was covered with iron plates which extended almost to midship.

The consul at St. John's, Mr. Molloy, replied to Washington that ships were already prepared to begin their sealing voyage and no owner would consider an offer of purchase. Some ship owners suggested that they would sell for delivery in May. This, of course, would be much too late to prepare the ship for the rescue of Greely. Fortunately, however, there was one ship, the steamer *Bear*, which had recently been completely overhauled at Greenock, Scotland, and was now on its way to St. John's. The *Bear*, a sister ship of the *Proteus*, was reported to be probably the best ship sailing out of St. John's. Mr. Molloy was instructed to negotiate for the purchase of the *Bear*.

In England attempts to purchase ships were made by Lieutenant Commander Chadwick, naval attaché at the United States Embassy in London. Chadwick was fortunate in having the co-operation and counsel of many English arctic explorers. Men who had successfully dared the dangers of the Arctic and who had left their names attached to capes and harbors and other bodies of land or water in the Far North, readily lent their assistance to Chadwick. This group included Sir George Nares, Sir Leopold McClintock, Captains Markham, Beaumont, and Aldrich, as well as Sir Leigh Smith and Sir Allen Young. At first, to avoid prohibitive increases in the price demanded for ships, the negotiations to purchase were handled by intermediaries. The intention was to keep secret the fact that it was the United States Government which was seeking the purchase. However, the plans of the United States for the rescue expedition were quickly a matter of general knowledge and such attempts at secrecy were immediately futile.

Chadwick's task was made more difficult by an increase in the price of whalebone. This price increase was reflected in the demand for whaling ships and Chadwick found himself in competition with private buyers.

There were about fifteen whaling ships sailing out of Dundee. Chadwick soon learned that the four best were the *Thetis*, the *Hope*, the *Resolute*, and the *Arctic*. The *Thetis*, the newest and best ship, was offered for sail at £27,000. The lowest price was for the *Hope*, for which £18,500 was asked. In the course of negotiations for the *Thetis*, the newest and best ship, was offered for sale at immediate delivery. After some discussion, however, Chadwick was able to obtain from the owners an offer to sell at £28,000.

During these weeks in late January, Congress was debating the question of a rescue expedition for Greely. The resolution which would provide for the purchase of the ships was tied up in a parliamentary tangle resulting from a division of opinion between the Senate and the House. The executive branch, aware of the necessities of the expedition and the complexities of the purchase of the ships, did not feel that it could wait for Congress to unravel its parliamentary tangle.

On January 23 Mr. Molloy at St. John's was instructed to purchase the *Bear* at $100,000 for delivery in New York.

When the purchase of the *Bear* became known in Washington, there was some general speculation about the legality of the action. The Secretary of War and the Secretary of the Navy were of the opinion that general authority existed for the purchase of the ship. But if such authority existed, why was Congress then debating the resolution for the purchase of the ships?

A newspaper reporter challenged Secretary Chandler about his action. What would the Secretary do, he was asked, if the resolution was not adopted by Congress? The Secretary replied, with mild humor, "I will, I suppose, become a part owner of a whaling ship."

Commitments had been made for the purchase of two ships. Chadwick in London was still seeking a third ship. With the skill and wisdom of a trained diplomat, Lieutenant Commander Chadwick on the morning of February 2 dropped in for a talk with Sir Cooper Key. In previous weeks Chadwick had obtained information about other vessels available in England suitable for Arctic navigation. He learned there were three such vessels, the *Pandora*, the *Discovery,* and the *Alert.* The *Pandora* was privately owned, but the *Discovery* and the *Alert* were in the service of the British Navy. The *Pandora* was found to be an excellent choice except that its engines were not powerful enough.

The *Discovery*, which Nares had sailed in 1875 through the very waters that Greely later navigated, was in use as a transport and could not be released by the Admiralty. The *Alert*, however, had been dismantled and was being considered for sale. The experienced arctic explorers all advised Chadwick that the *Alert* would be preferable to the *Pandora*. Accordingly, Chadwick decided upon an informal conversation with Sir Cooper Key.

In that talk on the morning of February 2, Chadwick made it clear that he had no specific instructions from Washington and could make no offer to the British Government. However, he believed there was a strong possibility that the United States Government would be interested in using the *Alert* for the expedition to rescue Greely.

The history of British diplomacy is often characterized by that familiar phrase "muddling through." It is a pleasure to report that in this instance the British Government demonstrated an ability to recognize the necessity of the situation and to act with a speed and a grace beyond comparison. The very evening of the day Chadwick had his conversation with Sir Cooper Key, James Russell Lowell, the American Ambassador in London, received a letter from the First Lord of the Admiralty:

February 2, 1884

Dear Mr. Lowell:

Commander Chadwick has mentioned, in conversation with Sir Cooper Key, that Her Majesty's ship, Alert, might be of use to the United States Government in an expedition to be dispatched in search of the expedition which is missing in the Arctic region. I write a line to say that we have not forgotten the very considerate conduct of the Government of the United States on the occasion of the recovery of the Resolute, and that if you should be instructed to make any suggestions through the usual official channels, that the Alert would be of any use to the United States Government, we shall be happy to ask you to accept her as a present.

Yours very sincerely,

Northbrook

Lowell was filled with gratitude at this splendid offer and immediately replied:

Legation of the United States,
February 2, 1884

My dear Lord Northbrook:

It is with an emotion for which the diplomatic phrase "peculiar satisfaction" is altogether too colorless, that I hasten to acknowledge the reception of your private note of yesterday, informing me of the offer by Her Majesty's Government of HMS Alert as a gift to the United States for the use of the Greely Relief Expedition. As I think the terms of your note more expressive than any that I could substitute for them, I shall this morning send a copy of it, in cipher, to Washington.

In the meanwhile I beg thus in advance to convey to you, and through you to Her Majesty's Government, the thanks of the President for this particularly timely and graceful recognition of that international courtesy which I trust will always characterize the intercourse of our respective countries.

Faithfully yours,

J. R. Lowell

After exchanges of communication between Lowell and Washington, the American Ambassador was instructed to make the request for the *Alert*.

Skilled diplomats of friendly countries had quickly recognized a common interest. In a single day, after an informal conversation and an exchange of personal notes, they reached an international agreement.

The passionate pleas of Mrs. Greely in San Diego had been heard, not only in Washington but across the seas in London.

CHAPTER THIRTEEN

HOPE RETURNS WITH THE SUN

After the death of Sergeant Cross on January 18, Greely watched the men carefully for its effect on their morale. They would face a great trial now, for Cross's death seemed but the first of several that were imminent. It would be a time of trial, too, for their commander. Greely knew his leadership would be tested even more severely. He could not feed their bodies but he would have to nourish their minds and their spirits. He had to keep alive in all of them the will to live and an interest in life.

Ellis, Jewell, and Lieutenant Lockwood were showing marked signs of depression. For some time Lockwood had been sharing Greely's sleeping bag. The commander found this "a great comfort to me mentally, although a tax upon my physical strength in assisting him to arise for meals and to change his position while in the bag."

Lockwood, in order to cease being a burden on Greely and to have the benefit of a little more sleeping room, returned to his own bag.

On the morning of January 21, Biederbick told Greely that he thought Lieutenant Lockwood was showing signs of mental weakness. Several times during the night Biederbick had heard Lockwood talking incoherently. That afternoon Lockwood crawled over to Greely's sleeping bag.

"Lieutenant Greely, I have something private I would like to say to you," Lockwood began.

"Of course, Lieutenant," Greely replied.

"I am in a very feeble condition. I have known for

several weeks that I am gradually breaking down," Lockwood said. "I have said nothing to you, Lieutenant Greely, for fear of the bad effect it would have upon the spirits of the party. I think I have improved slightly in the past day or two but I know I will never be able to cross to Littleton Island with you on March first, the day you propose leaving."

"That well might be," Greely broke in, "but in that case we will have to haul you as we will Elison."

"No, Lieutenant," Lockwood protested. "My weight added to the load you will have to carry will just destroy all of us. I want to ask you, Lieutenant Greely, as a favor to me that when the time comes to cross to Littleton Island, you leave me behind. You can leave me my share of the rations here. If there is a party at Littleton Island they can send a sledge for me before my food is gone. If there is no party over there we will all perish anyway."

"I am sorry," Greely replied sternly, "that you have such an estimate of my character as to make a proposition of that kind to me. As commanding officer of this expedition it is my duty to care for everyone in the party equally. If any favors are to be shown, or any sacrifices to be made, they will be done as we have done in the past, in favor of the sick and the helpless. I beg of you, Lieutenant, that you never mention such a subject to me again. I cannot think of abandoning any member of the party."

Greely, sensing that his sternness may have seemed harsh to Lockwood, continued, "I appreciate the sacrifice you offer to make, Lockwood, but to grant what you ask would be a change of policy that I cannot sanction. You know that I have persistently opposed any plan which indicates a desire to save part of our group at the expense of the rest. We must all work together and help each other."

After Lockwood returned to his sleeping bag, Greely realized he was quite shaken. The offer made by Lockwood had moved Greely deeply. Now the commander regretted that he had not insisted upon Lockwood's remaining to share his sleeping bag. Shaking off his own mood, the commanding officer turned to talk to Jewell who was extremely despondent over the death of Sergeant Cross. Greely spent a long time talking with Jewell and trying to inspire him with new courage.

Lockwood's decline deeply affected Sergeant Brainard. He confided to his diary:

> Lockwood is growing weaker and weaker. His fitful moods almost break my heart. As I watch him, tears gather in my eyes and there is a lump of sorrow which almost bursts my throat. That this should be the strong, daring and enthusiastic Lockwood with whom I went to the "Farthest."

Brainard could still remember the pride he felt when he was chosen as one of the party to accompany Lockwood on the sledge trip around the northwest coast of Greenland. The main party consisted of four sledges, a dog team, and ten men. The dash for the "Farthest North," however, and the attempt to reach the northernmost point of Greenland was made by Lockwood, Brainard, and Eskimo Fred. That memorable trip was made in the spring following their first winter in the Arctic. They started out from Fort Conger on April 3 with the temperature twenty-nine degrees below zero. During their first days of sledging the temperature fell lower. The third day out it dropped as low as forty-eight degrees below zero. Connell froze one of his toes while in the sleeping bag. Henry complained that he was suffering with rheumatism. Connell begged to be allowed to go on. In contrast, Henry warned that he would probably have to be hauled back to Fort Conger if he went any farther. Lockwood directed Henry to return and granted Connell's wish that he be permitted to continue.

After about an hour more of sledging, Connell was limping along so painfully that Lockwood concluded he would have to return to the station. Connell almost cried with disappointment.

Lieutenant Lockwood said, "Sergeant Brainard, you continue with the party. I will take Connell back as far as Cape Beechey on the fast dog sled. We ought to catch up with Henry at that point and Connell can return to Conger with Henry. I will catch up with you at tomorrow's camp."

When Lockwood caught up with them, he reported, "I took Connell back as far as Cape Beechey but we could not overtake Henry. In fact, we didn't even see him in the distance."

Brainard laughed, "That's certainly good sprinting for a man afflicted with rheumatism."

Day after day they moved farther north. As April passed into May the temperature rose with the sun. On April 17 Brainard noted:

> For the first time since daylight has been continuous, the sun did not disappear below the horizon at midnight. It dipped to the crests of the northern hills, rested there a short time, and then curving gradually upward resumed its course. It seemed such a queer thing for the sun to do.

On April 29 Lieutenant Lockwood dropped the supporting party and went on with Brainard and Eskimo Fred. They took a dog team, hauling provisions for twenty-five days. They were off on the last leg of their journey into the unknown.

At times they found smooth ice and the team and sledge moved ahead speedily. When they ran up against rough, hummocky ice they were forced to struggle, moving the sledge over the obstacles. If they ran into soft snow, the sledge runners sank into it, the dogs sat down, looked at the three men, and waited for the sledge to be lifted free. It was exhausting, frustrating work but they kept at it and, except during storms, they were able to keep moving north.

On May 10 they were stopped by a gale that lasted for three days. They spent the time repairing clothing, reading, sleeping, and rubbing their feet to stimulate circulation. When the gale subsided the sun came out briefly and they were able to take observation. In the northeast they could see a large dome-shaped promontory.

"If we can reach that point," Lockwood said, "I will be able to turn back satisfied with what we have accomplished."

Brainard said nothing. However, recording Lockwood's statement in his diary, he noted: "But our Lieutenant reaching one distant point has never yet been satisfied by just a glimpse of what lies ahead."

In that one line we can read so much of Brainard's affection and admiration for his companion on the trip to the "Farthest North."

They reached their goal the next day, May 13. Lockwood decided they would have to turn back or not have enough rations to sustain them on the return journey. They spent the day collecting geological and botanical specimens, mapping the area, sketching the profiles of mountains in the distance, and making latitudinal observations. They determined they were at 83° 24′ north. They were farther north than man had ever gone.

They built a large, conspicuous cairn and deposited a record of their journey in it. Then they climbed a small hill and there raised the flag that had been given the party by Mrs. Greely before their departure from the United States. Of this thrilling moment, Brainard wrote:

> We have reached a higher latitude than ever before achieved by mortal man, and on a land farther north than was supposed by many to exist. We unfurled the glorious Stars and Stripes to the exhilarating northern breezes with an exultation impossible to describe.

But the formal recording of their visit to the "Farthest North" was not sufficient. Brainard was moved by that irreverent spirit universal among American soldiers. He had never visited anywhere "without finding Plantation Bitters advertised conspicuously." On a slab in the face of the cliff he "carved the familiar characters: St 1860 X" ("Started trade in 1860 with ten dollars").

Watching Lockwood's decline in the hut at Cape Sabine, Brainard could recall painfully both the excitement and joy of their great sledge trip. Now the daring, courageous Lockwood, with whom Brainard had shared so much danger, was this near-skeleton who confessed weakly, "Brainard, I have lost my grip." Brainard fought to hold back tears as he thought, "It's true, too. He has lost the last hope of life."

To the threat of the growing despondency among the party was added the depressing news that twelve cans of milk had been stolen. Brainard's announcement of the theft stimulated intense bitter feeling among the group against the thief.

On January 21 Greely was happy to note that Lockwood's spirits had picked up. However, Jewell was still depressed and recalcitrant. He was reluctant to follow the doctor's orders and Greely had to tell him insistently that the doctor's orders must be obeyed. Greely also noted in his diary that Bender and Henry "were impudent and insubordinate in their language; the first instance of such spirit on the part of the enlisted men." However, in a couple of days he was able to report that the morale had risen substantially because of the increased rations. Striving to maintain the mental health of the party, Greely continued with the lectures and readings. He stimulated others, too, to contribute to the discussion program where they could.

Sergeant Brainard kept active and almost daily, when the weather permitted, he would be out to observe Smith Sound. It seemed to him that the sound was not freezing over, but for the sake of his comrades he kept his observations to himself. He thought it better "that their minds should remain in a hopeful state."

Sergeant Rice and Jens were to attempt the crossing of Smith Sound the first week in February. The little Eskimo was deeply touched that he had been chosen for this trip. Greely ordered that they be fed extra rations to increase their strength. Beginning January 26, Rice and Jens received each day a pound of bread and a pound of meat. Shorty Frederick and Schneider worked on the traveling gear of the two so they would be as well prepared as possible for the strenuous journey ahead of them. Privately, Greely regarded it as "a forlorn hope." The temperature had dropped to as low as thirty-six degrees below zero and the light from their returning sun was clearly noticeable in the sky. However, the frequent storms had tossed the ice back and forth in the channel and it seemed unlikely to Greely that the two brave souls would be able to make their way across to Littleton Island.

Most of the men believed that Lieutenant Garlington and his party were at Littleton Island with substantial supplies from the *Yantic*. Greely, regarding this as false optimism, emphasized that he hoped for nothing more than the discovery of a small cache. He did not believe that Garlington's record permitted them to hope for anything more. Even a small cache, he could not be sure of. The record left by Garlington reported a whaleboat at Cape Isabella, but it could not be found when Rice and his party made their trip to the cape.

Greely wrote letters for Lieutenant Garlington, General William Hazen, and for Mrs. Greely, all of which Rice was to take with him on his trip across the sound. The commanding officer also prepared a record of the expedition for Rice to leave in a cairn on Littleton Island if he found nobody there. He was given a list of rations and a list of medicines which the commanding officer and the doctor felt the group needed.

Rice, putting his own affairs in order, wrote a letter describing the disposition of his effects if he did not return. He crawled over to Kislingbury's sleeping bag.

"Lieutenant," Rice said, "take care of this for me will you?" He handed Kislingbury his diary and a note. In the dim light Kislingbury read the note.

Lt. Kislingbury—

Find letter addressed to you in back part of this book. Send copies of it to parties interested so that they may understand the position—rather embarrassing—in which I have placed you.

George W. Rice.

The lieutenant looked at Rice and said softly, "Certainly, George." They shook hands.

On February 1 all preparations for the journey were completed. If the weather permitted, Rice and Jens would leave the following morning in their attempt to find help at Littleton Island.

The cooks were up the next morning at 4:45 so that the two could leave early. Shorty Frederick and Brainard went out ahead carrying their packs to help Rice and Jens get off to a good start.

The packs weighed fifty pounds each, a very substantial load for men weakened by long days of a starvation diet and continual extremely low temperatures. Of the parting, Brainard wrote:

> A tremulous "God Bless You," a hasty pressure of their hands and we turned away in tears from those brave souls who are daring and enduring so much for us. We waited until their receding forms were lost to view in the bewildering confusion of the ice fields and then slowly retraced our steps to the hut.
>
> While watching their progress, I distinctly heard the hoarse grinding of the moving pack not far away. Of this I said nothing to my companions on returning.

Later in the day they saw clear signs of the sun which was expected to return to them within two weeks. The sky was so light that Henry was able to read the thermometer at noon by daylight. In the evening the temperature dropped to extreme cold and the mercury was frozen. The low temperature and the bright moonlight gave Greely hope that Rice and Jens would be able to make good progress.

The next day most of the talk was about Rice and Jens. The day was fine and the men were optimistic. However, in the evening the temperature rose from forty degrees below zero to eighteen degrees below zero, suggesting a threatening storm. To relieve the tension of the departure, Greely had ordered a special breakfast of the mixture they called a "son of a gun" made of lard, butter, and seal blubber. The richness of the dish seemed to affect Connell and Jewell. In the evening, coming in from outside, Jewell fainted in the passageway.

They could all notice the declining strength of the party, but in some it was more marked. Greely pressed them to keep up their spirits. The lethargy they all suffered was almost overwhelming. On Dr. Pavy's advice, Greely ordered the men during the daytime to keep their heads outside the sleeping bags. Too many of them were spending most of the day entirely covered up. Greely re-emphasized the importance of following strictly any instructions Dr. Pavy gave about the way they ate their food. Some of the men were saving their food and then eating a large amount at one time.

Greely resorted to various devices to break up the monotony of their menus. He announced they would begin having warm stews on Wednesday and Thursday, composed of two ounces of lime juice pemmican, two ounces of English beef, and three ounces of bread per man.

The announcement brightened the attitude of the party considerably, Greely was pleased to see. However, he was much concerned about Brainard's condition. His face, hands, and feet were swollen and he showed the effects of his trip to help Rice and Jens get started. Dr. Pavy advised Greely that he thought Brainard had serious kidney trouble and that possibly his chest was affected. Brainard would be in danger if he did not avoid exposure to the cold and vigorous exercise.

On February 5 Connell went out to view Smith Sound from the hill above the hut. He returned to report that he could see the other side of the sound and there were no signs of open water. This was promising. However, a storm blowing up later in the day raised their worries about Rice and Jens. The following day, February 6, was very windy and the air was filled with snow.

At two in the afternoon, the party was surprised by the return of Rice and Jens. They were both exhausted but otherwise in good condition. They had traveled out on the ice into the sound beyond Brevoort Island where they found open water running north as far as they could see. They then turned south and walked along the ice until they were opposite Baird Inlet looking for some point where they might be able to cross but the sound was open and they could not cross.

The night before they had been in desperate circumstances. Even though they were in their sleeping bag, Jens had frozen his fingers. Rice thawed them out by holding them against his own body. The temperature was so low, however, they were forced to get up and run back and forth in the snow to keep from freezing. Their cooking lamp was not working and for two days they were without water.

Thus, even their "forlorn hope" had failed them. What was left for them to attempt now? Lockwood wrote:

> Of course we are all very much disappointed; the party take a bold front, and are not wanting in spirit. Our rations have been counted on to last until March 10th, there being a ration of twelve ounces of bread and ten ounces of meat for ten days in March. So here is the upshot of affairs. If our fate is the worst, I do not think we shall disgrace the name of Americans and of soldiers.

Greely felt their doors were now all closed. Still, he would not give up. Over and over in his mind he wrestled with their situation. There was no hope for them now before spring, and yet it was such a long time for them to maintain their courage and their spirits. He concluded that the immediate problem was one of morale. He announced, therefore, that beginning next week the supply of blubber and lard would be raised to eighteen ounces per man per week. He confessed in his diary: "It is all a pitiful game of brag, and I shall have to reduce everything materially the coming week, but it had the desired effect."

The commander then announced plans for preparing to cross Smith Sound by March 6. It was more than certain that the sound would be frozen by March 1, he said. On March 6 they would have remaining rations for fifteen days, sufficient time for them to make the journey across to Littleton Island. To bolster the pretense, he detailed five men to special duty arranging everything for the proposed trip. He knew he was not fooling everyone, but the effort he was making did raise the hopes of some of the men.

However, Lockwood was still very weak, Jewell was low in spirit, and Jens was very depressed, apparently feeling guilt over his failure to cross the sound. Greely talked with the little Eskimo, praising his effort and trying to cheer him up. The commanding officer also conversed with Lockwood and Jewell, trying to raise their spirits, and he recorded that rousing Jewell out of his apathy caused him to display "considerable temper." The temper, Greely felt, was better than silence.

The temperature remained very low. Frequently the mercury was frozen, so that an exact reading could not be taken. The low temperatures raised their hopes that Smith Sound might yet freeze over. The dark days wore on and apathy, their chief enemy, seemed to be unrelenting. Lockwood wrote:

> I do little talking, finding it difficult to raise my voice. I am pursued by ennui, aimlessness, apathy and indifference, induced by hunger, cold, gloom, dirt and all the

miseries of this existence. I am very weak, both physically and morally, and find it impossible to shake these sad thoughts off; but my spirits today are better than usual, and those of the party very good indeed.

Greely was continually suggesting changes, making small revisions in the menu or proposing a different method of handling food. As another means of maintaining the men's interest, he asked each one to give his opinion about the best way to use their very poor equipment on the crossing to Littleton Island. Half-ashamed, he wrote in his diary: "It all seems to be a mockery, but the men are surprisingly cheerful, and enter into the spirit of it."

The little game Greely was playing had no success with Brainard. Almost daily he went out to observe Smith Sound and noted the roaring and grinding of the ice pack and the heavy water clouds hanging above the sound. Those heavy clouds were for Brainard "an augury of our future." He recalled Garlington's promise that "everything within the power of man will be done to rescue the brave men at Fort Conger from their perilous position." The words had once inspired them with hope but now he recognized that the promise was "made lightly and without a full knowledge of the difficulties to be encountered."

Since their water hole had given out they had had no drinking water and could not use fuel to melt ice. Some of the men were now begging for water but no one had the strength to find and dig another fresh water hole. Lockwood, particularly, Brainard recorded, was "pitifully persistent in his plea for water." Lieutenant Greely with the heat of his body melted some ice in a little rubber bag so that Lockwood might have the water he sought so plaintively.

Frequently, little contentions broke out in the group. At

other times silence would continue for hours at a time.

Brainard noted on February 14 that a small piece of butter had been taken from a can on the shelf overhead. He reported cryptically, "Henry keeps his candle molds on the same shelf." Henry and Schneider were the two chief suspects. Schneider confessed to Greely that he had taken a few pieces of bread the previous autumn but he had taken nothing else and he had no knowledge of the theft of the twelve cans of milk.

On successive days Dr. Pavy had bitter arguments, first with Lieutenant Kislingbury and then with Bender. Greely refrained from interfering in the latter argument because it did not "concern any official matter." At last, however, he had to break in to prevent the argument from disturbing the entire party.

According to Israel's calculations the sun returned to them on February 16. However, because of the water clouds, they could not see it. On the eighteenth the seemingly untiring Sergeant Rice climbed to the summit of the island for a view of the sun. He was not able to see the sun but he did get a good view of Smith Sound and he raised the spirits of the party by reporting that there was much open water but many large ice floes. Some good, cold weather, he thought, would solidify the ice from Cape Sabine to Point Cairn.

Bender, who on previous occasions caused discontent by various complaints, once more protested that he had been given a short bread ration. Brainard was much affected by Bender's accusations but Greely told his first sergeant to ignore such complaints.

The only hint of homosexuality during the expedition was reported by Greely on February 19. He wrote that Bender and Schneider quarreled in their sleeping bag the previous night "and came to blows, the first which have passed in the expedition. As far as I could gather, Bender was the aggressor."

Greely reprimanded both of them. He told them that "such a condition of affairs was outrageous, and must not occur again; that we were men, and not brutes." It seemed clear that the general attitude of the party condemned both of them for such behavior.

Storms continued to blow up, raising the temperature and depriving them of opportunities to hunt. Long went out at every opportunity but was having less success now in killing foxes. He saw no other game, except an infrequent bird.

On March 1 Smith Sound was still open and Greely had about abandoned even the wildest dream that they would be able to cross to Littleton Island. Lockwood's condition continued to fluctuate, some days good and some days bad. His mind appeared to be affected and he seemed unable to absorb any information. He talked almost continuously about food and repeatedly asked questions about their daily routine.

Biederbick worked diligently caring for Elison and Lockwood. Long continued hunting. Brainard, Rice, and a few of the others carried on the other necessary duties.

On March 3 a storm began which lasted for three days. The wind blew through their hut and drifted snow about them. After the storm abated, Long went hunting again. He saw the tracks of two foxes and two bears but no animals. Lieutenant Kislingbury went hunting later and ran across some bear tracks. However, he also was unable to kill any game.

Rice was feeling sick the morning of March 7 but it did not deter him from making a trip at noon time to the summit and there he saw the sun. It was the first time any member of the party had seen the sun for four and a half months.

Kislingbury returned from his hunting effort with his legs soaked through. He had walked on some thin ice and had broken through. There was no extra clothing for him to change to, and it was necessary for him to dry his clothing by the heat of his body. Greely and other members of the party offered to dry some of the clothing for him but he declined with thanks.

At the beginning of March and with the returning light, Rice resumed his diary. He had given it up at the beginning of the winter because of the difficulty of writing with such scarce illumination. "Our terrible life here, however," he wrote, "is indelibly marked in my memory. I only take this up again daily because the outlook indicates the possibility—nay the probability—of the whole party perishing, and I desire to leave some record of my last days, in justice to myself and friends."

He amused himself by writing down the menu he would choose if he were back in Washington. For breakfast at Godfrey's he would have chosen scrambled eggs, broiled smoked herring, baked Irish potatoes and butter, Parker House rolls, soft-boiled eggs, and a cup of chocolate. The breakfast he did eat that morning, he noted, was one twelfth of a can of tomatoes, a few grains of rice, desiccated potatoes, and some crumbs of dog biscuit made into a stew. For dinner at Godfrey's he would have chosen a half-dozen raw clams, bean soup, roast goose and apple sauce, cabbage, bread pudding, sweet potato pie, apples, oranges, raisins, nuts, cheese and crackers. His dinner actually consisted of four ounces of tallow and bacon and six ounces of bread.

Rice wrote with approval of the diligent effort that Frederick, Whisler, and Schneider were putting into pre-

paring their clothing and equipment for the possible crossing of Smith Sound. Like Brainard and Greely, Rice saw
little possibility of the group's getting across to Littleton
Island. He also shared their worry about the decline of
Lieutenant Lockwood. He worried more about the possible events of their last days. Recording an argument
which occurred on the evening of March 7, he wrote:
"Such men as Bender, Ellis and Schneider, of course, act
only as men of such dispositions and caliber can be expected to." He then concluded: "I much fear the horrors
of our last days here, as no doubt many, or at least some
of the party, will become completely demoralized."

A few days later, Rice, in conversation with Ellis,
learned that the latter had been "intimidated by the
other occupants of his sleeping bag." They had been talking about cannibalism. Their conversation, Rice wrote,
showed "a state of worked imagination which may result
in things too bad to contemplate."

Their morale was restored in part and much entertainment was provided by the first hair cutting session since
they had left Fort Conger. Their hair and beards were all
in the wildest, dirtiest state, so the barber had much to
work with. The method was simple, brief, and not entirely
effective. Those who wished to have their hair cut crawled
to the foot of their sleeping bag. The barber moved down
the alley through the middle of the hut and snipped hastily and raggedly at the matted masses of hair that hung
from their heads and chins.

Brainard recommended to Greely that Frederick be
promoted to the sergeantcy that was held by the late Sergeant Cross. Greely was glad to act on the recommendation. Frederick certainly deserved it for the work he had
performed for them and the promotion would serve to

keep "before the men the keener realization that there is yet a world and something worth striving for."

While these techniques for lifting morale had some effectiveness, Greely was well aware that the survival of the party was now a matter of very few weeks. The food on hand could not be stretched beyond the end of March. Somehow they would have to obtain more game if they were to hang on to life. Rice and Frederick volunteered to go after the English meat which had been abandoned at Eskimo Point at the time of Elison's trouble. Greely refused their offer, believing the journey to be too far for Rice and Frederick in their weakened condition. The journey was so dangerous for such little food. Instead, Greely decided to send Long and Eskimo Fred to Alexandra Harbor. The Nares expedition had reported that this area was well stocked with game. Perhaps the two hunters spending a few days there might be able to bag something.

Long and Eskimo Fred were to depart on March 11. In accordance with the usual practice, Rice and Ellis would get the hunters off to a good start by dragging their sledge out ahead of them. Greely was placing high hopes in this hunting trip. If this valley provided a winter pasturage for musk oxen and reindeer, as Nares had reported, he was sure that Long would bring back food. He had great confidence in Long's ability as a hunter.

As part of his effort to maintain morale and to keep the men's mind on something other than food even for a small part of the time, Greely had talked about the possibility of further explorations in the vicinity of Cape Sabine when opportunity afforded. Before Long's departure Greely went over a map of the Hayes Sound area with him. He impressed on Long the importance of noting anything he could see west of Mount Carey. Most important of all, of course, he told Long, they needed game but wherever possible the hunters should also make a record of the new land they discovered.

Greely knew his attempts at morale lifting were succeeding when Jewell, optimistically anticipating Long's return with ample supplies of game, suggested to Greely that he be given permission to go over to Hayes Sound for purposes of exploration in May. Greely was gratified by this indication. How responsive these men were to a call to duty even in these desperate circumstances! If only they could get food he was sure the party would survive and keep together. Jewell's spirit caught on and soon Israel, Brainard, and Dr. Pavy were also volunteering for the exploratory trip to Hayes Sound.

All of them during the past two years had tasted the intoxicating wine of discovery, the exhilaration of venturing into the unknown. Greely could recall so well his first sally out of Fort Conger to find the "Western Ocean." (Even as late as 1882 and as far north as Lady Franklin Bay, ever-curious man was seeking the fabled Northwest Passage.)

Greely had set out April 19, 1882, with Bender, Connell, and Whisler, dragging two Hudson Bay sledges. The weather was good and traveling conditions were favorable. The temperature was moderately cold, hovering about zero. As they went west, their interest heightened.

"The eye of civilized man," Greely wrote, "had not seen, nor his foot trodden the ground over which we were travelling. A strong, earnest desire to press forward at our best gait seized us all. As we neared each projecting spur of the high headlands, our eagerness to see what was beyond became so intense at times as to be painful. Each point reached, and a new landscape in sight, we found our pleasure not unalloyed, for ever in advance was yet a point which cut off a portion of the horizon and caused a certain disappointment."

They pushed on day after day, continually entranced by discovery. On the evening of April 30 they were following along a riverbank, struggling to pull their sledge through deep snow and over sharp rocks. After making a sharp turn around a projection of the hill, they were astonished by beauty. Before them was "an immense icebound lake. Its snowy covering reflected 'diamond dust' from the midnight sun, and at our feet was a broad pool of open blue water which fed the river. To the northward some eight or ten miles—its base at the northern edge of the lake—a partly snow-clad range of high hills (Garfield Range) appeared, behind and above which the hog-back, snow-clad summits of the United States Mountains rose with their stern, unchanging splendor. To right and left on the southern shore low, rounded hills, bare, as a rule, of snow, extended far to east and west, until in reality or perspective they joined the curving mountains to the north. The scene was one of great beauty and impressiveness."

Here seemed to be the culmination of all their discoveries. Connell, who had missed the trip north with Lockwood because of a frozen foot, exclaimed joyously that he would not "have missed the scene and discoveries for all the Polar Sea."

After some exploration around the lake Greely named Hazen, they returned to Conger. But Greely was not content. A few months later he led another, more fully supplied party in a second attempt to find the "Western Ocean." On this second trip their discoveries included the remains of an ancient Eskimo settlement. After examining the ruins of the two buildings, Greely observed that "these Eskimo had dogs, sledges, arrows, and skinning knives, and fed on musk-oxen, seals, hares, and occasionally fish." They left the mystery of the ancient settlement and went on westward. Eventually they reached a mountain so high as to be beyond attempting because of their exhausted state.

But Greely was burning to see the view from the top. He waded through snow four feet deep, crawled long distances on his hands and knees making his way upward. When he weakened and thought he could not go on, he threw his field glasses ahead of him. He could not abandon his glasses, and thus he forced himself upward. A half mile from the top he felt that his strength was completely gone. His eyes had weakened under the glare of the snow and he was tortured by thirst. He rested and ate snow, knowing full well the risk even in summer of lowering the body temperature. But he regained enough strength to proceed a hundred yards at a time. As he went higher he found he had to rest every fifty yards. He kept on doggedly, striving upward.

At last, he reached the summit. He was on a plateau higher than any land in sight. He rose to his feet and gazed slowly about. The view was extensive and magnificent. For a few moments he stood there enjoying the panorama and his conquest of the mountain. As he gazed the joy of his triumph was subdued. The "Western Ocean" was not in view.

He spent about twenty minutes mapping the area. Then he descended, returning to his men at the foot of the mountain, and began the journey back to Fort Conger.

He had not succeeded in crossing Grinnell Land but he had led the way. Where he had pioneered, Lockwood and Brainard followed the next summer. With the advantage of the discoveries made by Greely, they went all the way across to a height above the distant shore where they glimpsed the "Western Ocean."

It was by such means that Greely had hoped the mission of his expedition would be achieved. The work of one group would promote the work of another, and eventually the task would be done.

Now, two more of them were off on a more desperate journey that would mean so much to the rest of the party.

Long and Eskimo Fred had good weather as they started. The temperature was low, twenty degrees below zero, but the sky was clear and the long absent sun was now above the horizon. Those they left behind were keenly aware of the great dangers of this journey for two men in such a weakened condition. They made their parting, in Brainard's words, "with the kindest wishes of their grateful companions whose eyes will perhaps never see them again."

Long and Eskimo Fred at 11:30 A.M. caught up with Rice and Ellis, who were hauling the sledge in advance of them, at the east end of Cocked Hat Island. Rice and Ellis returned to the hut, and the two hunters, dragging the sledge behind them, went on toward Alexandra Harbor. The conditions were good for traveling, the ice being smooth, and by seven in the evening they made camp near Cape Rutherford. After cooking supper they attempted to get into their sleeping bag. It was badly frozen, however. They struggled for three hours and could cover themselves only up to their chests. The night was still, so they tried to sleep only partly covered; however, the cold was too much for them and at two in the morning they decided to get up and continue their trip. After reaching Cape Viele they stopped to make some tea, having eaten bacon raw as they were traveling.

Long and Eskimo Fred went on to Alexandra Harbor, continuing as far as Mount Carey. From the summit Long was able to observe with his field glasses for a great distance. He saw three capes which had not been seen before by any explorer. After making careful note of the lands he observed, he returned with Eskimo Fred to Cape Viele. Nowhere on their journey had they seen any signs of game, nor was there any vegetation which would serve as an attraction for game. Everywhere was ice and snow.

On March 13 they crossed to the west side of Alexandra Harbor. Long planned to make for the land beyond Mount Carey. They were blocked, however, by very steep cliffs rising two thousand feet above them. They then turned to the north and traveled all day in that direction. After nine hours of unceasing travel they reached a high point which gave them a good view of the area to the west. Still, as far as they could see everything was covered with snow or ice. Nowhere could they observe any sign of wildlife.

Eskimo Fred was becoming very depressed and exhausted by their long, unsuccessful journey. Long, therefore, agreed to his request to return to their camping ground at Cape Viele. They reached the cape at 10 P.M. having traveled a total of fourteen hours. During that time they had eaten only four ounces of pemmican and a bit of hard bread.

At Cape Viele they were able to restore their strength somewhat by making tea. Eskimo Fred then wanted to return immediately to the hut. Long agreed since they were unable to get into their frozen sleeping bag. After traveling for an hour, they found themselves too tired to continue, and once more struggled to get into the sleeping bag. The unyielding bag, however, would not permit them to cover their bodies above their chests, so they tried to sleep partly exposed to the bitter cold. In less than an hour Long was stricken with cramps. Poor Eskimo Fred, desperately worried lest he lose his faithful hunting companion and be abandoned in these desperate circumstances to face the Arctic alone, hastened to prepare some warm rum with spirits of ammonia. The drink served to relieve Long's cramps. Eskimo Fred then covered his sick companion with the flap of the sleeping bag and remained outside, walking up and down in the snow to keep warm. While Long slept, Eskimo Fred prepared some tea. About 5 A.M., after drinking some tea and eating four ounces of bacon, they felt strong enough to resume the return journey to the hut on Cape Sabine.

They traveled all day, their dead-tired bodies struggling to haul the heavy sledge after them. They reached Cocked Hat Island at two in the afternoon and paused for some tea and four ounces of pemmican. Their strength renewed by such little nourishment, they resumed the wearisome journey. It was 7:15 P.M. when they finally reached the hut, completely worn out but otherwise undamaged by their arduous and unsuccessful exploration.

It was a great disappointment for both the hunters and those remaining in the hut that the trip to Alexandra Harbor had not resulted in the killing of any game. However, there was some reason to hope for the future since that morning, March 14, Brainard had succeeded in shooting three ptarmigans. Brainard's success was hailed by Elison as breaking the evil spell. From now on, Elison predicted, they would have plenty of game.

Greely, however, was not so optimistic. He was fully aware of their desperate situation and the few days' supply of food remaining to them. For some time now, Rice had been pleading for permission to go to Eskimo Point after the 144 pounds of frozen meat abandoned there at the time Elison had to be rescued. Greely was very reluctant to have Rice and Shorty Frederick risk their lives on this very dangerous journey. These were two of their best men. Indeed, without question, Rice was the most highly regarded member of the party.

It would be an extremely hazardous mission, but 144 pounds of meat would mean several weeks of life for them. It was March 14. The remaining food might keep them alive until May 1. The dangerous trip would have to be taken, Greely knew, unless he could think of some other means of adding to their food supply.

CHAPTER FOURTEEN

ORGANIZING THE EXPEDITION

The administrator in American government is traditionally regarded as a bureaucrat, a man who knows the rules against doing anything, not an executive who gets things done. However, there have been men in the service of the United States Government who have performed their jobs as executives. There have even been a few whose abilities as executives were so superior as to win high praise. (General George C. Marshall, as Chief of Staff during World War II was such an executive, and was generally regarded as one of the heroes of that war although far removed from the battle lines.)

In 1884 Secretary of the Navy William Chandler went no farther north than New York Harbor, but his role in preparing the Greely Relief Expedition justified describing him as one of the heroes of that great effort.

While Congress was still debating the resolution providing for a rescue of Greely, Chandler arranged to purchase the ships necessary for the expedition. He also selected a commander. However, the formal appointment of Schley was not made until February 18, 1884. A letter addressed to Schley on that date directed him, as commander of the Greely Relief Expedition, to "make immediate and full preparation for the performance of your duty." Such preparation was to include a study of the voyage of Greely to Lady Franklin Bay in 1881 and the attempts to reach him in 1882 and 1883. Schley was also directed to familiarize himself "with the whole subject of Arctic exploring and relief expeditions." The commander of the expedition was ordered to inspect the *Thetis* and the *Bear* and to co-operate with bureau chiefs of the Navy in equipping his expedition, "giving particular attention to the special articles of outfit necessary in Arctic voyaging, including boats, sledges, dogs, houses, provisions, clothing, navigation instruments and the whole material of the expedition." Schley was also given authority to assist in the selection of the officers and crew of the expedition. In a sweeping conclusion to the letter, Secretary Chandler directed Schley that on all of the points mentioned he should "from time to time make to the Department all suggestions and recommendations which may occur to you as useful or important."

To ensure that Schley would receive the co-operation of the Navy's bureau chiefs, Chandler, on February 4, also sent a letter to all of them. In this letter he made it clear that he expected no delays or bureaucratic encumbrances to interfere with the swift preparation of the Greely Relief Expedition. He wrote the bureau chiefs:

> You will immediately familiarize yourself with the subject and be prepared to perform any work necessary from your Bureau thoroughly and without delay. Difficulty has been experienced in starting to sea vessels of the Navy at the date fixed for sailing. There must be no such failure in the case of this expedition. You will promptly call the attention of the Department to any questions upon which you wish decisions or explicit directions. You will give all practicable personal attention to the business, in all its details, trusting as little as possible to other persons. You will communicate freely with the Chiefs of other Bureaus, and with the commanding officer of the expedition.

Chandler closed with the expression of his conviction that every officer and seaman of the Navy would do his utmost to make the expedition succeed in its mission "to find and relieve our imperilled countrymen, for whose safety our whole people are full of anxiety." The Secretary of the Navy was making it very clear to all concerned that the Greely Relief Expedition would have their prompt attention. Red tape would not be permitted to entangle and delay the swift preparation and prompt departure of these ships.

In keeping with the directions that he issued to his bureau chiefs, Secretary Chandler did not delegate the supervision of the Greely Relief Expedition to anyone else. He made Commander Schley directly responsible to the Secretary of the Navy. He put full responsibility for the preparation of the expedition in Schley's hands and, as the commander later described it, it was his "business to call for everything that was needed, and to make sure that he got it." There is little doubt that these arrangements were very much to Schley's liking.

With the problem of procuring the ships settled, Schley's first attention was given to recruitment of the officers and men who would form the expedition. In ironic contrast to the debate which had taken place in Congress, there was an abundant number of volunteers for the expedition. Practically every noted American naval officer who had had any arctic experience wished to take part in the Greely Relief Expedition. All of the volunteers were first given a rigid physical examination. Many were rejected as not meeting the standards necessary to face the hardships of the Arctic.

Among the officers selected for the expedition was Lieutenant Uriel Sebree, who served on the *Tigress* when she cruised as far north as Littleton Island searching for the *Polaris* back in 1870. Schley named Lieutenant Sebree as executive and navigating officer for the *Thetis*. The *Thetis* would be the flagship of the three-vessel convoy under the command of Schley. Also aboard the *Thetis* would be Chief Engineer George W. Melville, who had so distinguished himself in the *Jeannette* expedition. Ice pilot for the *Thetis* would be James W. Norman, who had served as mate on the *Proteus* for both trips it had made to Smith Sound—in 1881 with the Greely expedition and in 1883 with the Garlington rescue party. Norman had also gone north in the *Neptune* in 1882 when Beebe attempted to reach Greely.

The second ship in the convoy, the *Bear*, would be commanded by Lieutenant William H. Emory, Jr. Serving with him would be Lieutenant John C. Colwell, the true hero of the abortive Garlington expedition.

Commander George W. Coffin was to be captain of the third ship, the *Alert*. Among his officers was Lieutenant Henry J. Hunt, who had been aboard the *Rogers* in its unsuccessful search for the *Jeannette*. Also on the *Alert* was Ensign Albert A. Ackerman, who had served on the *Yantic* when it had gone north the year before with the Garlington expedition.

In accordance with the recommendations of the President's committee, crews of the ship were kept to a minimum to provide the maximum space within the ship in case the expedition had to winter in the Arctic. There were to be eight officers and twenty-nine men on the *Thetis;* seven officers and twenty-seven men aboard the *Bear;* and seven officers and thirty-two men on the *Alert.*

Volunteers were called for from all the ships in the North Atlantic Fleet. However, most of the fleet was away from port and, therefore, three quarters of the crew of the expedition was made up of men from the one large ship in port, the *Powhatan.*

This was an era when there were a great number of

foreign-born among the enlisted men of the Navy. Apparently foreign birth was thought to lessen the homogeneity which was desired among the crew. Therefore, preference was given to native-born seamen. "After Americans," Schley stated, "the preference was given to 'north-countrymen,' that is, Scandinavian and Russian Finns." To imbue every member of the crew with a strong desire to make the voyage proceed as swiftly as possible, Secretary of the Navy Chandler ordered that pay would be increased $10 a month for the voyage. He also announced that there would be a bonus of two months' regular pay if the expedition were successful.

As soon as the officers and men had had their physical examinations, Schley put them to work. He assigned details and gave instructions for the inspection and supervision of procuring and loading supplies. Each ship commander and each officer had responsibility for some share of the particulars of the expedition. Schley held each officer responsible to report to him at eleven o'clock every morning on the progress of the preparations. Following Secretary Chandler's example, he directed them to be quick to note any improvements that might be made during the preparations and to suggest additional measures that might be taken to promote the success of their mission. The determination of the Secretary was being transmitted through the commanding officer to each officer in the party.

One of the first suggestions made to Schley was that Welsh semibituminous coal would increase the speed of the ships about twenty per cent over that produced by anthracite coal, the kind generally used by the Navy. Accordingly, Schley immediately ordered two thousand tons to be brought over from Cardiff, Wales, in a coal transport, the *Ybarra*, especially chartered for this purpose.

He also arranged for a contract with the English agent, Sutton and Company, to transport on the *Loch Garry* five hundred tons of coal to Littleton Island. The *Loch Garry* was to meet the convoy in St. John's and accompany it northward.

Each of the three ships in the convoy would carry a boat described as a steam cutter. These boats were built for three purposes. They could be used as boats, as sleds, and as living quarters for parties which traveled away from the ships. They were steam-powered for travel through water and could be converted to sleds by the attachment of runners. Each boat had oars and two paddles with ice chisels attached to the upper end, so the paddles and oars could be used as a means of cutting through small ice blocks. Each cutter was also supplied with sails and tents.

The expedition was also supplied with sleds of a special type designed by Chief Engineer Melville. Their runners were iron-covered and of the type called reversible so that the sleds could be moved forward or in reverse without turning the sled around.

Ample food supplies were loaded on each ship, which carried a two-year supply of rations for 115 men, the full number of the expedition. Recent advances in the technique of food packing permitted the expedition to be supplied with a great variety of foods well secured against deterioration.

In addition to checking the food supplies and the equipment, the commander of the expedition was faced with the responsibility of seeing that his ships were fully prepared for ice navigation. The *Alert* had been worked on in England before her departure, under the constant supervision of Lieutenant Commander Chadwick. He had the excellent advice of Sir George Nares, Commander Parr, and other British explorers who had served in the *Alert* on its trip to the Arctic. Indeed, the shipyard on the Thames became for a while a kind of rendezvous for the arctic men.

The *Thetis* and the *Bear* had been especially built to face the ice of Melville Bay and waters farther north, but upon inspection in New York it was decided by bureau chiefs of the Navy to take additional precautions. Supporting beams and truss frames were erected below decks. The ships were caulked and painted. The machinery was thoroughly inspected and put into first-class operating condition. The living quarters were remodeled to give the maximum air space for the officers and men. The captain would be the only one with a room to himself. The inner sides of the living quarters were lined with felt to insulate against cold and to prevent moisture condensation. In the officers' quarters and in the men's quarters there was placed a small coal stove. Thus, when the ship was not under way the quarters could be heated by these small stoves and make it unnecessary to use the ship's boilers. This would reduce the consumption of coal from two tons to 150 pounds a day when the ship was not cruising.

Nares had warned against a special arctic danger. He had found that a heavy pressure of extremely cold air in the flue sometimes prevented hot air from rising and escaping from the flue. There was danger of asphyxiation if some precaution was not taken. Accordingly, a special pipe was devised which would permit fresh air to come into the stove through an opening below the grate.

After giving the commander of the expedition one month to prepare himself and to organize his crew, Secretary of the Navy Chandler called on Commander Schley to report what his plan of campaign for the expedition would be. Schley replied to the Secretary on March 17.

He recommended that the *Bear,* whose preparations were most advanced, should leave New York on April 25 for St. John's. There it would take on coal and sled dogs and make inquiries about the condition of the ice in Davis Strait. As soon as possible the *Bear* would proceed to Disko and Upernivik. Schley expected that the *Bear* might reach these Greenland ports about the third week in May. The *Thetis,* the ship Schley would be commanding, would leave New York not later than May 1, also stopping at St. John's for coal and dogs and to meet the *Loch Garry,* which would be bringing the extra coal from Wales. The *Loch Garry* and the *Thetis* would proceed to Upernivik, arriving there about May 25. At Upernivik the *Thetis* would join the *Bear.* The two would then proceed northward for Cape York and Littleton Island. If the ice were too heavy, the *Loch Garry* would wait at Upernivik before attempting the voyage to Littleton Island.

The *Alert,* Schley recommended, should leave New York no later than May 10, take on coal at St. John's, and then proceed to Disko and Upernivik to meet the *Loch Garry* not later than June 1. The two ships should then proceed to Littleton Island, reaching there about the first of July. At Littleton Island they would land and build the winter house, unload their provisions, coal, and other supplies, and establish the base for the advance ships, the *Thetis* and the *Bear,* to retreat to in case of trouble. When these duties were completed, the *Alert* was to send a sled party northward along the coast on the east side of Smith Sound. If no word was received from the *Thetis* or *Bear* by September 1, the *Alert* and the *Loch Garry* were to return to St. John's.

It was possible for Schley to predict an arrival date at Littleton Island for the *Alert* and the *Loch Garry.* They would be coming up later and it would be possible for them to cross Melville Bay to Smith Sound in the time allotted. However, he gave no arrival date for the *Thetis* and the *Bear* at Cape York or Littleton Island. He could predict that they would be able to reach Upernivik by May 25 and then attempt to cross Melville Bay. He knew full well, however, that he could expect considerable heavy ice that early in the season. Garlington had not passed into Smith Sound until the middle of July and even that late he had lost his ship. Clearly, Schley could make no prediction about his own progress beyond Upernivik.

He was going out to face an adversary of unknown strength. All that he could reasonably report was that he would meet that adversary as early as possible.

CHAPTER FIFTEEN

HAPPY BIRTHDAY

The failure of Long and Eskimo Fred to obtain game in Alexandra Harbor was a great disappointment, but the depression which affected them all did not prevent Greely, Brainard, and Rice from devising other measures.

Rice and Frederick had volunteered to go to Baird Inlet after the English beef. Greely decided that he would first send Long and Brainard out to Bache Island to search for game. The commanding officer also considered sending Brainard and Jens over to Rice Strait. Brainard suggested they might well go down to Payer Harbor to hunt. On March 16, after only two days' rest from their exhausting trip, Long and Eskimo Fred went out to the open water, taking a kayak with them to hunt for seals.

Another idea for obtaining food was suggested by Brainard. He proposed devising a net for catching shrimps. Still another kind of hunting was tried by Brainard, who exposed a bit of meat on the rocks near their hut in hope of attracting a raven within gunshot.

These men were not giving up.

They still held hopes for crossing the sound to Littleton Island. The weather continued very cold and ice was piling up in the strait.

Long and Eskimo Fred had some success. They saw a small seal and fired at it, but missed. However, they shot four dovekies, small, plump little birds with black tips on their white feathers. These birds provided them with about four pounds of meat and improved the spirit of the group considerably.

The following day, March 17, Lieutenant Kislingbury and Eskimo Jens went hunting. They saw a seal but were unable to get a shot at it. However, Jens succeeded in killing a ptarmigan which weighed better than a pound.

This success of the hunters began to give the party new hope. All of them were very weak but most of them were not disabled. Only Elison, Linn, and Lieutenant Lockwood were unable to move about. Ever since the terrible experience on the trip to Isabella, Linn's mind had been weakened. Now it seemed to Greely that Linn was giving up.

On March 18 Rice went out to try the net invented by Brainard for catching shrimp but he succeeded in catching only a few ounces. These shrimp were so tiny that Brainard described them as "sea fleas." Small though they were, they would be a signicant addition to the food supply if enough of them could be trapped. Rice was hopeful that he could greatly increase his catch by modification of the net.

Brainard suggested to Greely that Long and Eskimo Fred should not tire themselves by hauling the kayak out to the water each day. Rather, others could perform this duty and relieve the hunters of some labor.

The determination of Rice and Brainard and a few others was infectious. Gardiner felt he, too, had to contribute to the effort to keep the party alive. He devised a rig which he suggested might be used for dredging up mussels or seaweed.

They were all aware of the alternative to such efforts. It was very clear that the party was near its end unless these attempts to gain food succeeded. Greely thought it surprising that they viewed death with such calmness. He wrote: "We have talked over the matter very calmly and quietly, and I have always exhorted the men to die as men and not as dogs."

Lieutenant Lockwood, weak and declining, was also impressed by the way the men were facing death. "We look on it with equanimity, and the spirits of the party, with this prospect of a miserable death, are certainly wonderful. I am glad as each day draws to an end. It puts us nearer the end of this life—whatever that end is to be. The fuel, except the boat, ends tomorrow. Talk all the time on the subject of food."

Rice was shrimping every day and improving his technique. On March 22 he brought back six ounces of shrimp and reported that he thought he would get about a quart on the following day. Brainard prepared a second net for him, and baited both nets with fox skins. They also learned that dovekie legs were excellent bait. In the future they would be saved for shrimping purposes.

Long and Jens went hunting in the open water off Cape Sabine but did not get anything. Long reported that the ice extended three miles farther out into Smith Sound than the week before. This seemed encouraging for the crossing to Littleton Island. But Greely had about given up the idea of getting the party across the sound. The men were too weak and the very limited rations would not permit such a strenuous journey now.

Greely announced the following week he would reduce the rations to a minimum which he hoped would keep them alive until May 1.

On March 23 Rice was up at 3 A.M. to renew his shrimping attempts, and Brainard was off for an examination of Rosse Bay, looking for a seal or a walrus.

He saw no signs of game but the party was delighted when Rice returned from his second shrimping trip with four pounds of shrimp. This startling success moved them all to burst out in cheers for their good comrade who would never stop trying and who was so frequently successful.

To aid Rice in his efforts, Whisler, Bender, and Salor prepared for him some rubber mittens, a scarf, and a large basket. Bender also made a fish hook, although Rice thought it was unlikely that they would be able to catch any fish with it.

Such efforts were gratifying to the commanding officer who had been trying for all the long dark weeks to build up a spirit of unity in the party. Linn had repeatedly sounded the keynote with frequent announcements of the slogan, "United we stand, divided we fall." Greely had impressed on them time and time again that their only hope for survival lay in working together. Now, the efforts of those who were hunting inspired those remaining behind in the hut to do something to contribute to the common good and to the success of the hunters. The physical strength of the individual members of the party was declining but the strength of the group, the feeling of unity, was growing and this growth gave the leader hope that they might yet survive.

On March 24 Rice was up at 3 A.M. again to catch the low tide for the placement of his nets. The temperature was down to twenty-two degrees below zero and a wind was blowing from the west. Rice reported: ". . . froze my nose as usual, and also my fingers." The effects of the cold were common to them now and the danger was little feared. Familiarity with the Arctic had taught them how to endure such discomforts and continue working.

A new and unfamiliar danger struck them that morning and the entire party was almost destroyed.

They had used all of their wood for cooking and were now using the alcohol lamp. The tin can funnel which served as their chimney was blocked with rags when they were not cooking in order to keep as much heat as possible within the hut. On the morning of March 24, while the cooks were preparing breakfast, Sergeant Israel began to feel nauseous. Greely asked Dr. Pavy about it, and the doctor advised Israel to lie down, saying that he would feel better in a few minutes. But then, on the other side of the hut, Biederbick fainted. While the doctor was going to help Biederbick, Israel also dropped unconscious. Greely turned to help Israel and another man fainted. Suddenly Gardiner yelled, "It's the alcohol. Open the door, open the door."

At once they realized that the rags had not been removed from the funnel and alcohol fumes were filling the hut.

Immediately, the door was thrown open. Those who could do so, tried to crawl down the passageway and out of the hut. On the way out, Greely saw Brainard stretched on the ground, white and apparently dead. Whisler fell and Greely tried to help him, but in doing so lost his strength and fell himself. Gardiner went to Greely, got the commanding officer to his feet and tried to put a pair of mittens on his hands which were already freezing. Whisler also tried to help but then Gardiner weakened and fell to the ground, and Greely and Whisler turned to help Gardiner. Brainard would appear to come to and try to raise himself, but then stagger and fall again. Dr. Pavy succeeded in reviving Biederbick and Israel. And so it went with the entire party, those who were able tried to assist those who were disabled.

The one exception was Private Henry. He showed no concern for anyone but himself.

As soon as they had recovered themselves they found they were freezing, and quickly returned to the hut.

Order was restored and breakfast was prepared. It was discovered that in the excitement a piece of bacon had been stolen. The men exploded with rage. It was almost incredible, Brainard thought, "that in our midst was a man so devoid of humanity as to steal food from his starving companions when they might be dying."

Curses roared and rattled around the dark, stone hut. Who could be so inhuman? Brainard suspected Henry. So did Rice and others. It wasn't long before Greely learned that there was a general suspicion of Henry. But the suspicious ones had no evidence to support an accusation. Greely could not accuse or take any action against Henry —not on suspicion alone. But what was to be done to stop thievery? Greely felt sick at heart. If they could not trust each other . . . ?

Those who suspected Henry kept a close watch on him. Shortly before dinner time Henry complained that he was feeling nauseous. Soon the meat for dinner was distributed.

"I'll just put this away," Henry said.

In a few moments Henry grabbed a can and started vomiting into it. Frederick quickly crawled over to Henry and examined the can. It contained a large amount of undigested bacon.

"There's your bacon," Frederick exclaimed, "out of the stomach of the thief."

With the crime revealed, the criminal was further indicted by Jens. Suddenly, and surprisingly, he crawled to the center passageway, pointed at Henry and said, "Me see. Me see."

In pantomime, Jens re-created Henry's crime. He acted out the morning's drama, the nausea that hit them, the fainting and the frantic scramble to escape from the hut.

Then, pointing to Henry, he demonstrated how the big, sullen man had moved over to the supply room, reached in to grab the bacon and tuck it in his shirt. When Jens finished the pantomime, he gazed at Henry with a fierce, cold look, and once more jabbed a finger at him.

The men had watched Jens in fascination and with growing anger. Words stuck in their throats and came out as growls. The commanding officer was partly fascinated by Jens's pantomime and partly seized by apprehension as he saw the hatred on the faces of the men. It was a hatred that sought vengeance—swift and violent vengeance.

As Jens concluded and, with artless, highly effective drama, pointed the accusing finger, one of the men burst forth, "Let's kill the thieving bastard."

Supporting yells were just beginning when Greely's voice broke in.

"Quiet. You men will be quiet. There will be no such talk.

"This is a military command. You are soldiers, not a mob. If anyone is to be punished for crime it will be done by order of the commanding officer.

"I am in command here. I will decide what is to be done in the morning."

The assertion of authority succeeded. The men muttered to each other, ate their meager meal, and then went to sleep. It had been an eventful, exciting, and exhausting day.

Greely lay awake trying to decide what he would do in the morning. They had caught their thief. He had to be punished. He had to be stopped. If action were not taken against thievery, it would spread rapidly. They would quickly cease to be soldiers and become vultures preying on each other. But what punishment could be added to the hardships they were already enduring? What could they do to Henry for his crime? What kind of punishment was worse than what they were already suffering?

In the morning Greely tried to deal with Henry's crime in an orderly manner. Henry brought up the question himself immediately after breakfast.

"You fellows made a lot of accusations last night and I want to tell you that you're wrong. I haven't stolen anything."

There was an immediate clatter of protest and, surprisingly, Eskimo Jens made the most vigorous objection. He got out of his sleeping bag and once more acted out the crime.

"That little Eskimo is a liar," Henry muttered.

"It's a funny thing that you didn't eat your breakfast yesterday, Henry," Biederbick said.

"I know why," Frederick added. "You just couldn't digest the bacon."

"And what about the rum, Henry?" asked Long.

Henry feigned a look of surprise. "What do you mean?"

After their near-asphyxiation, each man was given a cup of rum.

"Major Greely ordered that we each have one cup, but you stole a second, didn't you?" Long charged.

"Oh, hell, this isn't new," Ellis said, "he's been stealing for a long time. I saw him steal canned goods back in Fort Conger."

"I saw him a couple of months ago," Connell said, "with a new can of roast beef before any of the roast beef had been issued."

Lieutenant Greely quieted the violent talk and insisted on a calmer discussion of the question. He began by asking Henry's sleeping companions and friends their opinion of Henry's conduct. They declared him guilty. Greely then asked the rest of the party, one by one. Each of them gave the same verdict. "Guilty." When Greely had completed the poll, the verdict was unanimous. Henry was guilty.

"It's just about time," someone muttered, "for a lynch party."

Someone else said, "That's just what is needed to take care of that big bastard."

Greely quickly intervened.

"There will be no such talk and no such action. This is a military command. I am the commanding officer and I will take whatever measures are necessary."

"I think what we might do, Lieutenant," Rice suggested, "is to make Henry a prisoner within the hut and not let him outside except under guard. If he violates that confinement we will know how to deal with him."

Greely was conscious of the fact that he had taken no action against Dr. Pavy, although for many months the doctor had been stealing food. The commander had not acted against the doctor because of the need for his services, but he was unwilling to treat an enlisted man differently from an officer.

"Henry has been found guilty of an extremely serious crime," Greely said. "He is to be confined to his sleeping bag as a prisoner. He is relieved from all duties with the expedition and he is not to be permitted to leave his sleeping bag or go outside except under guard."

In reality, Greely realized, it was no punishment at all. It was hardly more than a pitiful attempt to maintain the appearance of military justice and discipline.

The ineffectiveness of this confinement was demonstrated the next day. The week before, Brainard had discovered twelve ounces of chocolate in the storehouse. It was decided then that the chocolate would be saved for the suffering amputee, Elison, to use as it seemed required. The morning after Henry's confinement had been ordered, Brainard discovered that the chocolate was missing. The circumstances, Brainard said, "point strongly to Henry as the guilty party."

By the last week in March the sun had risen high enough so that it was striking within their dismal hut. The illumination of the "scene of utter squalor and misery" about them made Greely feel that he was awakening from a nightmare. "For a moment the ennui and pain, the cold and hunger that had abided, the physical weakness and mental irritation which had come, the heart-sickness resulting from blasted and deferred hopes, and the impudent and maddening rage at our utter helplessness rose up before me."

The commanding officer turned to little Israel and asked, "How have we ever passed through this Hell on earth and kept our reason?" But, recalling the courage, the loyalty, and the unselfishness which had been demonstrated in the recent dark weeks, Greely added, "I shall ever think better of mankind for this ordeal."

The effect of the sun was to prove a great tonic for them. Brainard described it by quoting the words of another arctic explorer, Dr. Kane. After spending some hours basking in the sun on the rocks above the hut, Brainard declared, "It was like bathing in perfumed water."

A violent storm broke out on the night of March 26 and ended on the morning of the twenty-seventh. The abating of the storm seemed a happy sign, for March 27 was Greely's fortieth birthday. All of the men wished him a happy birthday and, jokingly, many happy returns. Greely declined to take the half gill of rum which it had been the custom to issue to a man on his birthday. But Rice and Long gave Greely a magnificent birthday present.

Rice made four trips to his shrimping nets that day and gathered in all twelve pounds of shrimp. Long and Eskimo Jens went hunting. For many weeks Long had been promising his commander that he was going to provide him with some special food for a birthday present. They returning in the late morning with fifteen dovekies. With pride and happiness, Long tossed the birds at Lieutenant Greely's feet and joyfully exclaimed, "Happy birthday, Lieutenant, happy birthday. I promised you a present."

Soon the whole group was buzzing with joy and excitement and cheers broke out for Long and Jens.

Inspired by this successful hunting, Lieutenant Kislingbury and Connell went out and were soon back with eight more birds. The party was now overflowing with good feeling and hope. This seemed to be the great change in their fortunes.

Feeling cheated by being kept out of the group, Henry pleaded to be allowed to do part of the daily duties. "You will kill me with injustice, if you do not," he told the commanding officer with tears in his eyes. This attempt to win sympathy failed, however. The men could not forget that a few days before this wretch had stolen food from them while they were within minutes of death. Henry's plea for sympathy was coldly ignored.

The hunters' success was repeated the next day. Long brought in fourteen more dovekies and Rice returned with twenty-seven pounds of shrimp. Eskimo Fred succeeded in shooting a ptarmigan up on Cemetery Ridge. The effort, however, seemed to be too much for him and he returned to the hut in great exhaustion. He was depressed and declared that he would never return to his home in Greenland. Brainard recorded solemnly: "Perhaps he is right."

Brainard also went hunting down at Payer Harbor. He found evidences of ancient Eskimo camps but did not succeed in shooting any game. He noted, however, that Smith Sound was open to the south as far as he could see. "Any vessel could steam up Smith Sound without difficulty or hindrance." There was, of course, no vessel to be seen.

The party, at last, was growing too tired to be interested in the evening readings which had been maintained through the winter months. Many of the men were inclined to go to sleep at this time rather than listen. Because of this general feeling, the readings were abandoned.

The success of the hunters enabled the commanding officer to increase the daily ration. On March 29 the party had for breakfast four and one-half ounces of bread, an ounce of bacon, and six ounces of shrimp, but no tea. For dinner the menu included one and one-third ounces of dovekie, one ounce of bacon, two and one-half ounces of bread, and eleven ounces of shrimp per man. These items mixed together made, Brainard declared, "a delightful stew. The solid content was more than we had been accustomed to eat for both meals. Although this makes only two full meals we are already able to note a change in our condition."

While this increase could make them all feel better, little could be done for the trouble Elison complained of that day. He turned to the doctor in the morning and said, "My toes are burning dreadfully, and the soles of my feet itch. Can't you do something for me?"

It was March 29, but he was unaware that his toes and his feet had dropped off back in January, more than two months ago.

CHAPTER SIXTEEN

THE SHIPS GO FORTH

The shores of upper New York Harbor were crowded with people the early afternoon of May 1, 1884. It was the day of departure for the *Thetis*, flagship of the rescue squadron going north to search for the Greely expedition.

Something of a miracle in ship construction and preparation had been accomplished during March and April at the New York Navy Yard. The three ships, the *Bear, Thetis*, and *Alert*, had been prepared for their arctic voyage in speedy measure under the constant supervision of Commander Winfield Scott Schley and the repeated prodding of Secretary of the Navy William E. Chandler.

As each ship had arrived at the Navy Yard it was given a swift inspection by a Board of Survey, which then issued a report recommending the work to be done on the vessel. The recommendation, however, was qualified by the statement: "It must, however, be distinctly understood that no work is to be undertaken on the *Bear*, or any other ship of the Greely Relief Expedition, which cannot be fully completed without delaying the expedition beyond the time which may be fixed for its departure from New York."

The time drew near for the departure of the *Bear* on April 25. The week before departure, the Navy Secretary sent a short, blunt letter to all bureau chiefs:

Navy Department,
Washington,
April 18, 1884

Sir:

You are requested to inform the Department whether the *Bear,* of the Greely Relief Expedition, is in all respects, so far as your Bureau is concerned, ready for sea. If she is not, what work yet remains to be done?

Very respectfully,

William A. Chandler

Secretary of the Navy

No bureau chief receiving such a letter could blithely assume that the men in his unit had accomplished their work. Each chief was forced to make certain every detail had been fulfilled so that he could report with confidence to the Secretary that the *Bear,* as far as his bureau was concerned, was ready for sea.

A small crisis occurred the last week before departure when it was realized that the departure date, April 25, was a Friday. According to the sailors' superstition, Friday was a very bad day for a ship to start a voyage. The sailing date of the *Bear* could not be delayed. It would, therefore, be necessary to leave a day early. Last-minute preparations were speeded up and the *Bear* left New York Harbor on Thursday, April 24.

Four days later Secretary Chandler once more sent to all the bureau chiefs a letter inquiring about preparations for the *Thetis* and asking once more the blunt question: if the *Thetis* were not fully ready for sea, "what work yet remains to be done?"

While the Navy Department was deeply engrossed in preparing its rescue expedition, Mrs. Henrietta Greely and her friends in Congress were not content that the government was doing all that was possible to promote the rescue of the Lady Franklin Bay Expedition. Mrs. Greely was convinced that the whaling and sealing ships which frequented the waters around Greenland and Ellesmere Island could aid materially in the possible rescue of her lost husband and his men. Continued pressure in Congress for more effort to be made to rescue Greely was successful. Mrs. Greely's plan to enlist the aid of the whaling and sealing ships won congressional favor. She proposed that a very substantial reward be offered by the United States Government to any ship outside of government service which succeeded in rescuing the men of the expedition.

In February the President had responded to Mrs. Greely's suggestion by sending requests to the consuls at Dundee and St. John's that captains of such vessels be asked to be alert for any sign of the Greely party as they cruised the northern waters. The consuls were authorized to say that any services performed by such vessels would be given substantial recognition by the Government of the United States.

A couple of months later Congress supported the President's action by adopting a resolution providing for a reward. The resolution adopted on April 17 authorized the Secretary of the Navy to offer a reward of $25,000 to any ship or person "not in the military or naval service of the United States, as shall discover and rescue, or satisfactorily ascertain the fate of the expedition of Lieutenant A. W. Greely, an officer of the United States Army, and his command. . . ."

The influence of the voices of caution were shown in the second paragraph of the reward proclamation which stated: "Unprepared vessels are warned not to incur extraordinary peril or risk in the effort to secure the re-

The harried men of the Expedition pause during their retreat. Here, near Conical Rock, they have drawn their boats up on the ice and are waiting for leads to open. Despite the terrible circumstances of the retreat, Rice is still diligently recording photographically the story of the expedition. (*The National Archives*)

The steam launch *Lady Greely* tows a small boat in Discovery Harbor, August 1882. One year later the launch, trailing three boats through heavier harbor ice, was to move through these same waters as the expedition began its retreat from Fort Conger to Cape Sabine. *(The National Archives)*

Arctic clouds over Bellot Island. The ice in foreground is stranded on the shore near Fort Conger. Greely and his men began their retreat by skirting Bellot Island and passing out through the western channel, seen at the right between the Island and Sun Cape in background at extreme right. *(The National Archives)*

Washington Irving Island in Kane Sea as caught by Rice's camera from the deck of the *Proteus* in 1881. Two years later he went ashore here in a small boat to examine the cairn made on the way north and to leave a record of the retreat of the Greely party. *(The National Archives)*

The pendulum cache. This silent, lonely sentinel is the eloquent appeal built by Lt. Lockwood on Stalknecht Island in Payer Harbor. Here in October 1883, he cached the records and instruments of the Lady Franklin Bay Expedition. The cache was found by Ensign Harlow of the rescue expedition on June 22, 1884. *(The National Archives)*

KEY TO RESCUE

A. D. L. Brainard, U. S. A.
B. H. Biederbick, U. S. A.
C. M. Connell, U. S. A.
D. Maj. A. W. Greely, U.S.A.
E. Elison, U. S. A.
F. Long, U. S. A.

1. W. S. Schley, Com'nd'r
2. W. H. Emory, Lieut.
3. J. Lowe, Chief Engineer
4. G. W. Melville, Ch. En.
5. H. E. Ames, Surgeon
6. J. Quevedo, Bo's'ns Mate

7. L. K. Reynolds, Ensign
8. J. C. Colwell, Lieut.
9. C. H. Harlow, Ensign
10. E. H. Green, Surgeon
11. E. H. Taunt, Lieut.
12. S. C. Lemly, Lieut.

The painting of the rescue of the survivors of the Lady Franklin Bay expedition, 1881–84, by officers and men of the United States Navy, at Camp Clay, Cape Sabine, June 22, 1884, was executed by Mr. Albert Operti, of the Arctic Club of America.

On the return of the Relief Expedition Mr. Operti was commissioned by the Hon. Secretary of the Navy W. E. Chandler, to paint the incident of the rescue historically for the Navy Department. The War Department detailed Sergeant (now General) D. L. Brainard, U. S. A., to assist Mr. Operti with details. General A. W. Greely and Mr. Biederbick also assisted. The Navy Department aided in every way possible. The officers, including Commander W. S. Schley, granted constant sittings for portraits and other details. The painting (3 feet 6 by 5 feet) was finally approved and accepted.

Commander Winfield Scott Schley, leader of the rescue squadron, at the wheel of his flagship, the *Thetis*. *(The National Archives)*

The collapsed tent at Cape Sabine and (at right) two members of the rescue party. *(The National Archives)*

The Six Who Came Back. Lt. Greely (right front) with Sergeant Brainard seated next to him. (Rear, left to right) Long, Frederick, Connell, and Biederbick. Aboard the *Thetis* on the way home. (*The National Archives*)

The commander of the Lady Franklin Bay Expedition aboard the
Thetis. Despite Greely's still very weak condition, the pride and
assurance of the successful military leader are apparent. *(The
National Archives)*

ward hereby offered; the United States will, in no event, be involved in any future liability or responsibility beyond said reward."

The energetic support of Secretary Chandler and the reward offer adopted by Congress were much in the mind of Commander Schley as he stood on the bridge of the *Thetis* the afternoon of May 1. If such energy and determination had been expended last year, Schley thought, the rescue might have been achieved with little trouble.

As the *Thetis* approached Governor's Island, the commander ordered the colors dipped to return the salute from the guns.

The Greely Relief Expedition was starting off with the hopes and expectations of all Americans. The Administration had achieved its goal. It had been shown that everything would be done in an attempt to rescue Greely. The Secretary of the Navy was on board the *Tallapoosa* following the *Thetis* down the bay to give a personal good-by to the men of the rescue expedition.

The Secretary had given Commander Schley his formal orders in a letter the week before.

Navy Department,
Washington,
April 21, 1884

Sir:

The *Thetis, Bear* and *Alert*, the ships of the Greely Relief Expedition of 1884, being ready, you are ordered to take command of them and to proceed to the coast of Greenland, or further north if necessary, and, if possible, to find and rescue, or ascertain the fate of Lieutenant A. W. Greely and his comrades.

All the officers and men under your command are hereby enjoined to perform any duty on sea or land to which you may order them. No detailed instructions will be given you. Full confidence is felt that you have both the capacity and the courage, guided by discretion, necessary to do all that can be required of you by the department or the nation for the rescue of our imperiled countrymen.

With earnest wishes and high hopes for your success and safe return, I am,

Very respectfully,

William A. Chandler

Secretary of the Navy

Commander Winfield S. Schley, U.S.N.,

Commanding the Greely Relief Expedition

There were no detailed instructions, and indeed that was sensible, for surely Schley would have to follow such course as circumstances indicated when he arrived in that strange world of the Far North.

The letter had an implied contradiction which was veiled, but very clear to the commander. Full confidence was felt that Schley and his men could do everything possible "for the rescue of our imperiled countrymen." But the possible accomplishment of the mission was stated quite boldly in the order to find and rescue or "ascertain the fate of Lieutenant A. W. Greely and his comrades."

As his ship steamed through the Narrows, past the booming guns of Fort Hamilton, Schley could reflect that the Secretary's accomplishment of getting the expedition to sea on time was a marvel of naval administration. But the irony was inescapable. What could be hoped for now? Schley could read it in the eyes of most of his officers. They discussed plans and they accepted orders in a spirit of determination. Each of them would do his utmost to make this relief effort succeed. There was an unspoken acknowledgment, however, that there was only the remotest possibility that they would find any of the Greely party alive.

Leaving behind the cheering crowd on the shore, the *Thetis* steamed out to the Sandy Hook lightship. There, Commander Schley stopped the *Thetis* and swung his ship to determine the deviation of her compasses. After this check had been made, the *Thetis* set out to sea on the afternoon of May 1 and headed for St. John's.

CHAPTER SEVENTEEN

THE BEAR HUNT

April opened at Cape Sabine with at least four of the Greely party in desperately weak condition. Lieutenant Lockwood, Linn, Jewell, and Eskimo Fred were obviously only days away from death. The rest of the party still had strength to move about, but all of them knew that their future depended entirely on the success of the hunters and on Rice's shrimping.

The sun was climbing higher in the arctic sky and they often looked wistfully to the south with the futile hope that a rescue ship might appear on the horizon. In a more rational condition they would have been well aware that a ship could not get that far north so early; but the ordeal they faced daily, their great hopes for food and rescue, enlarged their expectations.

March had gone out like a lion. A storm raged about the little stone hut for three days, ending at 4 A.M., April 1.

The ending of the storm permitted the ever-ambitious Sergeant Rice to make a trip with his shrimping nets. He spent the whole day at shrimping, going down to set the nets and going back a few hours later to bring in the shrimp and set the nets again. Long spent the day hunting. They were both very successful. In four trips Rice was able to collect thirty pounds of shrimp. Long succeeded in killing eleven dovekies. Even more exciting news was Long's report that he had seen four seals. Unfortunately, he was able to get a shot at only one of them, and even that one shot missed its target. But this was good news, very good news. If they could get a seal or two, or a bear, it would be such a substantial addition to their food supply they would dare hope again that they would survive until their rescue ship arrived.

But would they get such food? Would they be able to survive? Brainard wondered what their future would be. He was perhaps as strong and determined as any of them, and yet he could feel the weakness growing almost daily.

"Look at us," he thought; "four of us almost dead, the others barely able to walk."

He could feel his moral power diminishing with his physical strength. Only by intense concentration did he succeed in urging himself to move about, and when he did walk, he staggered like a drunk. He barely had strength to hold himself erect.

Rice and Shorty Frederick were in scarcely better condition than Brainard, yet they also continued their efforts to obtain food for the rest of the party.

On the morning of April 2, Rice said, "Come on, Shorty, let's go get some shrimp."

Off they went with the nets to the shrimping grounds and were gone most of the day. Out in the bitter cold they kept setting the nets, walking up and down for hours to keep their circulation going, lifting the nets, collecting the shrimp, and setting the nets again. They returned after seven hours with thirty-two pounds of shrimp. Although shrimps were a substantial addition to their food supply, they did not provide enough nourishment to make a significant change in the strength of the party. In fact, some of them found the shrimps difficult to eat.

Eskimo Fred showed noticeable signs of decline in the first days of April. Greely ordered that his ration should be increased to equal that provided the hunters. It failed to help him. His declining strength made him quarrel-some and irritable. It was especially painful for Brainard and Lockwood to see him slipping away. How many dangers he had shared with them on their many sledge trips out of Fort Conger. The little Eskimo had even been with them when they had made the most momentous journey to the "Farthest North."

The first week in April was for Greely a critical time. He could see that Eskimo Fred was dying and he knew that starvation would soon claim the rest of them. An inventory of their food supply on April 3 showed they had remaining for each man only five pounds of meat, three pounds of bread, and two pounds of stearine. Their days, truly, were numbered in ounces. Rice added to that number of ounces by the daily trips to his shrimp nets but this additional food could not suffice to keep them all alive.

On the evening of April 4 Eskimo Fred became delirious. It was clear the end was near. As the night wore on, his condition did not improve. In fact, it grew worse. At nine o'clock Eskimo Fred died.

Dr. Pavy and Biederbick made a close inspection of Eskimo Fred's body.

Greely asked, "Well, Doctor, what is your report?"

The doctor hesitated and then said, "Lieutenant, there are a few indistinct signs of scurvy, but it is my belief that he died from the action of water on the heart caused by insufficient nutrition."

"Insufficient nutrition."

The doctor avoided the word they dreaded to hear: "starvation."

The death depressed them all but it hit Eskimo Jens with a special force. The Eskimos, as a race, had a reputation for hiding their emotions in times of trial but Jens's emotions were too great for him to hide, or perhaps he was too weak to make such an effort. He was clearly deeply affected by the loss of his companion.

Out of concern for Jens's spirit and for his important role as one of their hunters, Greely ordered that Jens's ration be increased temporarily.

The death of Eskimo Fred removed from Greely's mind all doubt about the necessity for the desperate trip to be made by Rice and Shorty Frederick to Baird Inlet for the English meat abandoned there in November.

Eskimo Fred was dead, Lieutenant Lockwood and Jewell were in very bad condition, and Linn seemed on the point of death, too.

They dragged Eskimo Fred's body out on the sledge for burial at two in the afternoon. After a brief ceremony on Cemetery Ridge, the body was placed in a shallow grave, and a salute was fired above it.

When they returned to the hut, Brainard continued his work preparing the equipment for the trip to Baird Inlet. Rice and Shorty Frederick, the commanding officer said, would start out on their trip the next day.

The following morning Linn became even weaker and at 1 P.M. lapsed into unconsciousness. Linn's imminent death added to the feeling of urgency about the trip of Rice and Frederick. Lieutenant Kislingbury, Sergeant Brainard, and Ellis hauled the sledge with equipment for the trip out to the summit of the island. It was a relatively short distance, but their strength was at such a low ebb that it was unbelievably difficult for them to move their burden. It took them four and a half hours to haul the sledge the short distance. It took them another hour and a half to make their way back to the hut.

At noon on the day of departure, Rice crawled over to Greely's sleeping bag and joined him for a final conference.

Greely, still the commander concerned for formality and detail, told Rice: "Sergeant, you will have no written orders for this mission. It would obviously be very unwise for me to give you detailed instructions. All I can tell you is to go and do the best that you can. I must, however, warn you against overexerting yourself. I know your great ambition, Sergeant, to achieve whatever you set out to do but you must remember that none of us now has the strength he once had."

Greely paused for a moment and reflected on how to put the next question to this dedicated soldier of his.

"Sergeant, I want you to be fair with me and with yourself. I want you to be candid in your reply to my question. You know that this past Thursday you were not well. I am not sure that you have fully recovered now. I cannot send a sick man, an unfit man, on a journey so dangerous."

Greely continued, "You know that Sergeant Brainard is always anxious to serve us. I know that Brainard is willing, even more than willing, to go in your place. If you are not entirely well, it is wiser that you should not attempt this very difficult trip."

Rice immediately protested against the suggestion that he was not well. "No, Lieutenant, I cannot agree that Brainard should go. I have recovered from my illness. I am certainly as strong as Brainard. I was the one who originated the idea of the trip. I was the one who led the other mission to get this meat. I know more about the area around Cape Isabella and the route there than anyone else. I am the one who should go," Rice concluded.

"Very well then, Sergeant," Greely said, "but let me warn you again against overexerting yourself. Please don't attempt more than your strength will permit."

"We will be saving our strength, Lieutenant," Rice replied. "I have been out on reconnaissance during the past several days. Last week I found a way to avoid going all the way over to Rice Strait. We can go right across the island here directly to Rosse Bay."

"Yes, Sergeant, that is wise," Greely said.

While they were conferring, Biederbick looked up from Linn's side and announced in a dull tone, "I think Linn is dead now." The hut was silent for a moment, then a few of the men nearest to Linn raised themselves from their sleeping bags to glance at the dead body. No one seemed to have anything to say.

Brainard thought, "Death doesn't stir us any more. We may all follow Linn very soon but everyone seems resigned to it."

He thought of Linn as he was at Fort Conger in the days when they all had their strength. Linn had been a good-natured fellow, generous and willing, but in recent weeks with his declining strength, he had become petulant and irritable. Still, they all recognized that it was hunger that was speaking, not the man himself.

At last Greely said, "We will bury him tomorrow."

When Rice and the commanding officer had finished their discussion of the trip, Greely suggested that Rice get a few hours' sleep before leaving. They then both realized that Rice's sleeping bag had been loaded on the sledge which had been taken up to the ridge earlier in the day. The only remaining place for Rice to sleep was in the large sleeping bag with the body of Linn.

"That's all right, Lieutenant," Rice said, "I'll crawl in with Linn, it's as good a place as any to sleep."

For Greely, Rice's casual air about sleeping with the dead seemed symbolic of the spirit with which his brave men were facing their terrible ordeal. Death was accepted as their constant companion.

After a brief rest Rice stirred himself and then said

casually to Frederick, "Well, Shorty, I guess we might as well get underway."

There was little for them to do in preparation. Their equipment had been loaded on the sledge and taken out to the ridge earlier in the day.

By the standards of their earlier sledge parties their equipment for this trip was hardly adequate, but it was the best now available and about all the two men had the strength to haul. The load included a two-man sleeping bag, a rifle, an ax, an alcohol lamp, and a small cooking pot. They took no tent. There was none for them to take and, if there had been, it was doubtful that their strength would have been equal to the additional load.

Rice had tried to persuade the commanding officer that no increase in rations should be granted for the trip. He said the two of them could make the journey on the same quantity of food being given to the men remaining in the hut—four ounces of meat and four ounces of bread per man per day. Greely was torn between his desire to save every ounce of food and his keen awareness of the arduous journey Rice and Frederick were attempting. At last he decided that the two men should have on the trip a daily ration of six ounces of bread and six ounces of meat plus a small ration of tea. He also ordered that they take extra alcohol for cooking purposes as well as rum, spirits of ammonia, and some pills for medicinal purposes.

After a final adjustment of their clothing in the dark, crowded hut, Rice and Frederick were soon ready to leave.

Rice crawled over to the commanding officer for a final word before departure.

"We are going now, Lieutenant," he said. "I expect it should take us about four or five days, two days out and two days back."

"Yes, I would expect so," said Greely. He searched for something further to say. "Well, Sergeant, take care of yourself."

Rice smiled faintly in the darkness and said briefly, "Yes sir, we will."

The two men made their farewells to the rest of the group and then crawled down the center to the passageway leading outside. The good-bys were said to them in husky voices and with trembling lips. Each man in the hut knew what these two were attempting for them. Brainard looking around in the dim light could see the eyes of the men bright with tears as they watched Rice and Frederick leaving the hut.

"Well, there they go," Brainard thought, "hardly stronger than the rest of us, risking their lives to bring us a little food. God save them."

The hut was silent for just a moment and Greely could sense the feeling of depression settling about them. Then, suddenly, he said, "Let's give them a cheer, men."

Rice and Frederick, trudging away from the hut in the snow, heard the feeble voices of the men within raised in a husky cheer to speed them on their way.

It was 9:15 P.M., Sunday, April 6. The temperature was eight degrees below zero. Rice and Frederick headed for their sledge waiting for them out on the ridge.

The men in the hut awoke Monday morning to find snow falling heavily. After their meager breakfast, they hauled the body of Linn on a sledge out to Cemetery Ridge. It took eight of them to do the work, although Brainard noted, "Linn was literally a skeleton." Lieutenant Kislingbury scratched out a shallow grave for him. Now there were three mounds on Cemetery Ridge.

To raise the spirits of the party, Greely ordered that a small issue of alcohol be distributed. Biederbick performed his magic again and with a few ingredients was able to prepare a "moonshine drink" which warmed and revived them.

The death of Linn made them all conscious of how close the rest of them were to the end of their strength. They spent the day writing their last letters to friends or writing their wills. The snow fell heavily all day and high winds drove it into great drifts. Brainard thought, "My God, what's happening to Rice and Frederick in this weather."

On Tuesday the storm continued and Salor was too weak to take his turn at the shrimping grounds. Brainard substituted for him and went down after dinner. He returned in a few hours with fifteen pounds of the little "sea fleas."

Lieutenant Lockwood's condition worsened. It became apparent that death was imminent. At nine o'clock Wednesday morning the commanding officer made up his mind. He had long been apprehensive about Lockwood's death but had hesitated to restore Lieutenant Kislingbury to duty. It bothered him that Kislingbury had stubbornly refused to request being reassigned to duty. Greely, with equal stubbornness, had refused to make the request of Kislingbury. He had also hesitated to do it when Lockwood was stronger because, in the event of Greely's death, the command would then have devolved on Kislingbury as the senior officer. Lockwood had worked so hard and faithfully that Greely was reluctant to restore Kislingbury to duty when he necessarily would rank above Lockwood.

Now, such considerations were nullified. Lockwood was almost dead. Greely realized his own weakened condition and knew he had to provide for a possible successor to command the expedition.

Following breakfast, and in the hearing of all the men while they were resting in their sleeping bags, Greely called over to Lieutenant Kislingbury.

"Lieutenant Kislingbury, I consider it proper and my duty under the present circumstances, and also in justice to you, to restore you to the position of a member of the expedition. There is no telling what may occur in the future and it would be better understood, in the event of my death, that the command would devolve upon you.

"Your conduct, both at Fort Conger and since that time, has been upright, commendable, and manly under all circumstances. In fact, you have proven yourself, since we left Conger, a noteworthy man in many respects. I shall, when I return to the United States, make this report to the proper authorities giving you full credit for your creditable behavior throughout the time we have been together, and will, as soon as a more convenient opportunity offers for writing, issue the necessary orders.

"Until then, however, I announce to the party that you are now restored to your former position.

Lieutenant Kislingbury could feel that he had won a victory in his long battle of wills with the commanding officer. He had been restored to duty now and he had never requested it.

The snowstorm which had started Monday morning continued Tuesday and Wednesday. As the wind howled about the hut and piled the snow in huge drifts, Brainard's mind was frequently occupied with thoughts of Rice and Frederick. They must be suffering terribly. Would they be able to survive this weather?

While the storm raged, the life of Lieutenant Lockwood was ebbing away. On April 6 Greely had started giving Lockwood extra rations—four ounces of raw dovekie. This was all that the commanding officer felt he could justly allow Lockwood. The dying lieutenant was his brother officer who had served so well, so faithfully, courageously, and successfully. But Greely had to weigh

Lockwood's needs against those of the rest of his men. Four ounces of dovekie a day was the most that could be spared.

Surprisingly, the tiny bit of extra food seemed to help and for a day or so Lockwood felt better. But after Linn died, Lockwood was very depressed again.

"Oh, Lieutenant," Lockwood sighed to Greely, "I really wish that it was all over with me."

Despite his extreme weakness, Lockwood followed Greely's example and tried to keep up his diary. But on April 8 he fainted. His wanderings began and now they all knew that this was the end. The next day, April 9 at 4:20 P.M., Lockwood died.

This was the end of the man who had been the leader in winning the highest honor for their mission, the "Farthest North." He had dared so much and had done so much but this starvation hut had finally claimed his life. How could any of them hope to escape?

The storm ended about eight o'clock, Thursday morning, April 10. Once more they made the dismal journey to Cemetery Ridge. Lockwood was put to rest beside the others. The line of graves was growing.

Looking around the hut, Greely could see signs that others might soon follow Lockwood. Jewell was in very bad condition, although he tried to be cheerful. But he could not manage to eat the shrimps. Death by starvation was inevitable.

Greely had Jewell by his side. At mealtime he would feed Jewell, trying to pour strength into his spirit while he put the food into his body. "You must be determined to live, Jewell," Greely would say. "Make up your mind that you will live."

With each spoonful of food, Greely tried to instil in

Jewell his own spiritual strength. Greely could remember an incident when he had been wounded at Antietam. He had made his way to a field hospital. He would never forget the horror—the amputated arms and legs piled like cordwood against the side of a house. Dunham and Rich, both from Greely's company, were there. Each had suffered an amputation: Dunham, just above the ankle; Rich, at the knee. The surgeon looked at Rich and gravely shook his head. Dunham's condition was not serious and the surgeon was not worried about him. But Dunham was frightened and moaned, "I'm going to die. I know I'm going to die." Rich's attitude was just the opposite. "I'm going to get well," he vowed. "I won't die. I won't die."

In spite of the surgeon's estimate, each man fulfilled his own prediction.

Greely felt if he could inspire in Jewell the will to live he might keep him alive. So he held the little man in his arms and fed him, spoonful by spoonful. "Eat, Jewell. Eat and live."

The morning of April 11 was one of the most beautiful they had seen since the sun returned to them. At 4 A.M. the temperature was twenty-three degrees below zero, but the sky was clear, the sun was shining brightly, and the air was crisp.

Immediately after breakfast Long and Eskimo Jens went down to the open water to hunt for a seal, bear, or walrus.

Out in the sound, across several floes, they were thrilled to see a walrus resting on the ice. Jens got in his kayak and started to make his way to the walrus. Long moved out onto a floe near the shore, hoping to get closer for a shot at the walrus. Suddenly the floe Long was on cracked and broke in two, and he found himself on a small floe, drifting away from the shore.

Jens, seeing Long's situation, swiftly paddled to him.

Long yelled and gestured to Jens to move away and paddle back to the shore.

"Get out of here, you little fool, get out of here. Shore, go to shore." Long gestured toward the shore and made motions of paddling.

"No, no," said Jens, holding on to the edge of the floe with one hand. "You go, me go too."

They drifted along silently for a few moments gazing at each other. Then a shift in the current changed the course of the ice and it began to drift toward shore. In a few minutes Long was able to leap from the floe to some ice on the shore. He gave a hand to Jens and helped him bring his kayak out of the water. Long helped Jens to his feet and then threw his arms about the Eskimo. They stayed in the embrace, laughing and laughing.

They looked out to where the walrus had been but it was gone now. Exhausted, carrying the kayak between them, they made their way wearily back toward the hut.

In the hut they found Greely and Biederbick working to revive Jewell and Israel, both of whom had suffered serious weaknesses. Whisler had been down to make the first attempt at shrimping. He had brought back three pounds. Now Brainard was going out to catch the next tide.

The shrimping had become more tiring each day as their strength declined. Brainard, on reaching the point where he placed the nets, had to choose between resting and freezing or exhausting himself by walking up and down to keep his circulation going. He walked back and forth in the snow, occasionally glancing at the nets. Most of the time he devoted to daydreams about dishes he would like to eat.

He made his first haul of the net and collected about

five pounds of shrimp. Glancing casually in the direction of Beebe Point, he saw only two hundred yards away from him a medium-sized polar bear ambling directly toward him. He was startled and for a moment did not move.

His first thought was to hide behind a hummock of ice and then attack the bear with his hatchet and his seaweed spear. In the next moment he realized the insanity of such an effort. His strength was no greater than that of a child. How could he hope to attack a hungry bear?

He picked up his bucket of shrimp and moved as quickly as he could back toward the hut. The bear had not yet seen him. He tried to keep out of the bear's line of vision. It seemed to him that he moved with incredible slowness.

When he reached the rising land near Cemetery Ridge, he had to crawl to get over it. As he reached a point near the hut, he dropped the shrimp bucket and his heavy mittens and crawled rapidly to the front of the house. On his hands and knees he pushed open the door of the hut with his head and fell inside, exclaiming with a breathless voice, "Bear."

His strength completely gone, he collapsed in the passageway.

Swiftly, Biederbick poured a little bit of diluted alcohol down Brainard's throat. In a moment, Brainard revived. Long and Jens were kneeling next to him, the fire of the hunt burning in their eyes. Still breathless, Brainard poured out the news about the location of the bear. Long and Eskimo Jens, each with a rifle in hand, quickly left the hut. They were followed shortly by Lieutenant Kislingbury carrying the shotgun.

Those in the hut settled down to the tension of waiting for the return of the hunters. Were they to have a life-giving supply of meat or once more were they to be disappointed?

In a short time Lieutenant Kislingbury was back, completely exhausted and almost heartbroken. The shotgun he had taken had no ammunition and he had returned. Biederbick, noting his condition after this brief effort, doubted that he would have been able to pursue the bear much farther. Giving Kislingbury a short drink of his diluted alcohol, Biederbick sent the lieutenant to his sleeping bag to rest.

Long and Jens had not gone very far when they saw the bear coming toward them. Unfortunately, the bear also saw them, then turned and made for the shore and the open water about two miles away.

Long gestured to Jens, indicating that they would separate, Jens taking a route a little to the south and Long would proceed a little to the north. They would flank the bear as they pursued him. Moving as rapidly as they could, they found they were able to gain on the bear which was having trouble traveling over the rough ice. It was questionable, however, whether they would be able to get within distance for a good shot at the bear before he was able to plunge into the water. Luck was with them, however, and the bear stopped occasionally to look behind him. Even with such luck, however, he kept a good distance away from them.

It was not long before the bear was on the shore ice near the water. Once more he paused and looked behind him. The hunters were still 250 yards away but they realized this would be their last chance. Jens fired quickly and hit the bear in the right forepaw.

Long was more deliberate. He drew off his head covering, dropped the glove from his right hand, and took careful aim before firing. The shot hit the bear in the side of the head. As the animal was falling, both hunters fired again to make sure of their kill.

They hurried over to the bear as it lay on its side, its blood staining the ice around it.

The men in the hut were growing disheartened with every passing minute. The longer the hunters were away, the less their chances seemed of returning successfully. At last each of them retired to his sleeping bag filled with a deep sense that once more they were to be disappointed in their hopes. The hut was silent for some time.

About 9:50 P.M. they were startled to hear the joyful voices of Long and Jens approaching. Long, happily and accurately guessing the nature of the conversation in the hut, called out from a distance, "Make your bets, gentlemen, make your bets." In a second all of them raised themselves to a sitting position with surprise and anticipation on their faces. In a few moments Long and Eskimo Jens crawled into the hut, their happy faces telling all the news that was necessary.

Jens crawled over directly to the crippled Elison. In a voice filled with emotion, he said, "You all right now, Elison, you all right."

It was April 11. They now had 400 pounds of fresh meat. If Rice and Frederick brought back the 144 pounds of meat from Cape Isabella, they would feel that their larder was overflowing. They would have real hope of surviving until their rescue ship arrived.

The hut was alive with excitement as the large sled was made ready. Brainard was put in charge of all those strong enough to go out to retrieve the bear. Accompanying Brainard would be Dr. Pavy, Long, Schneider, Henry, Whisler, Ralston, Salor, and Ellis. Before departing, they were each given three ounces of bacon to fortify themselves.

Ellis proved to be a liability at the very beginning. He was able to go only a half mile from the hut when he was worn out and had to return.

It took them almost two hours to make the three-mile trip. When they reached the bear lying on the shore ice, they faced the incredibly difficult task of loading the four-hundred-pound beast on the sledge. None of them had any great strength. After much pulling, hauling, slipping, and cursing, the bear was finally moved onto the sledge.

The great amount of food did not divert them from their determination to save every bit of nourishment they could secure. The bear's blood had flowed into the ice and was frozen there. This frozen blood was chopped free with a hatchet and taken back with them.

It was 2:20 A.M. when they returned to the hut. The weakest men raised feeble cheers for those not much stronger who arrived at the hut with the bear. It was dragged into the center of the hut where Biederbick, Bender, and Jens immediately set about dressing the carcass. In celebration, Greely ordered a pemmican stew to be prepared.

As the bear was being skinned and quartered, the men looked with fascination on the mountain of flesh that meant so much to them. Eskimo Jens patted the bear tenderly, made admiring noises and smacked his lips. When the thick layer of fat was exposed, expressions of pleased surprise and eagerness escaped from the lips of the onlookers.

The commanding officer recognized that it was more than could be expected of human endurance to make the men wait any longer for a taste of this new delicacy. He ordered, therefore, that each of them could immediately be given one ounce of raw fat for sampling.

It was immediately decided that not a bit of the bear

would be lost. Everything would be used to add to their diet, the intestines, lungs, heart, and head. Even the blood would be used to thicken and to flavor the stews. The liver, windpipe, feet, and stomach were set aside to be used for shrimp bait. The teeth and claws were distributed as mementos of the great occasion.

It was an evening of great excitement and rejoicing. We have been expecting death for so long, Brainard thought, that our suffering made it something no longer to fear. Life had seemed a "vague something in the misty distance which was beyond our power to reach or control. Now, to believe that we will be enabled to reach our home, was sufficient cause for tears."

Their rising spirits were sobered later Saturday morning when Jewell quietly passed away. Greely had struggled vainly to keep the flame of life burning in Jewell. He had not been a strong man even before their months of ordeal. At 10 A.M., Saturday, March 12, he became unconscious and, a little while later, died in Greely's arms. He was buried that afternoon.

After the great excitement of late Friday night and early Saturday morning, the party spent the rest of Saturday resting, except for Bender who worked repairing the guns. The sudden increase in food made them all very listless.

Biederbick, the hospital steward, considered the party clinically and was conscious of their continuing critical condition. He felt very weak and tired himself and noted the low condition of a number of others. Ellis, Kislingbury, Israel, Gardiner, and Connell were all in a noticeably weak condition. Biederbick was most distressed, however, to notice Lieutenant Greely returning from outside after a bowel movement. (Their bowel movements were very infrequent, about once a week, and were accompanied by much exertion and great pain.) The commanding officer came in looking exhausted. He was shaking all over. It seemed to Biederbick that Greely was not aware of just how weak he really was.

Easter Sunday morning, April 13, they rested and many long periods passed without anyone's saying a word. The exhilaration of the successful bear hunt had passed. Jewell's death reminded them that in the past week three had died. The bear had been killed too late to save Linn, Lockwood, and Jewell. And what of Rice and Frederick? They had been gone for almost a week. They had started out last Sunday night. Rice had said he expected the trip would take them about four or five days. Where were they?

CHAPTER EIGHTEEN

A GIANT FALLS

When the brief cheer of the men in the hut had died down behind them, Rice and Frederick trudged silently side by side up toward their sledge on the ridge. It was the evening of April 6. They hoped to be back by April 10 or 11. They reached the sled and paused for a moment.

Frederick said, "George, we should watch each other carefully. If you see me getting tired, or if I see you getting tired, we should say so. We have to watch ourselves."

Rice smiled a little at his serious, conscientious comrade.

"You're right, Shorty," Rice said. "The lieutenant made me promise we wouldn't try to do more than we should. We're certainly not the men we used to be, are we?" Rice laughed.

Just as they started dragging the sled over the brow of the hill, the storm hit them. They caught their breath and dug their chins down into their chest as they butted their heads against the bitter wind. They fought their way down the hill struggling to keep going despite the wind, the eight-below-zero temperature, and the deep drifts of snow. They thought they would find some relief from the storm at the bottom of the hill, but when they reached the ice at the edge of the bay they found that the wind had increased. They could not see through the drifting snow that whirled through the air.

Their heads held down, their bodies straining to pull the sled along behind them, they battled on for as long as their strength would permit. When they stopped to prepare some food, they found that the wind made it impossible to light a cooking lamp to make their tea. They got into their sleeping bag, ate a few ounces of frozen pemmican, and rested while they waited for the storm to end.

They lay there huddled in the sleeping bag barely able to keep from freezing while the storm roared above them. The hours passed slowly and it seemed that the violent wind and snow would never be still. It was twenty-two hours before they were able to drag themselves out of their frozen sleeping bag.

They were so numb with cold that it was impossible for them to attempt to prepare any food.

"Shorty," Rice said, "we better move along and get ourselves warmed up."

Frederick nodded, being too full of cold to make the effort to speak. Painfully, they rolled up their sleeping bag and loaded it on the sled. Their stiffened limbs carried them uncertainly forward through the drifts of snow. They moved along in a wavering line, dragging the sled for about an hour before they felt sufficiently restored to stop and attempt to cook.

Carefully shielding the precious match and the wick, they were able to light the alcohol lamp on their first try. The warm tea and the pemmican they prepared for themselves were a small banquet after their frozen ordeal. With these few ounces of nourishment, their bodies felt surprisingly stronger. They went onward in their journey with more vigor.

They plodded side by side, hour after hour, scarcely speaking. All their strength was devoted to pushing ahead. Near the end of the day, wind and flying snow drove them back into their sleeping bag. Once more they shivered in their little shelter, waiting for the wind to stop so they could continue. Despite the cold and their wretched condition they were able to sleep. When they awoke, they found the day calm and clear.

They rose quickly, prepared themselves another meager breakfast, and started ahead with anticipation on the last lap of their journey toward Eskimo Point. In a few hours they reached the old camp which they had established when they were blown ashore by the furious storm at the end of the long retreat from Fort Conger.

"Shorty," Rice said, "I think we ought to unload the sled here. We'll leave the sleeping bag and the other things. That will make the sled lighter for us. We'll take just enough food for one meal. We should be able to reach the meat in a few hours. It's only about six miles from here."

Frederick agreed and they started out hopefully with a lightened sled. They soon started running into large pools of water, however, which made necessary repeated wide detours. When they wet their feet occasionally by stepping on the edge of a pool, their boots froze into solid blocks on hitting the dry ice. This added weight to their feet and made their steps slower and more uncertain. Still, they plodded onward.

Shortly another gale blew up and drove the blinding snow about them, chilling and exhausting them further. Now, however, they had no sleeping bag with them to retreat to while they waited out the storm. They plodded on through the wind and snow.

It was the middle of the afternoon before they reached the point where they thought the meat had been left. They began their search. They looked for signs of the up-ended rifle but could find none. They looked more carefully for their sled marks of the previous November, but of these, too, they saw no sign. They walked about in a pattern, separated to cover a greater area. Neither of them saw any indication of the meat which they had cached almost five months earlier. They searched and searched without success. The storm continued.

Finally, Frederick said, "George, I think we ought to quit and come back and look in the morning."

"Oh, no," Rice said, "not yet, not yet. This wind ought to stop soon and we should find it if we look a little longer."

They went on with the tedious seaching, tramping through the snow, looking vainly for some sign of the precious meat.

A little later Frederick noted great uncertainty in Rice's steps. Twice Rice had stopped moving about and swayed in his tracks. Frederick became alarmed and moved quickly to the side of his companion. He looked intently at Rice's face.

"George," he said earnestly, "we'll have to stop and go back to the sleeping bag."

Rice breathed heavily and gazed back at his friend.

"We promised, George, remember?" Frederick said. "We promised we wouldn't try too much, didn't we?"

After a few moments, Rice said, "All right, Shorty, all right. We will stop now."

They made their way over to the sled and then started hauling it back to the sleeping bag at Eskimo Point six miles away. They moved along silently with Frederick casting anxious glances at his comrade. He could see Rice growing steadily weaker. Concerned, he asked, "How are you, George?"

Rice replied, "I'll be all right, Shorty, but let's travel a little slower." They went on with Rice's weakness showing in every step.

Suddenly, Frederick, assuming command, said flatly, "We'll stop here and rest."

He sat Rice on the sled and gave him a drink of ammonia and rum. Then Frederick lit their alcohol lamp, made some tea and heated some pemmican. After this brief meal, Frederick urged Rice to move on so that they would not freeze. They were without a sleeping bag to protect them against the cold. They could not rest until they reached Eskimo Point.

Rice tried to rise but found he couldn't. He was too weak to stand up. He leaned against Frederick seated beside him on the sled and a great lassitude fell on him.

"Oh, Shorty," Rice said. "We're a long way from home, Shorty; we're a long way from home. I wonder what my folks are doing. Do you suppose they have given us up, Shorty?"

Frederick, holding his friend in his arms, felt the panic rise in him.

"I wish we were back in the States, Shorty," Rice said. "I wish we were in Washington. I'd take you to Godfrey's —buy you the best meal you ever ate . . . Shorty, how would this suit you right now?" Rice asked dreamily. "A half-dozen raw oysters, a great bowl of bean soup, a big roast goose with applesauce—cabbage—sweet potato pie —apples, oranges, raisins, nuts—cheese and crackers——"

"That would suit me fine, George; that would suit me fine," Frederick replied. "Won't you have some yourself? Sit down and join me."

"I think I will, Shorty," Rice said, "I think I will, since you ask me."

They were silent for several minutes while Frederick watched his friend closely. Rice made no sound other than his labored breathing. After a while, Rice said, "Shorty, have you ever been to Cape Breton Island? It's a great place, Shorty, a great place. They have some wonderful summers. They have fierce winters, of course, but they have some wonderful summers. There was one summer," Rice said, and then his voice trailed off to incoherent whispers.

Frederick changed his position on the sled and moved Rice so that his friend could stretch full length, resting the upper part of his body in Frederick's lap. Rice lay motionless for some minutes and then opened his eyes. Looking up at Frederick, he said, "I'm getting cold, Shorty; I'm getting cold. My feet are so cold. My feet are so cold." Then Rice closed his eyes again.

Trying to disturb his friend as little as possible, Frederick eased himself out of his sealskin jumper and reached over to wrap it around Rice's feet. He sat on the edge of the sled in the driving wind and snow, protecting his friend's face by holding his head in his arms.

After a while Rice stirred again and said, "Take care of my things, will you, Shorty? Kislingbury has some papers of mine and I left my will with him. I wrote him a letter giving directions about what to do with my things. Ask him to take care of things, will you? You and Brainard help him take care of them, won't you?" Rice took a deep breath and gave a great shiver. "It's all there in the letter," Rice said. "I wrote it all out in the letter."

He was still once more and Frederick cradled Rice's head in his arms.

Frederick sat there for uncounted minutes feeling that his whole body, even his mind was frozen. He couldn't move, he couldn't think. His eyes were closed, so he was startled when he heard his friend's voice saying, "Shorty, wake up, Shorty." He jumped slightly and looked down to see Rice smiling faintly up at him. "Have some more of that roast goose," Rice said; "then we'll have dessert."

Shorty smiled back at Rice and said, "I'd sure like to, George, but you ate it all up."

Rice smiled and said, "I guess I must have been hungry tonight. We'll have to order more."

Rice closed his eyes and was silent again. Then in a few moments he muttered, "Home, a long way from home."

The wind howled and the snow drifted up around the sled and the two motionless figures. Rice had been silent for a long time and Frederick was surprised, looking at him closely, to see that he was no longer breathing. He stared intently at the still face and it was some moments before his mind could grasp the fact that his friend was truly dead.

He sat there with the dead man's head in his lap and thought of the futility of their efforts. They had found no meat and Rice had killed himself in the trying. What good had it done? What good had it done?

Frederick raised the dead man's head from his lap and forced himself to rise. He stood by the side of the sled and gazed down at Rice's body. "What's the use of trying any more?" he thought. "It would be just as well to lie down here and die with George."

But if he did that the men at the hut would send a party after him—men who would risk their lives to save his. He could not throw away the life that they would try to save. His dead companion had never stopped trying. Rice spent every effort to the last ounce of his strength. Frederick knew that he would have to do the same. He had to make his way back.

He gazed for a lingering moment on the dead face of the body on the sled. Then, suddenly, he stooped and kissed it before turning away and beginning the journey back to the old camp at Eskimo Point.

Frederick did not know how long he traveled. He moved ahead, putting one foot in front of another, heading inexorably toward his destination and the security of the sleeping bag. He reached there only after seven hours of fighting his way through storm and snow drifts, too tired even to make an attempt to unroll the sleeping bag now frozen solid. Now, he thought, now he had reached the end. There was no strength left in him. He could not go on and there was no protection here. But he found in his pocket the small vial of spirits of ammonia which he had carried with him. He quickly drank the few drops remaining. They gave a faint revival to his strength. It was enough to enable him to force his way into the sleeping bag and there he slept. He awoke the next morning at 8 A.M. and after eating some food, found himself stronger.

He could, of course, make his way directly back to the hut at Cape Sabine but the body of his dead friend was out there unprotected on the sled. He could not leave it there unburied. Once more he made the journey back through the snow drifts and the rough ice.

Before attempting to bury Rice, Frederick went through the pockets of the dead man's clothing and removed each thing he could find that might be of value to Rice's relatives or friends. There were instructions, Rice had said, in the letter left with Kislingbury.

The only method Frederick had for burying the body was to bring small blocks of ice and pack it around the dead man. After building this white tomb, Frederick loaded the few pieces of equipment on the sled and started off on his long journey back to the living at Cape Sabine.

In a few hours he reached Eskimo Point and again rested there. When he awoke, he hastened out of his sleeping bag, loaded his few things on the sled, and once more started the weary business of dragging his sled over rough ice and deep snow back toward camp. After an hour of this exertion, he was sufficiently warm to prepare himself some breakfast. A cup of tea prepared over the alcohol lamp and some pemmican once more restored his feeble strength. The thoughts of despair, the temptation to give up and become a frozen corpse lost in the arctic waste, had been succeeded by a determination to make his way back. That determination was accompanied by a cold realization that he could succeed in making the return journey only by careful expenditure of the little energy he could muster.

Frederick worked out his method of getting back very simply. He moved on, dragging his sledge with him for only that distance which seemed reasonable in his weakened condition. When he reached the point of near-exhaustion he would stop, have a few ounces of food and rest. After a few hours he was up again, reloaded the sled and moved on for an hour before stopping for another tiny bit of nourishment.

Remembering the difficult time he and Rice suffered following the outside route around Cape Sabine to Payer Harbor, Frederick decided to take the inside route through Rice Strait. He could not help realizing that his dead friend was still helping him. Frederick would stand a better chance of returning to camp by following the route Rice had discovered for them back in October.

By careful stages he reached Cocked Hat Island before he doubted his ability to make it safely to the hut. He stopped at Cocked Hat Island for a little more food and more rest. On awakening from his sleep, however, he knew that his body was not equal to the task of dragging his sled as much as another hundred yards. The only chance he had for survival was to make the remaining journey to the hut in a single trip without stopping. He was much too weak to drag the sled or carry anything but a few ounces of food.

At Fort Conger, when one of their sledge parties had returned from an especially exhausting journey, a sled dog, completely worn out by the strenuous trip, had died of exhaustion within sight of camp. Frederick knew he, too, now was only a few miles from the hut but his strength was completely gone. He wondered if his fate would be the same as that of the sled dog. He summoned every bit of his spiritual strength and started out over the last few miles.

Each step was unbelievable labor but he locked his mind in the determination to keep moving ahead. His body moved waveringly over the ice hummocks, always onward toward the hut. He stumbled and fell repeatedly, but each time he dragged himself to his feet and moved on, always onward. He knew that if a storm should rise, as it had several times earlier in this tragic journey, he would not be able to survive. But fortune at last was with him and the weather held good. The sun was shining, no wind was blowing, and Frederick moved on across the ice back to his friends.

At last he rounded the final point of land and saw the hut off in the distance.

He stopped for a moment, breathing heavily as he gazed at it. His heart lifted as he realized what he had accomplished. He had come back. He had returned safely. But the brief moment of joy was immediately wiped from his mind as he realized the message that he would have to bring to his companions. He was not bringing them 144 pounds of beef. He was bringing them the tragic news that their beloved Sergeant Rice was dead out there in an ice tomb at Eskimo Point.

This heavy, dark realization slowed his steps as he moved forward over the last ground between him and the hut.

CHAPTER NINETEEN

THE "BEAR" LEADS THE WAY

Lieut. William H. Emory, Jr., captain of the *Bear*, in his early thirties, was a relatively young man to have command of a ship on such an important mission, but he was well chosen for the task. In addition to being a capable naval officer he had strong, personal motivation to share in the mission for the rescue of Lieutenant Greely. Lieutenant Emory's older brother, Campbell, and Greely had been close personal friends. Emory's brother had died during the past year. The rescue of Greely took on the aspect of a service to the memory of his dead brother.

Lieutenant Emory was a man filled with a sense of dedication to his mission. His determination had been fortified by a letter from the wife of the lost explorer. Mrs. Greely sent Lieutenant Emory a letter for her husband. Sending him this letter for delivery at some unknown place in the Far North, Mrs. Greely wrote Emory: "I know it is very possible when you do find him that he may be starving and close to death. I am sure this letter will renew his spirit and his determination to live."

Emory replied that he would deliver the letter. "I am going to keep it on me always until we find your husband," he wrote.

Emory was asked later about his plans for the search for Greely. He replied simply, "We will search until we find him."

"But what if you find no sign of the expedition?"

"Then," Emory said, "we won't come back."

The reply had the touch of melodrama that would be appealing to a youthful spirit, but burning in Emory was also the real determination that his mission would not fail.

The *Bear* sailed from New York Harbor the afternoon of April 24. Three days out of New York she ran into an extremely heavy gale. The bad weather buffeted the ship about and put her in real danger. The wild sea and the roaring wind tore away the bridge. Emory succeeded in retaining control of the ship and, when the gale had passed, pushed north rapidly to St. John's.

At St. John's he found that Consul Molloy had the extra stores ready for immediate loading. Emory did not permit the storm damage to the ship to delay their departure. Only the necessary iron work was completed during their two-day stay in port. Lumber was taken on board so that the remainder of the bridge could be built while the ship was at sea steaming northward. At St. John's they also took on sealskin boots and other extra clothing, Labrador sled dogs, and additional food supplies.

While the ship was being loaded, Lieutenant Emory sought information about conditions in the northern waters from the captains who had just returned from their sealing voyages.

On May 3 he cabled the Navy Department: "The strong northeasterly gales in the area may well have prevailed further north. It is possible that the northern ice started moving southward earlier than usual this year. An unusual amount of ice was reported off the coast of Labrador."

Emory reported that he intended to move to the Greenland coast as quickly as possible and move north from Disko along the foot ice to Upernivik. He would leave messages at these ports for Commander Schley. Emory also reported that he would attempt to go beyond Upernivik if the ice was open. His instructions said, "You may proceed beyond Upernivik if any special circumstances justify such movement." This justified, he believed, an attempt to cross Melville Bay if ice conditions would permit it.

Emory also reported that the whaling captains were much interested in the attempted rescue of Lieutenant Greely and all of them were planning to participate in the effort. He reported:

> It is not the intention of these whalers, nor have they authority, to go beyond Littleton Island. These steam whalers are ably commanded, and are efficiently fitted out. Their masters are ambitious to secure the Greely party; and, although the reward will not be a secondary consideration, they are one and all desirous of obtaining the prestige of the rescue. From information that I can gather, it would seem that the *Arctic* will be our only dangerous competitor. She is not stronger than the *Bear* or the *Thetis*, but has more powerful engines.

The whaling ships were regarded as competitors by the youthful lieutenant who was beginning to see this mission as something of a contest. The campaign of the previous winter in Washington and in the newspaper columns clearly had been successful. The whole world of north seamen was filled with the fever of the attempt to rescue Greely.

Emory reported to the Navy Department that by May 3 six whaling vessels had sailed north and intended as part of their voyage to make some search for the Greely party. Within the next week three more vessels in addition to the *Bear* would be leaving St. John's to go north and spend at least part of their time in the search.

After the swift work on the repair of the supports for the bridge, and after loading the additional equipment and supplies, the *Bear* was ready for sea. There were stormy weather and icy waters ahead but the *Bear* left St. John's on May 4. Emory was determined to get to the Far North as fast as possible.

The *Bear* ran into heavy weather almost immediately after leaving St. John's. It was rough going all the way. They had one advantage as they traveled north—the days lengthened. Soon they crossed the Arctic Circle and were enjoying the novel experience of twenty-four hours of sunlight.

The *Bear* arrived at Godhavn Harbor on Disko Island May 13, nine days after leaving St. John's. With the sea open north of him, Emory did not wish to delay. He steamed along the western shore of Disko Island but soon came up against the solid ice. A strong southerly wind was blowing behind him and Emory realized he was in a dangerous position. The prudence of a captain governed the impatience of the would-be rescuer. Emory ordered his ship to return to the safety of Godhavn Harbor until the wind changed.

As the *Bear* steamed into the harbor, Emory sighted two whaling ships, the *Polynia* and the *Nova Zembla*. These two ships were on their annual whaling cruise but the captains were also going to make a try for the rescue of Greely and the $25,000 reward.

The ships lay in the harbor for three days waiting a change of wind so that they might sail north once more. During this time Emory kept his men busy putting everything to order on board ship and purchasing from the Governor of Disko Island a team of seven trained Eskimo dogs. At St. John's the *Bear* had taken aboard eighteen Labrador dogs.

With the lesson of the *Proteus* in mind, Emory directed that food stores be brought up on deck and stowed there. The ship's boats were filled with food and supplies. The spare propeller was brought up and stored in the port gangway. Then Emory gave his men additional exercise by having them practice abandoning ship.

The morning of Wednesday, May 21, the waiting ships had the change of wind they had been anticipating. The whaling ships were away first and were soon out of sight. However, the *Bear,* steaming all afternoon and evening, passed the whalers at 10 P.M.

The ice pack was broken but still close and heavy, and Emory had a difficult time steering the *Bear* through the twisting leads. It was two days before they could work as far north as the Noursoak Peninsula. Here some Eskimos greeted the *Bear* in their kayaks. When they came on board, they recognized Lieutenant Colwell. The year before, when he was making his retreat in a small boat from Upernivik to Disko, these natives had helped him by speeding on ahead to bring the news of his approach to the *Yantic* at Disko Island. After a joyous exchange of greetings, Colwell presented them with gifts of bread and tobacco.

During the next several days Emory continued to fight his way northward by moving the *Bear* through openings in the ice close to land. The *Bear* passed several other whaling ships seeking to make their way north, the *Triune,* and *Aurora,* and the *Cornwallis.* After fighting the ice for almost a week, the *Bear* found on May 27 that the pack had moved away and open water lay ahead.

Emory started the *Bear* moving north early in the day and toward evening passed another whaler, the *Narwhal.* The *Cornwallis* and the *Aurora,* which had moved earlier than the *Bear,* were still ahead of him. However, he soon passed both ships and optimistically kept the *Bear* going across open water past Upernivik.

Emory had concluded back in St. John's that if he found

open water in Melville Bay he would try to cross to the north even though the *Thetis* had not then caught up with him. For a short time that day, Emory had a vision of sailing straight on to Littleton Island, walking ashore and shaking hands with Lieutenant Greely surrounded by cheering men. The vision was abruptly dissolved by the solid reality of the ice pack. Eighteen miles north of Upernivik the *Bear* was stopped by unbroken, impenetrable ice. In a short while the whaling ships, *Aurora, Cornwallis,* and *Narwhal,* caught up with the *Bear.* They, too, stood off impassively before the ice barrier.

The ships waited all afternoon while their captains hopefully searched for some sign of the breaking of the ice. After eight hours they gave up and turned back to the harbor of Upernivik. They arrived there about 11 P.M., May 28.

It would probably be the middle of June before they could hope to reach Littleton Island or Cape Sabine.

CHAPTER TWENTY

SUNSHINE AND DEATH

Frederick crawled into the hut Sunday morning, April 13. The news of Rice's death hit the men with the force of a strong blow. The entire party was shaken to its depths. One of them broke into great sobs. Moans escaped from his throat as though he were in physical pain. The rest of them shouted at him to stop it and told him he was behaving shamefully. The vigor of their expression revealed they were glad of a diversion to rescue them from the deep, tragic emotion they were all feeling.

Biederbick restored Frederick with some alcoholic stimulant and some food. Frederick then told the details of his story. When he was finished, he handed Lieutenant Greely a small package.

"What is this, Frederick?" Greely asked.

"That's the remainder of George's rations," Frederick replied.

Greely could not speak. Rice and Frederick had insisted on making the journey on six ounces of food per day. Frederick had finished his own rations but did not think it right to eat the food which had been given to Rice. Greely gazed intently at this man who had almost killed himself with exhaustion but would not violate the rules about food. He could find no words to utter other than merely, "Thank you, Frederick." Greely turned and handed the little bundle to Sergeant Brainard.

Later in the day Lieutenant Kislingbury took out the letter which Rice had given him back in February before the attempt to cross Smith Sound. The letter began, "My dear friend Kislingbury" and named the lieutenant and Brainard as executors of Rice's will along with M. P. Rice of Washington, D.C. Listing his effects, Rice mentioned a tin box with photographs, manuscripts and letters in the possession of Shorty Frederick, a trunk in the care of Mr. Hamlin, a barber in St. John's, Newfoundland, and a pocketbook which Rice carried on himself. Kislingbury was asked to inspect all of the effects Rice had at the camp and to destroy all of those "which from their nature or the rights of others should not be seen by my parents or others." Kislingbury was also asked to forward the manuscript which Rice had prepared for a newspaper along with his notebooks or other information which would add to the narrative. With wry humor Rice also asked Kislingbury to supply the paper with any information "which you think will add to an honorable reputation (if you can)."

Rice listed items to be distributed to his father, mother, brother, sister, and grandmother. He also asked, "Of my trinkets I desire a diamond ring, which will be found among my effects, to be sent to Miss Maud Dunlop of Baddeck, Cape Breton Island, as a souvenir of a few sunshiny days."

He was aware, Rice wrote, that "this hastily written paper" had no value as a legal instrument, but he felt sure "there will be no disregard of my wishes on the part of anyone interested in me or herein mentioned." The letter concluded with the hope "that we may joke over this in the sunshine of Littleton Island." It was signed "Your much obliged friend, George W. Rice."

Kislingbury put the letter back in the diary thinking, "Well, George, none of us now will ever see the sunshine of Littleton Island."

They lay in their sleeping bags deep in gloom. The

animation generated by the successful bear hunt had long since passed. The loss of Sergeant Rice weighed heavily on the mind of each of them. Their conversation was desultory. But suddenly the conversation was interrupted by the unbelievably loud chirping of a snowbird, the first they had heard or seen since fall. No one moved or spoke. It was perched on the roof of the hut, just above their heads. Their eyes widened and the continued song of the bird seemed to dissipate the gloom and inspire the entire party with renewed hope. Did not Easter mean resurrection?

Their ice prison might yet melt. They might yet escape to the green world of trees, flowers, and songbirds.

Their renewed hope was strengthened later that day. Long and Jens went hunting and joyfully returned with a seal to add to their supply. Long shot it out on a floe. Jens paddled out swiftly in his kayak and brought it to shore. Weighing only sixty pounds, it was a small seal compared with others they had brought in last fall, but it was a significant addition to their limited supply.

The seal, the bear meat, and the shrimp seemed to provide them with enough food to promise their survival. It was April 13. More game could be expected. If the hunters and the shrimpers continued successful, their prospects were bright. Because of their improved prospects, and also because of the depressed spirit of the party owing to the death of Rice, Greely increased the rations to one pound of meat a day. He also ordered eight ounces extra meat daily for Long, Jens, and Brainard who were doing the hunting and shrimping and for Ellison, the amputee. He expected that this increase in the meat ration, together with the shrimp stews, would improve both the strength and the morale of the party.

On the morning of April 14 Dr. Pavy made a check of

the physical condition of a number of the party, including Lieutenant Greely.

"Lieutenant," the doctor said, looking calmly into the commanding officer's eyes, "as you are probably aware, Lieutenant Kislingbury's mind is weakening. I must also tell you that your heart is in a very dangerous condition."

"Yes, Doctor," Greely said flatly, "I have had some pains."

They both knew the great significance of these symptoms. Greely had been aware for some time of his increased weakness. Biederbick had spoken to Greely on occasion and had suggested that he increase his own rations as he had done for others of the party who were suffering special weakness. The commanding officer had been unwilling to do so up to now but with the doctor's official warning he agreed to increase his own ration by four extra ounces of pemmican and two extra ounces of bread daily.

Greely, however, could not feel that this increase in rations was going to make a significant difference in his fate. He had seen what had happened to others once their decline had started. Kislingbury's condition was clearly unstable. At times he babbled incoherently. It was obvious that in the event of Greely's death Kislingbury would not be able to exercise command. Accordingly, Greely spoke to Brainard and wrote a letter naming the sergeant his successor in the event of the death of the commanding officer.

Kislingbury's behavior was often both pitiful and poignant. He would boast, "Well, tomorrow I will go out and hunt in Rice Strait. We could use another seal." Or he would promise to help Brainard with the shrimping and other work. Greely, fearful that he might actually attempt such labor, told Kislingbury that he was in no condition to attempt those things. The commanding officer ordered him not to put any additional strain on his weakened body.

The sun was climbing higher in the sky and the temperature was rising. By April 20 they would once more have twenty-four hours of sunlight. Many of the men took advantage of good weather to crawl outside the hut and indulge themselves in a sun bath. Greely lifted the arrest he had placed on Henry and permitted him to go outside the hut but not beyond the limits of their little peninsula.

Since the hunters had had no further success Greely felt obliged once more to reduce the rations. Instead of one pound of meat daily, they would receive only ten ounces of bear or seal meat. On April 18 Dr. Pavy gave Lieutenant Greely a detailed report on the physical condition of the party. He also recorded his report in his diary:

> Passages are generally the same, hard as musk ox beef. This proves torpidity of the bowels—the difficulty of the passages.
> The action of the heart is generally more fluttering, the decrease of rations seems to show itself already, the pulse is less strong and the force diminished with some, this is a bad sign, the end where the appetite begins to diminish, plus difficulty to collect thoughts; a strong tax upon the brain, that is to say, where the blood is poor.
> Jens—complains of feebleness in his legs, strength decreased.
> Long—complains of weakness and pain in the bowels, ordered alcohol compound. (Discussion with Greely)
> Schneider—has suffered much during the night at shrimping—weak, legs and face very much swollen. Heart fluttering. (Had him relieved) Constipation.
> Gardiner—Increased rations of four ounces since yesterday morning—heart very feeble, dropsical effusion around the heart—constipation. (weak stool)
> Salor—Very feeble, fluttering heart and pulse.
> Biederbick—Same thing, etc.

> Ellis—Grows better—diarrhea stopped—a little hard.
> Israel—A little better, still water around heart.
> Greely—Very constipated.
> Give quinine to Gardiner, Israel, Connell, Kislingbury,
> Salor, Biederbick.

Dr. Pavy, who was so conscientious in the performance of his medical duties, was also capable of the most reprehensible personal conduct. On April 19 Long caught the doctor drinking part of Schneider's rum allowance. Biederbick reported to Greely that the doctor had been stealing some of the bread belonging to his patient, Elison. Greely was at a loss as to what to do about the doctor. They desperately needed his professional services. There seemed to be no way of punishing him for his thievery without risking the loss of those services.

Greely's deepest concern now was to hold the party together, to continue operating as a military unit. If they did not behave as soldiers, as comrades, there was no hope at all. And worse, their last days might be spent in a nightmare of savagery. Greely knew that the evil conduct of the doctor was fearfully contagious. They needed the doctor to help them fight the effects of starvation, but the doctor's behavior might move others to cast aside moral restraint. What would happen to them if self-preservation became their only law?

Brainard continued to work very hard at his shrimping. Daily he brought in large quantities of the little "sea fleas." On one day he brought in as much as forty pounds. He was, however, overtiring himself and at times someone else would be sent in his place. No one else, however, seemed capable of working the nets correctly and the catch was always very small.

There was a large quantity of shrimp on hand and on the evening of April 19 Greely declared a party. Each man could have as many of the shrimp as he was able to eat. The shrimp stew, however, was nowhere near as palatable as the bear and seal meat. None of the men was able to eat more than a few ounces of the shrimp.

On April 22 both Dr. Pavy and Lieutenant Kislingbury strongly recommended to the commanding officer that the meat ration be raised to one pound per day.

"Do you realize," Greely replied, "that if we followed your recommendation our meat stock would be exhausted by May 7?"

Both Kislingbury and the doctor argued that the strength of the party was declining and an increase was essential.

Greely replied as he had so many times before that it was his intention to make the food last as long as possible by keeping the daily ration to the minimum necessary to keep the party alive. Pavy and Kislingbury continued to argue for an increase and at last Greely agreed to raise the daily ration from ten ounces to twelve ounces beginning April 24.

Once more Greely's heart was paining him and he felt his end was near. He conferred with Sergeant Brainard, reminding him that he would succeed to the command of the expedition upon the death of the commanding officer. He also gave Brainard detailed instructions about his personal effects and advised him that each of his items was labeled with directions for their disposition.

On the evening of April 22, Schneider, who had been doing the cooking in recent days, said, "Lieutenant, I'm sick. I'll have to be relieved from this duty."

Greely had Dr. Pavy examine Schneider and the doctor said that Schneider was not sick. Greely thereupon ordered Schneider to prepare supper. Schneider still refused and fell on his sleeping bag, crying.

"Well," Greely said, "if a commander cannot make his orders obeyed he must carry them out himself."

Greely crawled out of his sleeping bag and went over to the stove. Several of the men protested and said that the lieutenant should not be doing the cooking and one or two volunteered to do it. Greely rejected the offers and said once more, "No. If an officer cannot make his orders stand, he must perform them himself."

Schneider remained on his sleeping bag crying and saying, "I can't do it, I tell you, I'm sick. I'm sick."

While this scene was going on, Long and Jens returned from their hunting and crawled into the hut. The Eskimo, taking in the situation, was shocked to see the commanding officer at the stove. Jens quickly crawled over to Greely and pushed him away from the stove.

"No, no, Lieutenant," Jens said, "you no cook. Lieutenant no cook."

Greely smiled at the earnest little Eskimo they all loved so well. Jens said again, "You no cook, Lieutenant, me cook."

After a moment's hesitation, Greely gave in and said, "All right, Jens, you cook. All right."

Following supper Schneider seemed to be in a better frame of mind. He had stopped crying and seemed rational again. Greely talked with him, pointing out to him that he would have to perform his duties. He urged Schneider to take some pride in himself as a man, as a soldier, and as a German. Schneider kept insisting that he was too sick to do the cooking. At last Greely told him flatly that if he would not perform his duties, if he would not cook, he would not be able to eat. The following morning Schneider cooked breakfast.

The commanding officer might have felt that he was thus able to enforce his orders but this was a hasty conclusion. That evening while Schneider was preparing dinner Connell called out, "I saw him, I saw him. Schneider's eating food out of the mess pot."

"You're a liar," Schneider said hotly. "I didn't take anything."

"Yes you did, yes you did," said Whisler, "I saw you, too."

"You took some and you know you did," Connell said. "We both saw you do it."

Tempers were rising when Greely stepped in and said coldly, "Schneider, you're not going to get out of it that way either. You are going to continue cooking and I tell the rest of you men now: If any of you see him stealing food from us, you are to kill him at once."

The words had a shock effect that stopped the quarrel temporarily, but Schneider continued to glare periodically at Connell.

A little while later Schneider started to mumble to himself words obviously directed at Connell, one of which was "name caller."

"Name caller?" Connell said. "Name caller? I'll call you a name. The name for you is 'thief.' That's what it is, 'thief.' You're the greatest thief in camp and I just want to see you do it once more, just once more. Try to steal again and I'll put daylight through you."

The two glared at each other but Schneider said no more and the argument ended.

The commanding officer was much disturbed by these frequent contentions and the occasional thievery that went on. Conscious of the weakness of his condition and the continual danger of disunity, Greely felt impelled to remind the men of their responsibilities to each other as soldiers.

"Men," he said, "you know that we get weaker each day

and I have felt myself growing seriously weaker. Some of us have died and still more may die in the near future. It is possible that I may be one of the next to go. We need not fear death, but I do fear the possible consequences of disunity among us. We must not let that happen. We must have courage and we must have unity. Without unity, none of us stands a chance of surviving. Our only hope of coming through rests in all of us working together. It is my most urgent order, therefore, if anything should happen to me, that you maintain your courage and your unity."

Greely had prepared for his death earlier by instructing Brainard about disposition of his papers and other belongings. He had been conscious of Brainard's weakening himself by working too hard at his shrimping. He had assigned others to share in this task. Dr. Pavy and Schneider had attempted the shrimping but they did not seem capable of doing it correctly and were unsuccessful. So Brainard was kept at the shrimping and, it seemed to Greely, was literally working himself to death to keep bringing in food to the hut. The commanding officer, therefore, also instructed Israel and Elison about the disposition of his papers and effects.

By April 22 they had used the last of the stearine fuel. Bender, Henry, and Whisler set about ripping out the wooden lining of the boat which had served for the roof of the hut. Greely felt it better to use wood for fuel rather than alcohol. The alcohol was being used in the "moonshine" that Biederick concocted for them. Alcohol was more valuable as food than as fuel.

On April 27 Henry once more revealed himself to be an accomplished thief. While Biederbick was making the distribution of their daily drink of "moonshine," Henry contrived to steal some extra for himself. He crawled back to his sleeping bag but the drink was too much for him. Soon he had to vomit and Lieutenant Kislingbury saw that he was in a stupor and smelled strongly of alcohol.

"Look here," Kislingbury said. "Henry's drunk."

"He's been stealing again," Whisler said. "He must have stolen some of the moonshine."

"He's nothing but a born thief," Gardiner said. "We ought to pound him."

"That's right," Whisler said. "He ought to be given the beating of his life."

"Henry," Lieutenant Kislingbury said, "anyone who would steal from his comrades in these circumstances can have no principle at all."

Henry sneered at the lieutenant and said coldly, "Lieutenant, you can just go to hell."

Turning belligerently to Gardiner and Whisler he said, "You just try pounding me. You'll find out that I can take care of myself and that I can take care of the whole damn crowd of you, too." Gardiner growled deep in his throat and started to crawl toward Henry. "I'll kill him—I'll kill him." Gardiner was stopped by Whisler and Biederbick.

Greely was so sick and weak that he was unable to discipline Henry that day. The following morning, however, he ordered that, thereafter, Henry would not share in the daily "moonshine" drink and he would have the duty of emptying the urinal tub every day.

Greely devoted much of his time that day to cheering up the little Eskimo. The day before, Jens had had a rare opportunity for a shot at an oösuk seal. Although he was able to get within forty yards of the seal, his shot missed. He returned from the unsuccessful hunting trip with Long much disgusted with himself and the following morning was very depressed. The rest of the men tried to talk him out of his gloom and told him he would do better in the next day or two. He shrugged them off, muttering sadly, "Eskimo no good."

"Jens," Greely said, "you must not be unhappy about one failure. We all fail sometimes. We cannot always do as well as we would wish. Everyone sometimes misses what he aims for. This happens to all of us.

"You missed yesterday," Greely said, "but you have not always missed. You did not miss when you had the chance for the bear. You have succeeded so many times for us. You have done as much as any one to keep us alive. You missed yesterday, but you will try again. You will hit for us tomorrow or the next day. We know you do your best for us, Jens. You must not be unhappy."

Greely wondered if Jens, like so many of the rest of them, was losing his grip. But the encouragement from the rest of the men and the talk with the commanding officer seemed to have restored Jens's normal good spirits and he went out hunting with Long in apparently good humor.

Jens and Long returned from their trip without having seen any game. Greely watched Jens closely to see if there was any sign of his gloomy mood returning. He saw none. The next morning Jens's depression had disappeared completely. The party was awakened early so that breakfast could be served at 5 A.M. and the hunters could get off to an early start. The little Eskimo was in an especially good humor. He was smiling and laughing and before they went out he came over to the commanding officer and shook hands with him. Greely could see that Jens was optimistic about the day's possibilities. The commander thought, "He's determined to bring something back from today's trip."

Long and Jens went off to the point of Cape Sabine and spent the morning traveling along the shore looking

for seals. At last, a little after eleven o'clock they spotted
an oösuk seal out on a floe. They moved along the shore
for a while hoping the floe would drift in close to the
shore ice. Jens was obviously eager and impatient for this
second chance. Soon he said, "Me go."

Taking the Springfield rifle and the screen which he
used to hide himself from his quarry, he got into his kayak
and paddled out toward the seal.

There were several small floes intervening between
Jens and the large floe on which the seal rested. Jens
crossed the first lead of water and dragged his kayak
across the first floe. He was paddling his kayak across
the second lead when Long saw him suddenly start
paddling very rapidly. Jens leaped for the second floe. It
was new ice and broke beneath his weight. The kayak
capsized as Jens went underwater.

Long frantically tried to make his way out to the kayak
by leaping from floe to floe. After some time he was able
to make his way to within a few feet of the kayak which
was still floating upside down. He could see Jens's lifeless
body suspended from the kayak beneath the water but the
kayak was just out of his reach. As Long stretched for the
kayak the floe he was on cracked and he almost went
in the water himself. Long moved back cautiously to the
shore ice and helplessly watched the kayak drift away.

He made the long, slow journey back to the hut with a
grief almost too heavy to carry.

CHAPTER TWENTY-ONE

THE "THETIS" AT UPERNIVIK

After the *Thetis* set out to sea, leaving the Sandy Hook lightship behind, Commander Schley found fine weather and clear sailing. It was May 1. The spring sky was blue and the sun shone brightly on the blue-gray waters. The *Thetis* made very good time toward St. John's until the evening of May 4 when the connecting rod of the air pump broke.

This was bitter, hard luck to experience so early in the journey. The *Thetis* could proceed by sail, of course, but it would be a much longer trip to St. John's.

Schley now learned how fortunate he was in having as a chief engineer a man with the determination of George W. Melville. The engineer immediately went to work at the forge. All night long he worked, forging a new connecting rod. By morning it was completed and installed. The ship continued on her cruise to the north.

The *Thetis* arrived at St. John's without further mishap the morning of May 9.

The *Thetis*, as the *Bear* preceding her had done at St. John's, took on additional supplies and a team of Labrador dogs. Much attention was paid to preparing every detail of the ship for sea. Fresh vegetables and two thousand pounds of fresh beef were taken aboard. The beef was stored by the simple method of covering it with gunny sacking and hanging it in the rigging out of the reach of the dogs. It was correctly estimated that after one day's cruise out of St. John's the ship would be in freezing temperatures and there would be no worry about spoilage of the meat.

When the *Thetis* arrived at St. John's, Commander Schley found the coaling steamer, the *Loch Garry*, waiting in the harbor. The steamer, in accordance with the contract, was carrying five hundred tons of coal. She was to accompany the *Thetis* as far as Littleton Island. Thus, the *Thetis, Bear,* and *Alert* would have an adequate supply of fuel on hand in northern waters.

Among the last-minute measures taken was the overhauling of the engine of the *Thetis*. Bad luck again dogged Chief Engineer Melville. During the overhauling a small brass bearing was lost. They had no spares of this small, but essential, part. The engineer's crew searched frantically but the elusive brass bearing could not be found.

Early the next morning Melville went ashore to seek a replacement for the lost bearing. Melville was not surprised to find that all of the shops were closed on Sunday morning. It was an easy matter to hunt up the owners of the small shops around the harbor. However, the strict, religious people of St. John's were surprised and shocked that this peculiar, irreligious American would expect them to do business on the Sabbath.

Melville had a few bad minutes. He could imagine waiting twenty-four hours until the shops opened on Monday morning, all for the sake of the small, but crucial, part. However, the shopkeepers of St. John's did not require others to observe the Sabbath with the same strictness as themselves. If Melville were so indifferent to the sacred nature of the day, they would permit him to take the keys and open the shops himself.

And so Melville spent several hours hunting through the shops by himself looking for a brass bearing to replace the lost one. He was unsuccessful. However, he did succeed in getting enough brass so that he could make one. The next morning, Monday, May 12, the *Thetis* and the *Loch Garry* set out for Disko and Upernivik, leaving the people of St. John's convinced that little success could be expected for an expedition undertaken by a group of Sabbath-breakers.

North of St. John's the two ships immediately ran into heavy fog. This was complicated in the afternoon by a strong, northeast wind; it shortly developed into a gale which created a heavy sea. Later in the afternoon small pieces of floating ice were observed in the water. Not far from the ships, an iceberg was seen.

It was their first meeting with an iceberg and they cautiously avoided getting any nearer to it. A short time later the experience in the ice-packed waters of Melville Bay was to breed a familiarity with icebergs that was to make this initial reaction seem ludicrous.

The ship continued north, finding both good and bad weather on the cruise to Disko. Ten days out of St. John's, on the morning of May 22, they reached the harbor of Godhavn on Disko Island.

They found the harbor ice-packed and experienced some difficulty in mooring the ship to the ice. The next day a gale blew up from the south and packed the harbor full of ice. The ships were unable to move for another thirty-six hours.

The *Thetis* and the *Loch Garry* were able to break their way out of Godhavn Harbor on the morning of May 24. In a few hours they ran up against the solid ice pack of the previous year and their passage was blocked. Schley tried to ram the *Thetis* through the barrier but got no farther than fifty yards into the ice. The following morning a gale blew up from the southwest. For safety's sake, the

Loch Garry returned to Godhavn until the wind should change.

Meanwhile, the *Thetis* prepared for the exigencies she might have to endure fighting her way through the ice ahead of her. Selected stores were brought up on deck and each officer and man was ordered to keep at hand essential personal equipment and supplies in case the ship was crushed in the ice and had to be abandoned.

Now Commander Schley made the long climb upward to the crow's nest about 130 feet above the deck.

After climbing the long rope ladder almost to the mast head, Schley entered the crow's nest through the round trap door in the bottom. The crow's nest consisted of a heavy barrel with the top removed. It was held to the main mast by heavy iron bands. At this elevation Schley found that he had a view extending from twelve to fifteen miles if the weather was clear. The ice pack stretched away from him in a broad panorama.

At first the ice gave the appearance of being unbroken and impassable, but soon the commander learned to spot the small, significant signs which indicated leads, cracks, or water holes. Searching with the telescope, Schley could pick out stringy, black lines here and there. He learned how to force his ship through these small openings, breaking a way through to a point farther along where another lead might be found. The commander also quickly learned the great influence that wind and tide had on what at first seemed an immovable pack. For the ice, however seemingly immovable, did move, sometimes slowly, sometimes suddenly. A wind from the south or the west would force the ice into a denser pack, but winds from the north or the east would break it open and clear the way for the *Thetis* to make its passage farther north. A strong tide would move the ice away from the land thus making it possible for the ship to proceed in waters close to the shore.

The commander in the crow's nest also scanned the horizon anxiously looking for "water blinks" or "ice blinks." The dark cloud or spot on the horizon, "the water blink," was caused by the mist rising from an open pool of water. The "ice blink" was a band of light caused by the reflection from the ice pack. The "water blink" was a reason for joy and expectation that progress could be made in that direction, but the "ice blink" indicated that the pack was solid and the ship would be blocked.

All too often there were no water holes, no leads, or no cracks and the captain had to attempt to ram the *Thetis* through the ice. The ship was forced into a crack that opened even if only a little way. Then the ship would back off for a short distance, get up full steam and hit the ice as hard as possible. In this way the ship was forced into the ice, breaking it open as far as the full length of the ship or farther. The impact of the ship's bow hitting strong ice truly "shivered her timbers" and was felt by everyone on board. It was felt with special impact by the commander holding on to the metal bar around the top of his barrel perched on the mast 130 feet above the deck.

When ramming was not successful, ice torpedoes were tried. Men went out on the floe ahead of the ship to bore holes deep in the ice with ice-augers. Into these holes, small explosive charges were dropped. After the men had retreated to the ship, the charges were exploded. All too often, however, the ice torpedoes had little effect on the tough, elastic ice of the Arctic.

By searching out every lead, by ramming, and by occasional use of ice torpedoes, Schley forced the *Thetis* ahead toward Upernivik. On May 27 the *Loch Garry* came steaming up from the south and joined the *Thetis*. At two the following morning, May 28, a sealing ship, the *Wolf*, was seen approaching from the south. The captain of the sealer soon came on board the *Thetis* to pay his respects. In a few hours another whaler the *Arctic* came along. Both ships, sailing out of Dundee, were on their annual cruise along the western shore of Greenland. Both captains had some hope of participating in the search for and rescue of the Greely expedition.

There were now four ships searching for leads in the ice pack, seeking to force their way north to Upernivik Harbor. The weather on May 28 proved to be a special test of the navigating ability of the captains of the four ships. The pack broke in the morning and great masses of ice were in swift motion. The ships were forced into different routes and had to be moved quickly to stay out of danger from the fast-moving ice. Frequently, the *Loch Garry* and the *Wolf* were forced close together and the captain of each vessel had to be alert to avoid crashing into the other.

By noon the ships made their way into the ice-free water near Noursoak. Here it was learned from Eskimos fishing in kayaks that the *Bear* had stopped at that point a few days earlier.

A fog moved in during the early afternoon, followed by a heavy snowstorm and falling temperatures. The land was blocked from view and the ships made slow progress during the rest of the day and evening.

During this tense, trying period Schley was constantly in the crow's nest, deeply anxious about the safety of his ship in these dangerous circumstances. The entire night was spent with the *Thetis* dodging in one direction or another to avoid the moving floes on all sides.

At last, on the morning of May 29 the *Thetis* moved safely into Upernivik Harbor. The commander was able to relax.

Already in the harbor were the *Bear*, the *Polynia*, the *Triune*, and the *Nova Zembla*. Closely following the *Thetis* into Upernivik Harbor were the *Arctic* and the *Wolf*, and a little later the *Aurora*, the *Cornwallis*, and the *Narwhal*.

Mrs. Greely and her supporters who had worked so hard for the rescue effort to be made would have been thrilled could they have seen Upernivik Harbor on the morning of May 29, 1884. Here was a large fleet of ships ready to set out at the first opportunity to find the Lady Franklin Bay Expedition.

As soon as the *Thetis* had anchored, Emory came on board to report electrifying news. Eskimos had brought in a rumor that there were five white men near Cape York.

Schley immediately ordered: "We will move north this afternoon."

CHAPTER TWENTY-TWO

ANOTHER BEAR HUNT

The news of the death of Jens was received by the men in the hut with little display of emotion. There were a few gasps of surprise and some murmurs of grief. Then the men slumped back in their sleeping bags and the hut was silent again.

Greely wondered if the men had become indifferent to death, if there could be such little reaction to the death of one they all loved so well. The next day, April 30, he noted that the entire party was sunk in a deep depression. The death of Jens was having its effect. Greely ordered that Frederick and Long would now share the duty of hunting, Frederick to hunt at night and Long to hunt during the day. (There was no real night, of course, with the sun above the horizon for twenty-four hours. But daytime for them was when the sun was high in the sky and night time when the sun was closer to the horizon.)

They were now using turf, roots, and the few leaves they could gather to add to the wood chopped from the boat for their fuel. To increase their food supply Brainard made a rake out of iron barrel hoops which he used to scrape seaweed ashore at the fishery. The sergeant was hopeful that he would be able to bring in enough shrimp and seaweed to keep them alive until the birds returned in June.

Greely, still conscious of his critical condition, issued another order describing the succession of command in the event of his death. First to succeed would be Sergeant Brainard, followed in order by Ralston, Gardiner, Frederick, and Long. Lieutenant Kislingbury could not be expected to assume command responsibility. He continued to weaken. His mind still wandered occasionally and he often talked poignantly of his two little sons and of his desperate hope to see them again. On May 1 he was outside the hut futilely trying to saw some wood. His strength was not equal to the task, however, and he fell on the sled nearby crying, "Oh, it's hopeless, hopeless. I cannot fight any longer." Brainard helped him gently back into the hut to his sleeping bag.

Their supply of bear and seal meat was running out. The commanding officer once more turned over in his mind the cruel problem of how little food he could authorize and still expect the party to stay alive on it. He told the men that Dr. Pavy had submitted written recommendations about a change in diet. The doctor, Greely said, advised reducing Brainard's extra rations from eight ounces to four ounces, and also recommended an increase for everyone else of one ounce daily.

Greely announced that he had decided to alternate their diet. One day for breakfast they would have a stew of shrimps, plus one ounce of blubber and one ounce of meat per man, as well as four ounces of dry pemmican and a cup of tea. For dinner there would be a stew of shrimp and seven ounces of meat per man with a cup of tea. The next day they would have the same shrimp, blubber, meat stew with four ounces of bacon for breakfast. At night they would have bacon, pemmican, and seven ounces of meat.

The doctor argued with the commanding officer that this was not what he had recommended. He insisted that Greely read his written recommendation so the men could understand his proposal. Greely, irritated by the doctor, refused to read the letter and told the doctor to be quiet.

The following day while the doctor was out of the hut

chopping ice for their drinking water Greely spoke to the men.

"In looking over the letter from the doctor I spoke of yesterday," the commanding officer said, "I find he recommends only four ounces extra meat for Brainard to support him while he is doing the shrimping for us. You know how hard Brainard works for us and how we depend on him for the shrimps. It is so important to keep Brainard strong that I disregarded Dr. Pavy's recommendation and I have ordered eight extra ounces of meat daily for Brainard.

"I mention this during the doctor's absence," Greely continued, "so as not to have any further altercation with him such as occurred yesterday. It was in part, I believe, due to my weak condition, but it also shows the selfish nature of the doctor."

Lieutenant Kislingbury thought, "What's the matter with Greely? Why must he always be running the doctor down?"

A few days later the doctor and Lieutenant Greely had another squabble. The doctor, speaking in French, tried to advise the commanding officer about the men who should be given the duties as hunters. Greely, resenting the doctor's interference in what he regarded as the responsibility of the commanding officer, curtly rejected the advice.

The next day, while the doctor was out of the hut, Greely again spoke to the men. "I wish to tell you that the altercation last night between the doctor and myself was over who I should decide on for hunters. The doctor has no right to interfere in these matters and I only mention it to show how disagreeable and unpleasant he is making it, interfering in what does not concern him. But you must try and bear with him."

Once more Kislingbury was irritated by Greely's "back-biting." "The doctor is irascible," Kislingbury thought, "and has made himself mean and disagreeable and has done me great injuries in various ways, but I cannot tolerate the sneaky, underhanded, low-minded, cowardly work of Greely. He just seems intent on setting the men against the doctor who, for all his faults, is doing his best."

On the morning of May 3 Long went off for the extended trip to Rice Strait in search of seal or other game. Frederick went out hunting too and Brainard went down to the fishery after shrimp and kelp. He was now using the bear's liver for bait but there was not more than a few days' supply of it left.

Brainard was seriously worried about Lieutenant Greely's condition now. He seemed to be losing his appetite and had been able to eat only a few spoonfuls of the stew. This was one of the symptoms that seemed to precede the final decline. Speaking with Brainard that morning, Greely said, "Sergeant, I think that I am near my end."

The strongest member of the party was Private Henry, who was still regarded as a prisoner but who was doing considerable work gathering the saxifrage which they were using as fuel.

During the day Lieutenant Greely's condition worsened and he felt he was not going to last much longer. Brainard, Long, and Frederick were away hunting and shrimping so the hut was virtually without anyone in command. Suddenly, those inside the hut heard cries from outside.

"You thief, you dirty thief, what have you taken?" Bender and Henry had caught Whisler outside the storehouse. The door was open and Whisler had almost a pound of bacon in his jacket. Some of those inside the hut crawled out to join the scene. Whisler was soon surrounded by a small group of infuriated men. He was hanging his head and crying.

"I couldn't help it, I couldn't help it. The door was open and I couldn't help it."

With angry shouting and threats they dragged Whisler back into the hut to face the commanding officer. Greely, sick and confused and hearing the cries of "a thief," asked weakly, "What is it, Henry stealing again?"

"Me," Henry shouted, "are you accusing me? I caught him. Whisler's the thief, I caught him. Don't accuse me again," Henry said.

Whisler retorted, "The door was open. He's probably the one who broke open the door. I saw the food and I just couldn't help myself."

Whisler's counteraccusation modified the fury of the men. All were aware that Henry had gone outside before Whisler. All were intensely suspicious of Henry because of his previous thievery.

Whisler, still crying spasmodically, said, "I'm guilty, I know I'm guilty. Go ahead and do whatever you want. I'm sorry I did it but I couldn't help myself."

The men were still angry but were now restraining their threatening remarks. Greely said weakly, "Everyone go back to his sleeping bag." Some of the men were still angry and muttering but the commanding officer was obeyed.

The miserable day ended with depressing reports from the hunters when they returned that they brought back no game. Long had shot a seal in open water in Rice Strait but it sank before he could reach it.

The next day Greely found himself feeling a little better but he was still not able to eat all his food. Long, too, now had difficulty in forcing down his shrimps.

Dr. Pavy added to his previous recommendations that

Greely should increase the rations for everyone. A few days earlier Greely had put the question to all of the men to see if they wanted him to follow the same principle of stretching the food out as far as possible. The men were unanimous in support of this plan.

Listening to the doctor once more making his recommendation, Ralston thought, "Oh Lord, he's at it again. If we had listened to the doctor's advice we would have all been dead long ago. As it is we have ten days before us yet."

The contention between Dr. Pavy and the commanding officer reached a crisis the morning of May 6. A heavy storm had blown up about 3 A.M. and continued through the rest of the morning, turning to snow a little after noon. The men were all huddled inside when the doctor once more raised the question of increasing the rations. The doctor reminded the commanding officer of other recommendations he had made. Greely replied that the statements the doctor was now making contradicted recommendations he had made earlier.

"No, no, no," the doctor replied. "Why do you continually misrepresent what I say?"

Greely replied coldly, "We will not discuss it any more, Doctor."

Undeterred, the doctor went on. "If you would listen to what I say and put it to the men fairly they would know that what I recommend is right."

"Doctor," Greely said, "we will have no more discussion of this."

The doctor's continued insistence and the implication that he was lying infuriated Greely. Twice more the doctor attempted to press his views on the commanding officer and Greely rejected them each time. His fury mounted at the doctor's arrogance and insolence. The doctor continued until Greely, almost beside himself, said angrily, "Doctor, I tell you this, that if you were not the surgeon of this expedition I would shoot you for insubordination."

Bender came to the doctor's defense and began arguing with the commanding officer. Greely told him, "Be quiet, Bender."

Bender ignored the order and said, "The doctor is trying to tell you what he thinks is best for the party."

"You will not tell me what I am supposed to do, Private," Greely stated.

"All right," Bender replied heatedly, "you don't have to listen to me but why don't you listen to the doctor? Do you think you know it all?"

"Private Bender, you will shut up," Greely said.

"You can't shut me up just because you don't like to hear what I have to say," Bender said. "I'll talk if I feel like it. What are you going to do about it?"

Greely, fury blazing from his eyes, reached for Long's gun and said, "If you won't obey my orders I'll shut you up permanently."

Sergeant Brainard concluded that the affair had gone far enough. As Greely lifted the gun to aim it at Bender, Brainard reached over and took it out of the commanding officer's hands. Brainard then turned to Bender and said, "All right, Bender, that's enough from you. Crawl back in your sleeping bag."

Bender stared at Brainard for a moment, stole a quick look at Greely, and then decided to obey Brainard's order. The whole party was held in silence by the nearness of violence. It was immediately clear that neither Dr. Pavy nor Bender would oppose the commanding officer with Sergeant Brainard at his side.

The moment of frozen silence passed. The men slumped down in their sleeping bags again and all was quiet.

During the next several days Dr. Pavy increased his activity in caring for the sick, cutting ice for their water, and even occasionally giving lectures to stir the men's minds again. The commanding officer devoted himself to putting his effects in order, and helping Whisler and Salor prepare their wills. Frederick and Long continued hunting without success, but Brainard daily brought in shrimps and kelp.

On May 7 a storm was blowing when Brainard went out at 2:30 P.M. to visit the fishery. He reached the crest of Cemetery Hill only to be blown down by the wind three times. At last he had to concede that his strength was not as great as that of the wind. He crawled on hands and knees back to the hut.

The storm subsided the next day and Brainard returned to his shrimping. He spent six hours at the fishery on May 10, dragging up ten pounds of kelp and catching thirty-six pounds of shrimp. The effort greatly exhausted him. When he was climbing the ice foot, he was suddenly startled to find blood gushing from his nostrils. He sat down on the ice and held his nose to stop the bleeding. He found himself very faint and took deep breaths through his mouth to restore his strength.

After a short time the hemorrhage stopped and the faintness passed. Eventually, he made his way slowly back to the stone hut.

They were getting some good weather now. The sun was very high in the sky. Most of them tried to crawl outside for some part of the day to enjoy the warmth of the sun. The temperature was not always above freezing, but it was a great change from the temperatures they had experienced during the long, dark months. The sun melting the snow on what remained of the roof of their hut caused a great deal of dripping and made it very uncomfortable for those inside.

Greely sought unity for the party but there was still conflict. He knew he could not permit himself such outbreaks if he was to hold the party together.

Long returned from another unsuccessful hunting trip to report that from the summit of Cape Sabine he saw open water north and south as far as the eye could see. Perhaps their rescue ship would be able to arrive early.

The men's spirits were good despite the fact that there were but a few days' rations left. The temperature was rising. It was close to zero during the night but rose to almost forty degrees in the sun during the day.

On May 12, Greely consulted with Brainard. They agreed it would be best to divide the remaining rations which would probably last only until May 15. They were afraid that one or two of the stronger members might be tempted to steal the few remaining rations and keep themselves alive at the expense of the others. They had discovered that a few ounces of Elison's bacon had been stolen and someone had stolen food from Long.

After these discoveries, Greely felt impelled to make another plea to the men.

"We may not have much longer to live," he told them. "During these last few days we should remember that we are men and not brutes. Let us remember our obligation to one another. If any of us are to live it will only be possible by maintaining our unity and if we are all to die, is it not better to die by living up to our responsibilities?"

After Greely's plea, Elison asked to speak to the commanding officer. The amputee could remember the harsh things he had thought about Greely during the hectic, difficult days of the retreat from Fort Conger to Cape

Sabine. He could remember the contempt which he had felt in his mind for Lieutenant Greely and, in contrast, he could remember the treatment which the commanding officer insisted be accorded Elison during the long winter months after the disaster at Cape Isabella.

"Lieutenant," Elison said, "I want to thank you for all you have done for me during the past months. In spite of my helpless condition you have given me favored treatment. I have been no help to the party at all, but you have insisted I get as much food and more than the others. I cannot tell you how much I appreciate the consideration you have shown me."

Greely, surprised, and touched by Elison's words, said, "But, Sergeant, we have given you nothing more than is due you. I have tried to see that everyone is treated fairly."

Elison nodded his head. "You have, Lieutenant, you have. You have been fair with all of us."

By May 15 all the food was exhausted except for the shrimp and kelp which Brainard supplied daily. The hunters had no success until May 18 when Long shot a raven. Greely gave Long the bird's liver and ordered that the rest be used by Brainard for shrimp bait.

A wild storm kept everyone in the hut except Brainard, who doggedly went out to the fishery after shrimp.

Ellis, who had been declining in recent days, was extremely weak and irritable. Bender responded with even greater irritation and abuse. The others were shocked by Bender's callous treatment of a man who was obviously dying. Even Henry joined in the general rebuke of Bender for his shameful conduct. Greely added his reprimand by saying to Bender, "Have you no feeling at all for a man who is dying?" Then, thinking to himself that they were all dying, Greely wondered whether Bender was any more to blame than Ellis. How could he hold Bender responsible for his weaknesses when the man was hardly sane?

The following morning, May 19, Frederick was up early and went out for ice to use in cooking breakfast. He returned immediately and breathlessly gasped, "Bear outside." He and Long swiftly put on heavy clothing, grabbed their guns, and went out for the hunt. Brainard followed them with the shotgun. The bear, sensing the pursuit, had moved away quickly. Brainard, after traveling for an hour, prudently returned to the hut afraid of wearing himself out and becoming unable to continue his shrimping. They then waited quietly, filled with tension over the long hours, until Frederick and Long returned.

Frederick came in at 10 A.M., breathless, exhausted, and depressed. Long followed about an hour later. Neither of them had been able to get close enough to the bear for a shot. They were deeply depressed and disappointed by their failure. Frederick suffered special agony which he conveyed to the others when he said, "When I first saw him outside this morning he was only a few feet away from me. If only I'd had the gun with me. He was only a few feet away."

CHAPTER TWENTY-THREE

DISHONOR

The failure of the hunters to kill the bear sighted by Frederick on May 19 seemed to be the end of the last hope of the party for survival. There was now a general acceptance of the fact that the only relief for them would be that provided by death. It was merely a question of how they would meet that inevitable fate.

The morning of May 19, shortly after Frederick returned with the sad news that the bear had escaped, Private Ellis quietly passed away. He was buried the following day at noon on Cemetery Ridge. There were scarcely enough men with the strength necessary to drag his body up the hill.

Those with strength enough to do so were spending many hours outside collecting saxifrage for fuel and scraping Tripe de Roche (rock tripe) from the rocks. This small lichen was the latest pitiful addition to their diet.

They were all extremely weak and not more than a handful were strong enough to walk without support. A number of them, like Lieutenant Greely, although too weak to walk, crawled the distance of some fifty yards to the rocks to spend several hours each day collecting the lichen. They had strength only to crawl but they were still striving to live.

On May 19 Ralston went outside in a futile attempt to saw wood. He was too weak to stand, however, and Shorty Frederick helped him back to his sleeping bag. The next day Ralston wrote in his diary: "The game is or must be nearly played. Thank God when the aid comes, as the men are getting quarrelsome and growl a great deal. The commanding officer is very patient."

Except to sign his name the next day, they were the last words he wrote.

Dr. Pavy, while Lieutenant Greely was out of the hut, prepared a paper testifying to his medical skill and his devotion to his duty. The doctor then prevailed upon Sergeant Israel, who was too weak to leave the hut, to copy the words the doctor had prepared. "I would like my family to know that I have done my duty here," the doctor pleaded. To oblige him, Sergeant Israel wrote out the statement in his own hand and signed it. The doctor then circulated it among the rest of the men for their signatures.

When Greely returned to the hut, Israel informed him privately of what the doctor had requested. This action of the doctor angered Greely, who viewed it as another method of the doctor for exploiting his position at the expense of dying men. Greely wrote out a statement which he inserted in Israel's diary recording that "everyone is at the mercy of Dr. Pavy, all being nearly starved, in the lowest possible condition physically, and being daily treated with medicine. The value of such a certificate is therefore evident." Greely's statement repeated the indictment of the doctor as a thief. "I have distinct sworn evidence," Greely wrote, "from five members of this party that Doctor Pavy has stolen bread at various times from his crippled patient, Sergeant Elison. Also other sworn evidence that he has stolen meat from the same patient, and extract of beef from the medical stores."

Knowing the doctor to be a thief, Greely could still recognize that he was performing some valuable work. He recorded: "Doctor Pavy is working wonderfully hard getting ice for water, and, strange to say, is making a collection of stones covered with lichen. His strength and energy lately are quite surprising. I am glad to write something good of him."

Greely was devoting himself to Ralston who seemed to be in the last stages. At each mealtime Greely would hold Ralston in his arms while he fed the dying man the few mouthfuls of food that constituted their meal. On May 22 Ralston was able to eat only part of the pitiful portion of food that was his. In the morning he had eaten a large amount of saxifrage and had sung a song. This behavior was of dire significance. Curiously, many of the dying men felt impelled to sing a few hours before their end. When tea was prepared at three-thirty, Greely leaned over Ralston and said, "Ralston, tea is ready now. Do you want some?"

In a weak voice, Ralston replied, "Yes, Lieutenant, I think so."

Greely raised Ralston in his arms to spoon-feed him the tea. As he did so, Ralston fainted. Greely gently lowered Ralston to the ground again. A little while later Ralston regained consciousness but became delirious. It was obvious that death was only hours away.

The stronger men spent the day erecting the tent upon the hill so that it would receive sunlight all of the time. It was a great struggle because most of them were hardly strong enough to stand.

At 1 A.M., May 23, Ralston died. Like the others he passed away quietly, apparently without pain.

The manner of death was recorded graphically by Henry, who wrote:

> It is remarkable to notice the way all of our starving comrades passed away from this earth. The terrible struggling of death by starvation actually had no terror for us, we looked with stolid indifference upon our coming fate,

and were glad that a death bed by such gradual starvation was not so painful or terrible as the one represented by those familiar with the scene where the victims were suddenly cut off from all sustenance and food.

(The following personal observations regarding such case might be of some interest to the medical fraternity)

A few hours before death, instead of a craving for food, they instead kept calling for water and could hardly be controlled or satisfied. All with but one exception were unconscious for hours before dying, and that exception was the native, Fred, who at seven A.M. received his quarter of a raw bird and ate it, and at nine A.M. he was a corpse.

After the tent had been erected, those who were in the weakest condition were moved into it. Whisler was able to walk the distance alone, but the effort so exhausted him that he fell into unconsciousness later in the evening. Israel attempted to walk, but halfway there had to be carried along. Lieutenant Greely managed to struggle the distance unaided, carrying the afghan which he was using as a sleeping bag. He was disappointed that the move resulted in the accidental breaking of the barometer. He had hoped that they would be able to continue their daily observations until the last man died. The most exhausting part of the change was carrying Elison on his mattress from the hut to the tent. After the change was completed, Frederick continued to work erecting a shelter in front of the tent opening. Brainard went off for another effort at shrimping.

Brainard was able to catch only ten pounds of shrimp. His baits were almost worthless. Their diet now consisted solely of saxifrage, lichens, a handful of shrimp, and a little tea.

The strongest of the group, Dr. Pavy, Brainard, Long, Henry, Salor, and Frederick, still slept in the hut but took their meals at the tent with the others. Frederick and Schneider worked putting together blankets and old canvas so as to make the tent large enough for all.

The tent made them more comfortable but the increased comfort could not keep them alive. They began to supplement the shrimp stew by the addition of sealskin. Thongs of sealskin were cut into small pieces and boiled with the shrimp stew. They also took small quantities of sealskin from old sleeping bags and burned them over the fire. The crisp cinders of sealskin were then eaten as though they were great delicacies.

It was clear that the end was only a short time away for all of them. The commanding officer tried to show them by example how they should meet death. He devoted his attention to the weakest member of the group. When Israel was failing and unable to sit up, Greely raised him and fed him, although the effort was almost beyond the commanding officer's remaining strength. Israel reminisced poignantly of his family and his younger days. This loss would be especially painful for Lieutenant Greely because for many months Israel had been his sleeping bag companion. The commanding officer had found the young sergeant a great comfort during their desperate trial. Israel had been unfailingly kind, considerate, and cheerful. His sweet character had made him a favorite with all of the party. He was sometimes referred to as "our Benjamin." Greely thought the Biblical description of Israel as the favorite younger brother precisely accurate. Now Israel was dying. In his last hours he pleaded for a little rum. There was almost none left. Greely was torn between yielding to the plea of a dying man and saving their remaining resources for those whom it would benefit. Greely knew it was not fair to the rest of the party and yet he found it impossible to refuse Israel's plea. Holding the pitiful figure in his arms, the commanding officer gave Israel his last nourishment, a spoonful of rum. Israel swallowed the precious liquid and then gazed up at Greely with a ghastly smile. He soon passed into unconsciousness and eleven hours later he was dead.

In four days, from May 23 to May 27, three of the party had died, Ralston, Whisler, and Israel.

Greely's conduct had fully impressed itself on most of the party. Despite his irritability and his occasional pettiness, he was the acknowledged leader of the dying band. Biederbick thought, "He has shown himself to be a man of more force of character and in every way greater than I believed him to be." The hospital steward deeply regretted that he had not "sooner found out his full worth." Biederbick reflected that at Conger and on the retreat he had so frequently thought critically of the commanding officer. "I was wrong," Biederbick thought. "During the whole winter Lieutenant Greely has done everything for us that one man could do to keep us up and alive."

Greely's word and example, however, were not sufficient to persuade all of them to be kind and good to one another in their last days. The afternoon of May 27 Dr. Pavy removed all of the remaining iron pills from the medicine chest. Biederbick reported the doctor's action to Lieutenant Greely. The commanding officer said, "Doctor, you will return the iron to its proper place."

The doctor replied insolently, "This is a medical matter, Lieutenant."

"The medical supplies are the property of the expedition, Doctor, not your personal property," Greely responded heatedly.

There followed another bitter exchange with Lieutenant Kislingbury joining in to defend the doctor. Greely then turned on Lieutenant Kislingbury and ordered him to stop criticizing and interfering in the actions of the commanding officer. At last the argument dwindled off to an inconclusive ending.

Long and Frederick were still hunting and Brainard still making his daily shrimping efforts. Occasionally, Long was able to secure a dovekie. Greely ordered that such food be divided among Long, Frederick, and Brainard to keep up their strength and that part of the bird be given to Brainard to use as shrimp bait.

Brainard also ordered that all scraps and pieces of sealskin were now the property of the party and would be turned in for use as food. The following day, however, Bender was caught chewing on a piece of sealskin. He confessed he had failed to turn it in as ordered and pleaded that he could not resist the temptation. Brainard then ordered Frederick to make a full check for all sealskin that might be edible and to lock it in the storehouse.

A storm blew up the afternoon of May 29 while Long and Brainard were down at the fishery. They struggled through the gale back to the tent with their catch of one dovekie and eight pounds of shrimp. Brainard then went over to the old hut to collect some wood for their fire. After fighting his way back through the wind and snow, Dr. Pavy and Salor would not admit him to his place in the sleeping bag they shared.

"There's no room in here," Dr. Pavy said. "We're too crowded."

Brainard gazed down at the two of them and slowly shook his head. He went outside the tent and found one of the abandoned sleeping bags. It was frozen stiff and covered with snow but he managed to crawl inside. The storm had not permitted them to make any fire. So, after the long day's work, Brainard went to sleep that night without dinner.

The storm raged all night and most of the next morning, drifting snow into the tent and covering their sleeping bags. Brainard found his feet and face swollen from exposure and he suffered severe rheumatic pains. The gale died down during the day on May 30 but blew up again that evening. The heavy storm kept them in their sleeping bags for the full day so that they had nothing to eat or drink.

The morning of June 1 they were able to prepare a breakfast consisting of three ounces of shrimp per man and a cup of weak tea. They had been without food for thirty-six hours.

This latest ordeal proved too much for Lieutenant Kislingbury. In his last moments of consciousness, he began to sing. In a weak, thin voice, which had once been strong and vibrant, he sang the words of the Doxology. As his voice gave forth the words, "Praise God from whom all blessings flow," they all recalled how he had led them in song two years ago at Fort Conger during their first Christmas services in the Arctic. The group was still while Kislingbury completed the singing. As soon as he had finished, he fell back unconscious.

Lieutenant Kislingbury died that afternoon and was buried the following day, June 2.

The graves they had prepared for their dead companions were exceedingly shallow. In his daily trip to the fishery across Cemetery Ridge, Brainard at first had been deeply affected by the sight of the resting places of his former comrades. As he walked by he could see the bright brass buttons of Lieutenant Lockwood's blouse sticking up through the gravel. The wind had also blown away the light covering of earth from Linn's feet so that now they were fully exposed. Once Brainard had thought that he would rebury the dead flesh. But he had become so weak that the effort was beyond him and, indeed, the familiarity of the scene now made it possible for him to view it without emotion.

On June 3, they lost another man. At 3 A.M., Salor died. Brainard was in the same sleeping bag with him but the sergeant had neither the strength nor the inclination to move himself or the dead man. He shared the sleeping bag with Salor's corpse until 9 A.M. when the party arose for breakfast.

That morning it seemed that Dr. Pavy would be the next one to go. He was talking incoherently and recommending a number of queer prescriptions.

Occasionally, Long was able to get a dovekie. Greely continued the practice of dividing it among the hunters only and ordering that a portion of it be used for shrimp bait. However, on two occasions Henry again displayed his thieving ability and stole part of the bird. He was also caught stealing some sealskin.

They knew now they were all going to die. They were reconciled to it. For the commanding officer, there remained only the task of holding up the morale of the party for another few days so that they might die honorably and without injustice to one another, but problems still arose. On June 4 Long was able to shoot another dovekie and, as previously, Greely ordered the bird to be divided among the hunters who could barely walk. However, Bender, pleading and crying, insisted he was entitled to one twelfth of the bird. There was great discussion among the other eleven members of the party as to whether Bender should receive the morsel of food he was pleading for. Greely ordered that Bender should be given the food and immediately wondered if he had done the right thing. He, therefore, again told the men that it was essential to keep the hunters going. If they were not able to obtain birds and shrimp, all of them would die immediately.

They struggled to hang on to life but death was no longer feared. They had seen too many die. Those who had died had done so without great pain or suffering. As soon as the unfortunate member started his first wanderings, they would all look at each other aware of the dreadful significance. The mental wanderings were followed by singing or pleading for water, then unconsciousness and a quiet death.

June 5 was a clear, calm, warm day. Greely crawled out to the rocks once more to collect a can of rock tripe. While he was outside, the lieutenant had a private talk with Henry about his stealing. Henry frankly admitted his guilt. Greely managed to raise himself to his feet to talk to the sullen man who stood before him.

"I have been convinced," Greely said, "that you have no conscience, that you seem unable to share a feeling of responsibility with the rest of us. But, at least, you should have common sense. Can you not see that no one will survive if we do not work together? The only way for any of us to live is through unity and fair dealing with one another," Greely said. "I want you to promise to stop this stealing."

Henry stared back at the officer and then said, "All right, Lieutenant, I promise."

The flat tone of Henry's voice left Greely unconvinced that this man intended to live up to his word.

"And I will promise you, Henry, that if you do not live up to your promise you will come to grief."

Greely watched Henry's face closely and wondered if his warning had made any impression.

Greely returned to the hut and wrote out an order:

Near Cape Sabine,
June 5, 1884.

To Sergeants Brainard, Frederick and Long:

Private Henry, having been repeatedly guilty of stealing the provisions of this party, which is now perishing slowly by starvation, has so far been condoned and pardoned. It is, *however, imperatively ordered* that if this man be detected either eating food of any kind not issued him regularly, or making caches, or appropriating any article of provisions, you will at once shoot him and report the matter to me. Any other course would be a fatal leniency, the man being able to overpower any two of our present force.

A. W. Greely, / Lt. 5th Cav. / A.S.O. & Asst.

Comdg. Lady Franklin Bay Ex.

The following day, June 6, the weather still held good. It was a fine, warm, clear day. The warm weather was melting much of the snow and water was trickling down the hillside. Reindeer moss was appearing in various places and other vegetation was adding some green to the bare land. The saxifrage, grass, poppies, and lichens were becoming more evident. Vegetation was coming to life but everything human was dying.

While breakfast was being prepared, Frederick saw Henry stealing shrimps out of the mess pot. Frederick reached for a gun but there was none in the tent. A little later Henry went off by himself down to the old hut. Frederick reported to Greely that he had seen Henry stealing. Greely went out and found Henry making a second trip to the old winter quarters. Henry was carrying a small bundle on his shoulder.

"Henry, what have you been up to today?" Greely asked.

"What do you think I've been up to?" Henry replied.

"Frederick saw you stealing from the mess pot and I think you've been stealing from supplies in the old hut," Greely charged.

"Well, Lieutenant, you're exactly right," Henry said. "I've got some sealskin right here, as a matter of fact. And another little bundle tucked away for myself."

Greely turned away from Henry and walked slowly back to the tent. Inside, he wrote another order:

Near Cape Sabine,
June 6, 1884.

Sergeants Brainard, Long and Frederick:

Notwithstanding promises given by Private C. B. Henry yesterday, he has since acknowledged to me having tampered with seal thongs, if not other food at the old camp. This pertinacity and audacity is the destruction of this party, if not at once ended. Private Henry will be shot today, all care being taken to prevent his injuring anyone as his physical strength is greater than that of any two men. Decide the matter of death by two ball and one blank cartridge.

This order is *imperative* and *absolutely necessary* for *any chance* of life.

A. W. Greely,

1st. Lieut., 5th Cavalry, U.S.A., and Ass't.,

Commanding L.F.B. Expedition

Greely, describing the usual manner of military execution, had forgotten that the only usable rifles were of different calibers. Thus, the rifle with the blank cartridge could not be disguised. The three sergeants walked a little way from the hut and then each in turn read the order that Greely had written out.

"We cannot follow the lieutenant's method. How will we do it?"

"Only one of us will shoot. We will each swear to keep forever secret the name of the one who did the shooting."

The other two agreed. Then, each in turn, said, "I swear I will keep this secret forever."

After each of them had sworn the oath, their thoughts turned to the manner of execution. The sergeants well knew that Henry was a strong and dangerous man. Greely's warning to take care to prevent Henry from injuring anyone was justified.

"I don't suppose we could shoot him in the back."

"No, of course not."

"We will tell him plainly that he is to be executed by order of the commanding officer. He may want a minute to pray before he dies."

Henry was up near the tent on Cemetery Ridge. One of the sergeants went up and said to him, "Henry, come on down to the hut and help us carry up supplies."

Henry went without suspicion. The other two sergeants were waiting behind the old stone hut. As soon as Henry saw them, one of the sergeants cradling a rifle in his arm, he knew that something dire was imminent. He stopped in his tracks.

"Private Henry, for repeated thievery of supplies of the party you are to be executed by order of the commanding officer. You may have a moment to pray before you die."

Henry stood still. He saw an ax on the ground nearby. He leaped for it. One of the sergeants put his foot on the ax as Henry grabbed at it. The two were close together, but the sergeant with the rifle took quick aim and fired. The shot caught Henry in the chest.

Henry rose and whirled, shouting, "You have tricked me. You have tricked me."

The sergeant fired again. This shot caught Henry in the head. He dropped to the ground, dead. The lifeless body lay on the rocky ground. The sergeants looked at it and walked away.

The expedition was now unmistakably marked by dishonor. It had been necessary to kill one of their own. They could not be certain now whether it was comradeship or the threat of violence which would hold them together in their last days.

It was two in the afternoon. A little later the execution order was read to the rest of the men. They were unanimous that Henry deserved to be executed. A search of Henry's bundles revealed large quantities of sealskin, scientific instruments, a silver chronograph of Greely's, and a pair of sealskin boots stolen from Long two nights earlier.

Later in the day, at 5:45 P.M., Bender died. Fifteen minutes later Dr. Pavy also passed away. On that day, June 6, three of them had died. Only nine were left.

CHAPTER TWENTY-FOUR

THE PUSH THROUGH MELVILLE BAY

The *Thetis* and the *Bear* left Upernivik Harbor at five o'clock the evening of May 29. Schley knew that the push across Melville Bay was not going to be an easy one. He would probably have to fight for every mile of advance through heavy, dangerous, ice-filled waters. Other ships had crossed Melville Bay in a comparatively short time. Greely, in 1881, going north in the *Proteus*, had crossed the bay in thirty-six hours, the *Neptune* in 1882 made it in eighty hours, and the *Proteus*, with Garlington aboard in 1883, had crossed the bay in seventy-two hours. But these crossings had been made in July or August. Schley was trying to cross Melville Bay at the beginning of June. It was a different time and Schley knew that it would likely be a very different story.

By 9 P.M. the *Thetis*, the *Bear*, and the whaling ships had reached the island of Kingitok, a small Eskimo settlement and a former Danish trading post. Here the ships were forced to wait for an opening in the ice. It was two days before such an opening occurred. The ice was broken by a storm which blew up on Sunday, the first of June. When the storm had passed, leads through the ice were discovered running north and west.

All of the ships were quick to seize the opportunity and were soon picking their way through the openings in the ice pack, heading north in their search for the Greely party. By that afternoon the leads had closed and the ships once more were stopped.

Searching for a way through the seemingly impassable ice, Lieutenant Emory brought his ship, the *Bear*, close to shore. He found a small lead and started through it, followed by the *Thetis*. The lead led between two icebergs which rose forty feet above the water. Employing the usual ratio of seven to one, Emory concluded that the icebergs must reach down at least 280 feet. He was confident, therefore, that there was enough clearance for the keel of the *Bear* and the *Thetis*, although they were close to land. Emory could not know that there was a submerged rock rising to within fourteen feet of the surface of the water. The *Bear* hit the rock with a shock that shook everyone aboard.

There followed some very bad moments for Emory with the inevitable worry that he might be losing his ship. However, there was no immediate indication of serious damage. Examination later proved that the leak caused by the accident was not a serious one and it was soon repaired.

Commander Schley was now spending long hours without relief in the crow's nest. He was looking endlessly for every lead that would provide an opportunity for him to move his ships farther north. The crew was kept constantly on the alert, ready to move whenever an opportunity opened. The *Thetis* and the *Bear* worked closely together to assist each other's progress. By seemingly untiring diligence, Schley was able to keep the *Thetis* out in front of the whalers most of the way. However, the whalers kept a good pace and stayed close to the *Thetis* and the *Bear*. Sometimes they were even able to move out ahead of Schley and Emory. The whaling ships had not been re-enforced for ice ramming as strongly as the *Thetis*, but the shrewd, experienced captains were ever ready to take advantage of the openings made by the *Thetis*. Occasionally, by a different choice of maneuver they were able to win a lead on the *Thetis* and the *Bear*.

The competition between the whaling ships and the *Thetis* and *Bear* was all in good spirit and in the best tradition of the sea. However, after several days the competition began to wear on Schley a little. He found himself beginning to resent the advantage that the whaling ships were taking of the efforts he and his crew were making. The fever grew in him to keep his ship in front.

A strange thing began to happen on board the *Thetis*. The fever that burned in Schley was caught by the rest of the officers and crew. The distant, lone figure 120 feet above the deck communicating with the others by staccato signals was able to fill them with the same drive that possessed him to go north, go north. Schley's intensity was soon seen in the conduct of each man aboard as he attacked his duties with fervor.

The captain of the *Thetis* was well aware that his competitors, the whaling ship captains, had the advantage of far more experience in the strange, ice-filled waters of the North. But he had a quarter century of sea experience himself, and he maintained his determination to keep pushing ahead by recalling the advice of the successful arctic explorer, Army Lieutenant Schwatka. Before departing on this arctic voyage, Schley had studied his subject well. He had been especially impressed by Schwatka's warning "against too much reliance on the subject of experience as applied to arctic affairs. The whole history of continued arctic expeditions under one commander showed retrogression rather than increased success." Lieutenant Schwatka had advised against "a too rigid application of principles of experience." Arctic experience, in other words, seemed to breed timidity in a commander.

Schley found this true in his conversations with the whaling captains. All of them had advanced so many cautions about the dangers of arctic navigation. Schley acknowledged that the warnings they gave were valuable in hunting whales, but he wasn't hunting whales. He was making a dash to rescue Greely and his party. The *Thetis* had to get north as fast as possible.

Somehow the unspoken assumption that this voyage could not succeed in rescuing Greely—the belief that they would inevitably be too late—dissipated to nothingness under the ramming of the forefoot against the ice pack. Schley was filled with the fire to advance every mile, every yard, every foot, just as rapidly as he was able. They could not delay one unnecessary minute. They must go forward. He would get his ship through.

And so they searched for every lead and rammed against every promising ice crack, worked diligently with the ice torpedoes that seemed so ineffective against the arctic ice. They worked ceaselessly to keep their ship moving ahead.

This method of fighting their way through the ice was frustrating for an impatient commander. The first sixteen days in the ice pack north of Upernivik they made only fifty miles. On the seventeenth day, however, they were astonished as the pack opened in front of them and free water stretched out ahead.

The crew of the *Thetis* and the *Bear* worked swiftly to break out of the pack into the open water. Once in the open water the ships flew north. After the days of crawling through the ice pack, a speed of eight knots seemed a magic change. The men felt they were traveling aboard an express train.

Most of the whalers had been working closer to shore and were thus unable to break free as the *Thetis* and the

Bear had done. However, the *Wolf*, the *Arctic*, and the *Aurora* were offshore. They soon followed the two relief ships in speeding across the open water.

After several hours of express train speed, the five ships soon were stopped again by another ice barrier, but they had made thirty-five miles to the north in a matter of hours.

Once more they settled down to the tedious business of waiting for a promising lead, butting their way into it and hoping to make progress through the heavy ice. The following day the ice once more opened for them and again they sped north through open water. Traveling at full speed for more than seven hours, the ships were able to progress more than sixty miles.

There were only five ships left in the competition now, the *Thetis*, the *Bear*, the *Wolf*, the *Arctic*, and the *Aurora*. They were now about sixty miles south of Cape York and were once more blocked by an apparently solid ice barrier. The way to the north was blocked but on the afternoon of June 16 several tempting leads opened leading off to the southwest. Schley declined to attempt this method of rounding the ice barrier to the north of him. He felt sure that the best method of progress would be to wait for a lead to the north in along the shore.

The rest of the afternoon of June 16 was spent in waiting for a lead. About seven that evening Captain Guy of the *Arctic* grew too impatient and accepted the temptation of one of the leads running out to the southwest. The *Arctic* had progressed only two miles through the lead when the ice closed about her. The *Aurora* and the *Wolf* had started to enter the same lead but, seeing the predicament of the *Arctic*, they quickly escaped the nip. The next day was spent in waiting. At 9 P.M. June 17, leads once more appeared and the four ships quickly seized the openings. The *Arctic* was still beset in the ice to the southwest.

There were now only four ships left in the race to rescue Greely, the *Thetis,* the *Bear,* the *Wolf,* and the *Aurora.* For several hours the ships forced their way through narrow leads making slow progress. By eleven o'clock, however, the ships had reached more open leads and were able to move ahead. The two whalers, having the jump on the *Thetis* and the *Bear,* put on full steam and moved off ahead of them.

They were not far from Cape York now and Schley was determined that the whalers would not beat him to that point. The crews of the *Thetis* and *Bear* worked at a fever pitch fighting for every advantage through the ice leads. By 1 A.M., June 18, all of the ships were stopped by another ice bar. The next hour and a half was spent by their vigorously pounding away, trying to crack their way through the bar. At half past two in the morning the ships almost simultaneously broke through the last barrier and slid into open water. As each ship cleared the pack, its crew gave a rousing cheer. They moved off at full steam toward Cape York.

The *Bear* was a faster ship than the *Thetis,* and Schley immediately gave Emory permission to move out as fast as he could for Cape York. The *Bear* soon overtook the *Aurora* and went into the lead. The *Thetis* and *Wolf* brought up the rear. An hour later, at half past three the morning of June 18, the *Bear* reached the ice four miles off Cape York. In a short while the other three ships joined her.

Now, here at Cape York, they would learn if there was any truth in the rumor which had reached Upernivik that there were five white men at the cape. Lieutenant Colwell, who was here the year before, was put in charge of the landing party. Preparations for the landing party had been made on board the *Bear* as it was proceeding northward so that Colwell and his men were dropped on the ice with little delay.

The landing party took a dog team, a sled, and a dory. They pushed across the ice for several miles until they came to open water which extended to the land ice. They then put the dory in the water, loaded themselves and their sled into it, and rowed across to the land ice. Ashore, they soon picked up some sled tracks which they followed until they met an Eskimo who was seal fishing.

Eagerly they questioned him about the existence of any white men in the area. With great disappointment they learned from him that he knew of no white men near Cape York. He also assured them that none of the other Eskimos in that area had seen any white men. With this disappointing news, they made their way back to the ship.

While the Colwell party was ashore, Schley ordered Emory to sail off to the south and west to see if there was a way of getting around the ice barrier in that direction.

The captains of the *Aurora* and the *Wolf* now decided that they had pushed as far north as they could hope to in the face of the very heavy ice found in Melville Bay this year. They decided they would turn off to the southwest and the fishing grounds in Lancaster Sound. Before leaving, Captain Fairweather of the *Aurora* came on board the *Thetis* to bid Schley good-by. With a warm handclasp and wishing him Godspeed, Fairweather said to Schley in a rich, Scottish accent, "Gud-bye, Captain. We may live without fesh, but those poor fellows up there must have breed. God bless you. It's na use for us to go further."

With that warm farewell, Fairweather returned to his ship and the *Aurora* and the *Wolf* departed to the southwest.

About one hour later the ice pack suddenly and unexpectedly moved out from Cape York leaving an open lane about fifty yards wide running off to the north. The *Thetis* quickly lifted anchor and headed along the lane, staying close to the land ice as Colwell's party was approaching the ship in the distance. Stopping only for a moment to pick up Colwell and his men, the *Thetis* moved rapidly northward. By four in the afternoon the *Thetis* reached Conical Rock, a barren island half a mile long with a sugarloaf peak.

Here Lieutenant Sebree took a landing party ashore and built the first cairn of the expedition. On a rock three hundred feet above the water, messages were left for the *Bear* and the *Alert*. Stones were placed in a large pile and a flagpole set atop the stones.

While the *Thetis* was waiting for the Sebree party to return, the ice pack moved in again and the way north was blocked once more. Again Schley experienced the frustration of delay, when there was nothing to do but wait or look futilely for leads which failed to appear.

The changing tide in the afternoon of June 19 loosened the pack and the *Thetis* made its way through the ice past Cape Dudley Digges. Pushing northward with every man working furiously, Schley brought his ship close to the open water of Wolstenholme Sound. Only five hundred yards of ice remained between the ship and open water. Schley bent every effort to have the *Thetis* break her way through this ice. They were making some progress until the *Thetis* rammed violently into a narrow crack and was stuck fast in the ice.

Schley found that he could move his ship neither forward nor backward. Every man was put to work on board the ship or on the ice trying to free her. It was here that Schley found that the ice torpedoes could be effective.

They were planted in the ice ten or twelve yards away from the midships of the *Thetis*. The fractures caused by their explosion released the ship from the tight, icy grasp.

Schley pushed his ship ahead, ramming on through the remaining ice. In a short while he broke through to Wolstenholme Island.

Once more Colwell was sent ashore with a landing party. He built a small cairn, again leaving messages for the *Bear* and the *Alert*. When the party returned, the *Thetis* pushed on for Saunders Island, arriving there at about 2:30 A.M., Friday, June 20.

At Saunders Island there was a settlement of about fifty Eskimos. Colwell again went ashore to learn if they had any news of Lieutenant Greely and his party. Colwell recognized some of the Eskimos he had met the year before at Cape York. They were friendly and remembered him but they had no news of Greely. One old man with a wooden leg, apparently the chief of the Eskimo settlement, reported that earlier in the season they had sent a hunting party over the ice toward the Cary Islands. No signs of white men had been seen. It was clear that the *Thetis* would have to push farther north.

The *Thetis* left Saunders Island about 5 A.M. and headed for Cape Parry. The water was filled with ice and caused some trouble in navigation. Various maneuvers were taken to avoid collisions with bergs. The *Thetis* moved forward. Many walruses were seen on the larger floes and the air was filled with thousands of screaming birds. The *Thetis* went north all day, stopping at Cape Parry, Northumberland, and Hakluyt islands. No sign of Greely was found at any place. By 9 P.M. the *Thetis* was pushing north from Northumberland Island through enormous icebergs huddled closely together. The wind blew up from the south bringing with it flurries of snow. During the night the strength of the wind increased but, since it came from the south, it aided the progress of the *Thetis*. About twenty miles above Northumberland Island the *Thetis* finally broke into the long expected North Water.

On June 20 near 12 P.M., with the midnight sun trying to break through the clouds, Captain Schley in the crow's nest had before him a view he had waited so long to see. His heart filled with expectation and exultation. The way was open as far as Littleton Island. Now they would travel!

CHAPTER TWENTY-FIVE

THE LAST DAYS

They ate their remaining supply of shrimp for breakfast on June 7. It was the first time since Rice and Brainard had started catching the shrimp that they were without any supply of them. Everyone who could move crawled out to collect reindeer moss, rock tripe, and saxifrage.

They had no strength to bury the bodies of Bender and Dr. Pavy. Lieutenant Greely read the burial service for them and then Biederbick, Brainard, Long, and Frederick dragged the bodies off some distance from the hut.

Brainard made another attempt at shrimping but succeeded in bringing in only two pounds. He also gathered together all the sealskin that could be used for food. Schneider was unable to move out of the tent but spent long hours burning the hair from the sealskin clothing that was to be eaten by the remaining members of the party. Lieutenant Greely, Connell, and Biederbick devoted themselves to collecting lichen and saxifrage. They were finding the saxifrage blossom sweet and palatable. A small but significant addition to their supply was made by Biederbick who discovered a small cache of bear meat in the rocks near the tent, apparently made by Henry. On June 9 they breakfasted on a few shrimps and a cup of tea. They had no stew for dinner, however, only tea and a piece of burned sealskin and some raw lichens. They gathered enough strength to drag the bodies of Bender and Dr. Pavy to the tidal crack at the ice foot and there tumbled the bodies into the icy grave.

Long continued hunting and Brainard shrimping with little reward. On June 11, however, Long succeeded in killing two guillemots. One of the birds was used in a stew for the party, the other was divided among the hunters, Long, Frederick, and Brainard.

For weeks they had been expecting the death of Gardiner. Back in April, Dr. Pavy had predicted that Gardiner would be the next to die, but there was a strength of spirit in Gardiner which they all admired. He seemed to live solely on will power and a great desire to return home to his wife and his mother. A picture of these two loved ones was constantly in his hands and often he spoke to them. Early the morning of June 12 Gardiner became partly delirious. They found him half out of his sleeping bag with the beloved pictures in his hand. They heard him whisper, "Mother, wife," before lapsing into unconsciousness. At 11 A.M. it seemed he was dead and his body was moved out of the tent. However, a little later it was noticed that there was still some life in Gardiner's body and they placed him on an old buffalo robe. He died about 5 P.M.

They suffered a second loss that day when the ice, breaking up at the shrimping grounds, carried away Brainard's nets and baits. Brainard returned from the fishery with the bad news but found the party asleep. He had not the heart to wake them. He pitied them, anticipating their disappointment when they learned in the morning that no breakfast awaited them.

In the next couple of days, the weather turned bad. A southeast wind brought in mist and dampness and then rose to a gale. They were unable to crawl out to collect their lichen and saxifrage. Their meals consisted of roasted sealskin.

The storm ended early the morning of June 14 but the weather remained cloudy. The temperature was now up above freezing during the day. Brainard with new nets and a bird skin for bait returned to his shrimping but caught only one pound.

In the next couple of days the pitiful baits Brainard was using became utterly useless. On June 16 Brainard worked five hours at the fishery and caught only two or three ounces of shrimp. The disappointment and the exertion so weakened him that he was barely able to crawl back to the tent.

Greely knew that there was nothing much left for them to try, but he would keep them trying as long as life remained. Elison was helpless but Biederbick continued tending to him, dressing his wounds and feeding him. Schneider was almost equally helpless. In fact, he was unable to raise himself without assistance, but Long and Brainard would lift him to a sitting position so he could sew on the boots or write in his diary. Following the commanding officer's example, they all still kept their diaries, although the entries became shorter.

Greely was startled when Connell remarked, "Well, it's just about over. It's every man for himself now, I guess."

"No, Connell, no," Greely said. "There's not much time left for us, I suppose, but we are all here together. We have come this far by working together. We must continue to do so in the last days. If we must die, let's do it helping each other to keep alive."

And that is how the next few days were spent. There was literally almost nothing left now. They had roasted and eaten the sealskin covering of the sleeping bags. Brainard could get no more shrimp. They tried making saxifrage tea and only half of them could drink it. It was bitter and distasteful. With the sealskin almost gone, they tried to make a stew of the lichens but this was not very satisfactory, either.

Long was still attempting to hunt but could barely support himself on his feet. Brainard, Greely, and Connell were attempting to collect lichens. Schneider did what little he could in the hut. Frederick was doing the cooking.

They found it remarkable that, although they dreamed of wonderful meals, the actual physical sense of hunger had left them. They ate now to keep alive, not out of any real desire for the distasteful food available to them. The weather on June 17 was exceptionally warm. The sun shone brilliantly and the temperature rose to sixty-three degrees. But the next morning they woke to find the temperature down to thirty degrees, the sky clouded and a fresh wind blowing.

After eating his breakfast, Schneider became delirious and then unconscious.

Biederbick suffered severe rheumatic pains and was unable to leave the hut. However, he devoted some of his time to Elison's wounds. Later, when his pains abated, he crawled out with Connell and Brainard to pick lichens. They returned to the tent in the evening. Schneider was still unconscious and at 6 P.M., he died.

There were seven of them left now—the commanding officer, Brainard, Long, Frederick, Biederbick, Connell, and Elison. Only a few mouths to feed but almost nothing to use for food. All that remained were a few pieces of sealskin and the lichens they could collect.

The weather was clear on June 19 but a west wind was blowing. In the afternoon the wind rose to a stronger force. Long dragged himself out to go hunting. He succeeded in killing two dovekies and two eider ducks but they fell in the water and the ebb tide carried them away from the shore. He watched helplessly as the precious birds drifted away from him.

The wind subsided on June 20. The weather was clear,

calm, and cold. The temperature was down to twenty-nine degrees. It was Greely's sixth wedding anniversary and just three years since he had left his wife and two daughters and sailed away for the Arctic.

The wind blew up again in the afternoon and continued through the night. They woke the morning of June 21 to find a strong gale raging from the south and the temperature down to thirty-one degrees. The wind shook the weak supports of their tent and threatened to collapse it. Occasionally snow fell, was whirled about by the wind and drifted into their tent. They were unable to go out but, fortunately, they had a small supply of lichens with which they made a stew for breakfast. A few pieces of sealskin served for their supper. The wind blew all day and all night. On the morning of June 22 the storm was still raging.

Connell reported that he was paralyzed from the knees down. Biederbick was once more suffering from severe rheumatic pains.

They had no food on that day but Frederick succeeded in providing them each with a small drink of water.

Greely tried to read to them from the Prayer Book, for it was Sunday. He was still trying to be conscientious about their religious devotions. The roaring wind made it difficult for his weak voice to be heard. After several tries he gave up the effort as too exhausting.

The wind slapped and tore at their tent and the supports began to give way. Brainard, Frederick, and Long each made an attempt to strengthen the supports but they were futile. The wind roared unrelentingly, forcing the tent down. By the end of the day, June 22, the front end of the tent had collapsed. They were pinned inside, a helpless few, too weak to stir.

The storm continued.

The *Thetis* had arrived at Littleton Island at 2:30 A.M., June 21. Schley had his ship steam around to the north side of the island to get protection from the gale blowing from the southwest. He took ashore one landing party and sent others under the command of Colwell, Melville, and Norman. The entire day of June 21 was spent searching Littleton Island for any sign of Greely's appearance there. They found caches made by Beebe in 1882, by Nares in 1875, and by Commander Wildes in 1883. None of the caches had been disturbed. It was clear that Greely and his men had not reached Littleton Island.

At the end of the day the parties returned to the *Thetis.* The storm continued during the night.

Schley gave orders that a landing of provisions be taken ashore as soon as a break in the storm permitted. About eight o'clock the morning of Sunday, June 22, the storm subsided for a while. Lieutenant Sebree went ashore in a small boat and made the cache of 760 rations. He also left messages for Lieutenant Emory in the *Bear* and Lieutenant Coffin in the *Alert.*

Schley now faced two questions. Where was Greely, and where was Emory in the *Bear?*

The commander turned over in his mind the possible actions that Greely might have taken. Greely could have stayed with his party at Lady Franklin Bay. Schley was convinced, however, that Greely would not have done this. Greely's last instructions were that, before the beginning of the third winter, he would move to the south if no relief ship had arrived. Schley peered through the storm looking over toward Cape Sabine. His thoughts rested on that point for a moment. It was hardly possible that Greely would have reached Cape Sabine and not have sent a party over to Littleton Island. There was no substantial amount of rations on Cape Sabine. Arriving there, Greely would have sent someone over for the caches on Littleton Island. What seemed most likely to Schley was that Greely had been unable to make his way all the way to the south. His party had probably been stopped somewhere between Lady Franklin Bay and Cape Sabine. It would be necessary for the *Thetis* to push farther north in its search.

The commander of the *Thetis*, however, was reluctant to move on from Littleton Island without knowledge of what had happened to Lieutenant Emory and the *Bear*. It had been four days since the two ships had parted at Cape York. There had been heavy ice on the way north. Schley wondered if the *Bear* had met the fate of the *Proteus*. He was reluctant to move on without the *Bear*. Yet the fever still gripped him to move north as fast as possible. Somehow he felt he could not lose one minute in his search for Greely and his party. Should he wait here, or should he push on? If the *Bear* was crushed like the *Proteus* . . . ? The thought of the *Proteus* reminded him of Garlington's mistake. Schley concluded he certainly could not push north of Smith Sound without making a substantial deposit of supplies at Cape Sabine.

He made up his mind.

He would leave messages on Littleton Island for Emory stating that he had decided to go over to Cape Sabine to make a deposit of supplies before pushing north to search for Greely.

After the messages had been placed Schley sent two men to cast off the lines which held the *Thetis* to an iceberg. When they came back on board, they reported that they had seen a steamer in the distance. Through the midst of the whirling snow Schley was able to make out the familiar outline of the *Bear*, covered with frost and ice, coming toward him.

In a few minutes Lieutenant Emory was on board the *Thetis*. He told the commander of several days of fighting through heavy ice and narrow escapes with icebergs. The *Bear* had suffered some close calls in the fog and storm of the past few days. Emory had landed briefly at the southeast Cary Island and examined the cache there. It had not been disturbed. There was no sign of Greely or his party having visited the island. The whalers had steamed away to the southwest and the *Bear*, running before the southerly gale, had made fast passage up to Littleton Island.

Schley informed Emory of his plans. At 3 P.M., Sunday, June 22, the *Thetis* and the *Bear* cut across Smith Sound toward Cape Sabine.

The two ships made the passage across the twenty-three miles of water without difficulty. The obvious anchorage was Payer Harbor, surrounded by Brevoort, Stalknecht, and Payer islands. Schley found the harbor frozen over. The ships were anchored to the edge of the ice near Brevoort Island. To avoid losing any more time than necessary, Schley ordered several landing parties to inspect simultaneously the several caches in the area. One party was to go to Brevoort Island, another to Stalknecht Island, and a third to the coastline at the head of Payer Harbor. Lieutenant Colwell was to take the *Bear's* steam cutter, nicknamed the "Cub," to run around Cape Sabine and look at the wreck cache that Colwell himself had made the year before after the escape from the sinking of the *Proteus*. Accompanying Colwell would be Chief Engineer Lowe of the *Bear*, the two ice masters, Norman and Ash, a coxswain, and two sailors. Schley ordered that as soon as the examination was completed, a substantial depot would be landed. They would then proceed north into Kane Sea.

Taking advantage of the time necessary for the parties to complete their inspection, Schley went below to his cabin for a short rest. As he lay down on his bunk, he heard what he thought was cheering. He leaped to his feet and rushed up on deck. The deck officer said he had heard nothing but the sound of the wind blowing through the rigging. The storm was continuing with some force and nothing could be seen of the parties which had set out. Colwell's party was just preparing to board the cutter. They had heard nothing either. Schley returned below to his cabin and once more lay down. As he once more heard the cheering, he realized his bunk was on a level with the water line, or what was now the ice line. The voices were being carried across the ice against the ship's side and transmitted into his bunk.

By the time Schley reached the deck a second time, it was possible to see Ensign Harlow signaling by semaphore from Stalknecht Island. "Have found Greely's records. Send five men."

Before any action could be taken, Yewell was seen running over the ice toward the ship from the party which had visited Brevoort Island. He stumbled on deck breathless, gasping out the news that Greely's party was at Cape Sabine and that they were all well.

The men on deck were immediately afire with excitement.

"We'll go to Cape Sabine immediately," Schley ordered. "Recall all parties."

The recall signal was given, three long blasts of the steam whistle.

In the collapsed tent Greely and his few survivors had ⸺in for hours saying little and unable to move. The storm had given no sign of stopping. The wind was roaring about them when suddenly Greely felt himself electrified. He was certain he was not mistaken. He had heard three blasts of a ship's whistle. How could a ship be moving along this coast in such a storm?

"Did anyone hear that?" he asked. "I heard a ship's whistle." No one else had heard it. They shook their heads sadly. They were not excited. They were sure, although they did not say so, that the lieutenant's mind was playing tricks on him.

"Brainard," Greely asked weakly, "I wonder if you and Long have the strength to go out and look."

"Well, Lieutenant, we'll do our best," said Brainard.

"Sure, we'll give it a try, Lieutenant," said Long.

A spark of pride glowed in Greely at this response. These were his soldiers!

"Sergeant," Greely said to Brainard. "If you do see a ship one of you should return immediately with the news."

"Yes, sir," Brainard said as he and Long struggled to make their way out through the collapsed front of the tent.

Long and Brainard crawled along on hands and knees against the wind up toward the ridge overlooking the sea. After long minutes of effort they finally reached the crest.

They peered through the storm but saw nothing other than the rocky coast and the broken ice pack stretching away in the distance. The expected nothing more. Still, they were bitterly disappointed.

They turned away to return to the tent. Long noticed that their distress flag had blown down. He crawled back to set it up again.

Before Brainard crawled into the tent he noticed that the top was off one of their water cans. The wind blowing over it made a whistling sound. He dragged himself back into the tent and reported there was nothing to be seen. Perhaps the lieutenant had heard only the wind blowing over the open water can.

Schley had all of the recovered records brought down to the officers' ward room. There the officers gathered around the table while the records were hurriedly read aloud. They listened breathlessly while the entire saga of the Lady Franklin Bay Expedition was told in simple, staccato language. The records told of the trip north, the explorations at Fort Conger, Lieutenant Lockwood's achievement of the "Farthest North," Greely's exploration of the interior of Grinnell Land, and finally the retreat from Fort Conger to Eskimo Point. In addition to the reports by Greely, there was the report deposited by Sergeant Rice on his reconnaissance trip from Eskimo Point to Cape Sabine early in October, 1883. Rice told of his difficulties in making his way through the strait and past Cocked Hat Island to Cape Sabine, of finding the cache made by Lieutenant Garlington and his intention to search for the English cache. He closed "but it is now a dense fog and the ice not very secure, and it is possible I may have to return to my party without the information regarding the latter cache. . . .

"Too cold to add further particulars. I start back at once. George H. Rice, Signal Corps, Lady Franklin Bay Expedition. October 6, 1883."

The final message included in the records was from Lieutenant Greely.

> My party is now permanently encamped on the west side of a small neck of land which connects the Wreck Cove or Bay and the one to its west. Distant about equally from Cape Sabine and Cocked Hat Island. All well.

A. W. Greely, 1st. Lt. 5th Cavalry, A.S.O. & Ass't. Commanding Expedition, Sunday, October 21, 1883.

Schley marveled at the story. What these men had achieved! And Greely had been able to bring his command all the way south to Cape Sabine without loss. But the latest document was dated October 21, 1883. The party then had rations for only forty days. What was to be expected eight months later? Could anyone still be alive?

Colwell and his party in the "Cub" had not departed for Cape Sabine before the messages were discovered, but they were all ready to go. Schley said, "Colwell, take your men and get to Cape Sabine just as fast as you can."

Colwell and his little group hurried down into the cutter and prepared to leave. He attached a boat flag to the end of a boat hook and erected it in the stern of the cutter.

As Colwell went off to the north toward Cape Sabine, Schley hurried over to the *Bear*, the faster ship, and ordered it underway to follow Colwell and his few men. It was only six miles to the point where they could hope to find Greely. Eight months, thought Schley, as he stood on the deck of the *Bear* with the storm blowing about him. Eight months, forty days' rations—what could they hope to find?

Long erected the distress flag with some difficulty in the driving wind. He gazed out at the rocky coast and the endless line of broken ice. The wind caught the flag and knocked it down. He stood there trying to work up the strength to pick it up again. He gazed almost unseeing at the sea when—he stared in unbelief—the cutter came round the point of land.

As it rounded the point of land, Colwell caught sight of the figure of a man standing on a ridge. Instantly, the coxswain waved the boat flag. The man on the ridge stooped, picked up a flag, and waved back at them.

As they brought the cutter into shore, they watched the man hurriedly make his way toward them down the steep slope. He stumbled, picked himself up, started down again and fell. Colwell called to him from the boat, "Who all are there left?"

The man replied feebly, "Seven left."

Colwell leaped from the boat onto the ice and went up to the man. His cheeks were hollow. His hair and beard were matted. His eyes were wild. He was wearing an army blouse over several thicknesses of shirts. All his clothes were ragged and dirty. On his head was a little fur cap and on his feet untanned, rough moccasins with the leather tied around the leg.

His voice was thick and his jaws worked convulsively as he tried to talk. Suddenly, he took off his glove and shook Colwell's hand.

Colwell asked, "Where are they?"

"In the tent—over the hill—the tent is down."

"Is Mr. Greely alive?"

"Yes, Greely's alive."

"Any other officers?"

"No—the tent is down," he said again, vacantly.

"Who are you?" asked Colwell.

"Long."

While Colwell was having this brief exchange with Long, Lowe and Norman leaped from the cutter onto the shore ice and started up toward the ridge. Colwell returned to the cutter briefly and hastily filled his pockets with bread and cans of pemmican. He told the coxswain to take Long into the cutter and then Colwell started up the hill. Ash accompanied him.

On the ridge they saw a rocky, desolate expanse. Beyond was a range of hills rising to about eight hundred feet. The wind blew furiously through a gorge.

Colwell and Ash caught up with Lowe and Norman as they were talking to a man. Norman turned to Colwell and said, "This is Sergeant Brainard."

Sergeant Brainard drew himself up and was about to salute but Colwell grasped his hand and shook it warmly.

Inside the tent there was a rising murmur of inquiry. "Who's there? Who's there?"

"It's Norman—Norman who was in the *Proteus*."

From the tent came a weak cheer. Ash was trying to loosen the flap of the tent. He was crying with excitement, on his hand and knees trying to roll away the rocks at the base of the tent. Colwell saw the fumbling, asked for a knife and cut open the tent. He looked in at a sight of horror.

On the ground almost in front of Colwell was an apparently dead man; his eyes staring glassily, he lay there motionless, his mouth half open. On the other side lay another figure, motionless, with haggard face. He had neither feet nor hands. Tied to the stump of his right wrist was a spoon. In the middle of the tent were two men pouring a few drops of liquid from a rubber bottle into a tin can. They offered it to a man on his hands and knees directly opposite Colwell. The man shook his head and said in a whisper, "Give it to Connell." They turned and gave it to the motionless figure lying on the ground in front of Colwell.

The man opposite Colwell on his hands and knees was dark-complexioned and his beard was long and thick. He wore a ragged, filthy dressing gown and a dirty red skull-cap. His eyes were bright and staring. As Colwell looked at him he attempted to raise himself, and he put on a pair of glasses.

"Who are you?" asked Colwell.

The man stared at him.

Colwell repeated, "Who are you?"

One of the sergeants said, "That's the major—Major Greely."

Colwell began to take in the squalor which surrounded him. The castoff clothes, the dirty sleeping bags, two or three cans of an evil-looking jelly (the product of boiled sealskin). Connell was barely breathing and there seemed to be no life in him. The miserable figure without hands or legs was hardly alive, either. The other two men were obviously so weak they had difficulty holding themselves erect or even talking. One of them leaned over Connell to tell him that the rescue party was here.

"Leave me alone," Connell said. "Can't you let a man die in peace?"

Colwell sent Lowe back to the cutter for the surgeon and for stimulants. He gave Frederick and Biederbick a little biscuit and then gave some to Greely and Elison. They ate the biscuit slowly, methodically, and without any interest. Norman opened a can of pemmican and handed it to Colwell. Colwell scraped off a little of the pemmican with his knife and fed it to the men by turn. They could not stand up for the food, so they knelt and held their mouths open like puppy dogs. After the first taste of pemmican their sense of hunger returned and they begged for more.

Colwell fed them each a bit twice and then refused them more for fear they might become sick. Their hunger had been aroused, however, and they begged for more, insisting that the food would not hurt them.

Colwell threw away the can of pemmican. Greely then turned and took out a can of boiled sealskin which he had carefully saved. He said it was his and he had a right to eat it now, but Colwell took it away from him.

Colwell tried to cheer them up while they waited for the arrival of the surgeon. He told them about some of the things that had happened in the world since they had been away. He was surprised that they were informed about so many events. They had read some newspapers, they told him, which had been left behind by Lieutenant Garlington.

Greely was now outside the tent and he complained of the cold. Colwell talked to him gently and persuaded him to get back in his sleeping bag.

In a short while a landing party arrived from the *Bear*, led by Commander Schley, followed by Lieutenant Emory, Ensign Reynolds, Dr. Ames, and Chief Engineer Melville.

Schley went directly to Greely. He leaned over the pitiful, skeletonlike figure and said, "You are all right now, Major; we have come to rescue you.

Greely looked back at Schley and asked, "Are you Englishmen?"

"No, Major, we are Americans, we are Americans."

"I am so glad to see you," Greely said.

"Major," Schley said, "your wife and family are all well."

"Thank you," Greely said. "This seems so wonderful."

"We have pictures of your wife and children on board ship," Schley told him.

"Thank you," Greely said again. "It is so kind and thoughtful."

Schley, knowing of Emory's message, turned to the lieutenant and said, "You speak to the major, Emory."

Emory knelt down by Greely's side and, with his face close to the weakened man, said slowly, "Major, I am Emory."

Life came into Greely's face and he almost smiled as he said, "Oh, yes, you are Cam." (Campbell Emory, Greely's good friend had died before Greely went to the Arctic. Greely had obviously forgotten in his weakened condition and Lieutenant Emory did not remind him now.)

"No, I am William," Emory said. "I have a letter from your wife—she and the children are well."

Greely's eyes glistened with tears. He replied weakly, "Keep it for me." And then added, "Put your hand in my sleeping bag and under me you will find my diary. Keep it."

Emory reached in, found the diary, and put it inside his jacket.

There was considerable activity beside the tent now as the doctors and others arrived to prepare stimulants and food for the stricken men. A small fire was prepared under the shelter of some rocks and milk punch and beef extract were heated. Soon somebody brought up an alcohol stove from the cutter and this too was used to prepare nourishment for the survivors.

Under the direction of the doctors each of the party was given a few mouthfuls of the milk punch and beef extract every ten minutes or so.

While the doctors were devoting their attentions to the survivors, Schley looked about the desolate scene. On top of a slope about fifty yards from the tent he saw ten graves. One of the graves was marked by a row of stones around it. Two of the other graves also were apparently made with some care. The remainder, however, were obviously made with less preparation. The bodies which had been buried latest, Schley could see, were barely covered with a small amount of gravel and rock dust. From a few of the graves a hand or a foot rose out of the thin covering. In the other direction from the wrecked tent was a small rock hut with the roof almost gone. Beyond the hut the rocky ground, partly covered with snow and ice, ran down to the ice foot. And out from the ice foot stretched the broken ice pack across to the sea leading northward. Wherever Schley looked he saw nothing but barren rock or, in the lower places, snow and ice. In a few places on southern slopes there were some scant patches of vegetation. At the bottom of the slope that led up to the graves lay the body of apparently the last man to die. He had been dragged toward his grave, Schley thought, but no one had been able to dig it for him. Scattered all about the hut and the tent were broken cans, abandoned cooking utensils, and worn-out clothing.

Schley walked over to Emory and said, "Lieutenant Emory, have those bodies uncovered and prepared for transfer to the ship. Also, have a group of men make a search of the surrounding area. Everything of any value or interest will be packed and returned to the States. Keep a careful inventory of everything that is recovered; especially note any possible identification of the bodies."

Before Emory could reply, Greely, who was lying in his sleeping bag nearby, raised his head to protest feebly.

"Sir, I must ask you to reconsider your decision about the men in those graves. This is barren and forbidding ground but it is the ground consecrated by their great achievements. I think it would be well if they could be permitted to remain here."

Schley gazed at the pleading figure on the ground and then impulsively knelt beside him and placed a hand on his shoulder.

"Lieutenant Greely, I can appreciate the reasonable nature of your sentiment. You have served here with these men and know what they did here. However, can you not understand that the friends of these brave men would wish that their bodies were returned home? I think you will agree with me, Lieutenant, that we must first consider the feelings of the friends and families of your comrades."

After about two hours of the careful nourishment of the survivors, the surgeons decided they were in strong enough condition to be carried to the ship. Stretchers were brought for all of them but Frederick, who stoutly declared that he was strong enough to walk. After taking a few steps, it was clear that he needed help and two sturdy sailors walked along with their arms about him. The stretcher bearers led the way in single file and the two sailors, with Frederick's arms on their shoulders, followed along behind.

In the area surrounding the tent and the hut, Emory and his men were busy sorting through the debris, picking out everything of value or interest. At each sleeping bag within the tent, they found a little package carefully packed and addressed to a friend or a relative at home. Each of the dead men and each of the survivors had prepared such a little package.

The bodies on Cemetery Ridge were removed from their graves with no great trouble. Lieutenant Emory carefully made a drawing of the burial ground and gave each grave a number. A corresponding number was placed on the body removed from that grave. The bodies thus removed, as well as Schneider's, which lay in the open at the foot of the slope, were wrapped in blankets and carried to the ship.

In transferring the survivors and the dead from the shore to the ship, the rescuers had great difficulty. The storm was still raging and the sea was choppy. Several times the boats doing the ferrying were nearly swamped. At one time, as one of the boats came alongside the *Thetis*, a strong wave tipped it and two of the dead bodies were dumped into the sea. One of the seamen, acting swiftly, was able to recover them before they sank.

It was midnight before all of the bodies were transferred to the ship.

Colwell and Ash made a tour of the area surrounding the tent and the hut. As he looked through the abandoned equipment, Colwell, with a quick stab of recognition, came upon a uniform coat which he had abandoned on this shore after the wreck of the *Proteus*. What would they have done then, Colwell thought, if they had known the consequences of their precipitous retreat last year?

Colwell and Ash walked on down beyond the hut toward the ice foot. There was a dark object in the white snow. They followed a path through the snow to the object and found a body with a bullet hole in the head. Colwell secured a blanket, wrapped the body, and carried it over to the waiting boat.

All those who had gone ashore were now back on ship. The *Thetis* and the *Bear* steamed back to Payer Harbor so they might anchor in safety from the storm.

Schley decided that the ships would lay up in Payer Harbor for the rest of the night so the men could have some rest after the strenuous effort and excitement of recent days.

The following morning at eleven o'clock Lieutenant Emory was ordered to return with the *Bear* to make a final search of the area around the tent and the hut. Two landing parties went ashore and made an extensive search lasting several hours. Schley also sent another party to Stalknecht Island to bring off the remainder of Greely's records and equipment.

The *Bear* and the search parties returned to Payer Harbor about 5 P.M. The wind that had been blowing so strongly from the south during the storm had now slackened. The ice was moving down swiftly from Kane Sea and the *Bear* was not far ahead of it. As Emory turned his ship into Payer Harbor the ice, with a rush, closed the narrow passage which the ships had used to move around the point of Cape Sabine to the camp.

Schley knew it was now time to give the order to start the return voyage. From the bridge he looked across the water to the north. Probably never before had sailors so well equipped been as far north as early as June 23. How far might they be able to go if they now went north across the Kane Sea and up through Kennedy Channel? The prospect was almost irresistible for the commander. He gazed north a moment longer. Then sober reason and duty wiped the vision from his eyes. He had performed but half of his mission. He had found and rescued the Greely expedition (or what was left of it). Now he had to bring them home. He gave the command. The ships moved away from the desolate coast of Cape Sabine and began their journey to the south.

Neither Schley nor anyone else who shared in the rescue would ever forget the few hours spent on Cape Sabine or the story revealed by the scene and the few skeletons of men still living.

The accolade for the Lady Franklin Bay Expedition had been offered by its commander at the moment of rescue. In the squalor of the collapsed tent, the leader of the tragic, determined band had stared back at the strange face before him.

"Greely, is this you?" the face asked.

At the edge of death but with his spirit still undefeated, Greely gasped, "Yes—seven of us left—here we are—dying—like men. Did what I came to do—beat the record."

The effort of talking had exhausted him and he fell back.

Indeed, they had beaten the record and won for their nation the honor of the "Farthest North." But Greely would never be able to tell fully of the greater victory they had achieved in the long, desperate months at Cape Sabine.

In spite of the failure of their relief ships, the unrelenting cruelty of the Arctic, the jungle instinct they all felt and two had succumbed to, in spite of the frailties of the body and the temptations of self-preservation, they had devoted themselves to each other.

Despite conflicts, irritability and irrationality that verged on madness, they had worked together, shared their last bit of food, sacrificed for weaker comrades, repeatedly risked their lives, and some had given their lives, in efforts to secure food to keep the rest alive. These—the spiritual achievements of the men of the Lady Franklin Bay Expedition—were their greatest triumph.

EPILOGUE

The rescue squadron arrived back at St. John's the morning of July 17. Schley immediately telegraphed to the Secretary of the Navy the news of the rescue. Elison had died on the return voyage after an attempt to save his life by secondary amputation. Only six of the twenty-five members of the Lady Franklin Bay Expedition returned alive.

Secretary Chandler by telegraph sent congratulations to Schley and his command and said that "the hearts of the American people go out with great affection" to the survivors. He wired Schley:

> Care for them unremittingly, and bid them be cheerful and hopeful on account of what life has yet in store for them. Preserve tenderly the remains of the heroic dead; prepare them according to your judgment, and bring them home.

The survivors had improved steadily on the way home and their strength was increased during a week's stay at St. John's while metallic caskets were prepared for the bodies of the dead.

The squadron arrived in Portsmouth harbor on August 1 where an elaborate welcome was staged. The ships of the North Atlantic Squadron were there for the ceremonies. There was a tremendous ovation from the ships and the crowds on the shore as the rescue fleet arrived. The band on the battleship *Tennessee* played "Home Again." Flags and signals were displayed on warships and merchant vessels. Aboard the flagship, the *Tennessee*, was Mrs. Greely and relatives, Secretary Chandler, General

William Hazen, and other distinguished guests. (Significantly, Secretary of War Lincoln was absent.)

Schley arranged for the meeting of Lieutenant and Mrs. Greely in the privacy of his cabin. While Greely waited below, Schley went on deck to meet Mrs. Greely. The tall, young, and extremely beautiful brunette carried herself with great poise and dignity although she was obviously under much strain of anticipation. After Mrs. Greely entered the cabin, Schley heard her cry, "Dolph, Dolph." As she flew to her husband's arms, Schley closed the door behind him, leaving them alone.

Schley returned with his squadron carrying the bodies of the dead to New York Harbor. Present to take part in the ceremonies were Major General Winfield Scott Hancock, commander of Governor's Island, Secretary of War Lincoln (he would not be embarrassed here by the presence of Greely), Lieutenant General Philip Sheridan, and Brigadier General Hazen. Here Commander Schley and his men performed the last solemn duty of their mission: they formally delivered the caskets to the Army. The ships then proceeded to the New York Navy Yard and the crews were discharged.

A few days later President Arthur came to New York and gave an audience to Schley and his officers at the Fifth Avenue Hotel. After congratulating Schley and his officers on their splendid work, the President told the commander that he was being promoted to chief of the Bureau of Equipment and Recruiting in the Navy Department.

Schley, taken unawares, stammered his thanks and added, "I believe, Mr. President, you are rewarding me far beyond what my services merit."

The President smiled faintly and replied with mock seriousness, "I can appreciate your sentiments, Commander, but you will forgive me, perhaps, if I say that in this instance, at least, I believe that I am the better judge. I only wish the law permitted me to reward you more substantially for your great work."

Thus, after a brief experience at a sea command, Schley found himself once more ordered to a desk job ashore.

A few days later a report in *The New York Times* told of rumors of cannibalism at Cape Sabine. Schley refused to answer questions put to him by newsmen. The reporters would have to look to the Navy Department which had his official report.

As the rumors continued, the family of Private Whisler had his body exhumed and inspected. It was seen that a square of flesh had been cut from the back. Schley's report told that six of the dead bodies had been cut, Lieutenant Kislingbury, Jewell, Ralston, Henry, Whisler, and Ellis. In one instance, the skin had been cut neatly along the line of the ribs below the shoulder. The cut had been made so that a flap of skin could be lifted, the flesh beneath removed and the flap replaced. This had been done with the precision of a surgeon, the *Times* reported.

Eventually, Greely at Portsmouth was questioned about it and he replied emphatically that he knew of no cannibalism at Cape Sabine. Writing of his arctic experiences later, he said he knew of "no law, human or divine, which was broken at Cape Sabine, and do not feel called on as an officer or as a man to dwell longer on such a painful topic." In the privacy of his family, he commented, "I don't know who did it. I know I didn't and I know Brainard didn't."

On August 11 Greely wrote to the War Department his report on the execution of Henry. He asked for a court of inquiry. The Adjutant General replied that because of "extracts from the diaries of several members of the Lady Franklin Bay Expedition, and also in connection with the diary of Private Henry himself, the Secretary of War entertains no doubt of the necessity and the entire propriety of your action. . . ." There was no question about the need for Greely's order. No court of inquiry was appointed.

The official story of the Lady Franklin Bay Expedition was ended.

The principal figures in the rescue drama at Cape Sabine, Schley, Greely, and Brainard, went on to serve their nation in military service. All three participated with some distinction years later in the Spanish-American War. Both Schley and Greely received considerable renown for their arctic service but the enlisted men of the Lady Franklin Bay went unrecognized for some time. In concluding his account of *Three Years of Arctic Service*, Greely noted the neglect of Sergeant Brainard whose "manhood, courage, and self-sacrifice . . . would have gained him a commission at once in any other service of the world." Referring to the other members of the party, Greely extended his indictment of official Washington. The promotions Greely had made during their days of trial were not approved by the War Department. Greely commented bitterly:

> Two men, with broken health, have adventured their private fortunes; and one, a most self-sacrificing, soldierly, temperate, and loyal man, lies, as these lines are penned, helpless in a city hospital, aided by private charity, his pension not even awarded.
>
> Even the meager allowances originally promised for Arctic service have not been fully paid and the widows of the dead are generally as yet unrecognized.

The publicity resulting from Greely's book had its effect. Lethargic, official Washington responded to the pressure of public opinion. Biederbick was awarded an appointment as Inspector of Customs in New York City.

Frederick was named an observer in the Weather Bureau at Indianapolis. And some time later Long and Connell also received appointments in the Weather Bureau. In 1886 President Grover Cleveland commissioned Brainard a second lieutenant "as a recognition of the gallant and meritorious services rendered by him in the Arctic."

Greely, after a period of recovery from his trials in the Arctic, and after a tour of Europe where he was highly honored by various scientific and geographical organizations, returned to duty in Washington. In 1887 as the senior officer next to General Hazen in the Signal Corps, he succeeded to the head of that unit and was automatically promoted to the rank of brigadier general.

Schley served in Washington for some years and later had various posts of sea duty. He held the rank of commodore in 1898 at the beginning of the Spanish-American War. He was named to the command of the Flying Squadron. The Flying Squadron played a significant role at the Battle of Santiago Harbor which resulted in the defeat of the Spanish Fleet under Admiral Cervera. His actions at this battle, however, years later were questioned by his superior, Admiral Sampson. Schley indignantly asked for a court of inquiry to settle the matter. The conclusions of the court of inquiry were not definitive but they did leave a question mark about Schley's action. He retired from the Navy after forty-five years of service and devoted his later years to writing a book about his many adventures and defending his actions at Santiago. It is remarkable that the naval officer who had completely defeated the enemy fleet with the loss of only one American life should find that his conduct of the battle was subject to criticism.

Greely had some subsequent experience in the Arctic for the Army. He was active in the development of the telegraph system in Alaska and was one of the first to make use of wireless. Later, he was in charge of the military forces at San Francisco during the earthquake and fire in 1906. He received much acclaim for his swift restoration of order and his caring for and feeding the many thousands of homeless. His own home was burned during the fire and his diary and other records of his experience with the Lady Franklin Bay Expedition were lost.

Greely remained a prominent figure in Washington for many years. He was one of the founders of the National Geographic Society and won a reputation as an authority and a writer on meteorology and geography. He retired in 1908 as Chief Signal Officer of the Army with the rank of major general.

Brainard also had a distinguished career in the Army, serving in the Spanish-American War, the Philippines, Cuba, and in World War I. He retired with the rank of brigadier general in 1918. He, too, made his home in Washington.

Brainard and Greely remained lifelong friends. Each year, whenever possible, they would meet on the anniversary of their rescue. They would dine on one of the menus which Lieutenant Lockwood had collected in the hat during those dark days at Cape Sabine. They would reminisce about their arctic experience and the valor of the men who had shared the hazards of the Arctic with them.

Greely lived a long, full life. It was not until October 1935 that his splendid physical mechanism showed the inevitable signs of decline. Under the advice of his physician, he entered the Walter Reed Hospital in Washington. Brainard visited the hospital every day to see his old comrade. He would not permit himself to believe that Greely was in his last days. "I have seen Greely much worse off than this and get through it," he said. "I am sure he will do it again."

This was the end, however. Greely died October 20, 1935, and was buried two days later in Arlington National Cemetery.

Brainard survived him by eleven years. When Brainard died, March 22, 1946, there was little public notice. It was more than sixty years since the desperate days at Cape Sabine and the achievements at Fort Conger. The last survivor passed away with little attention from the nation he had served for so many years. America had forgotten the Lady Franklin Bay Expedition and the winning of the "Farthest North."

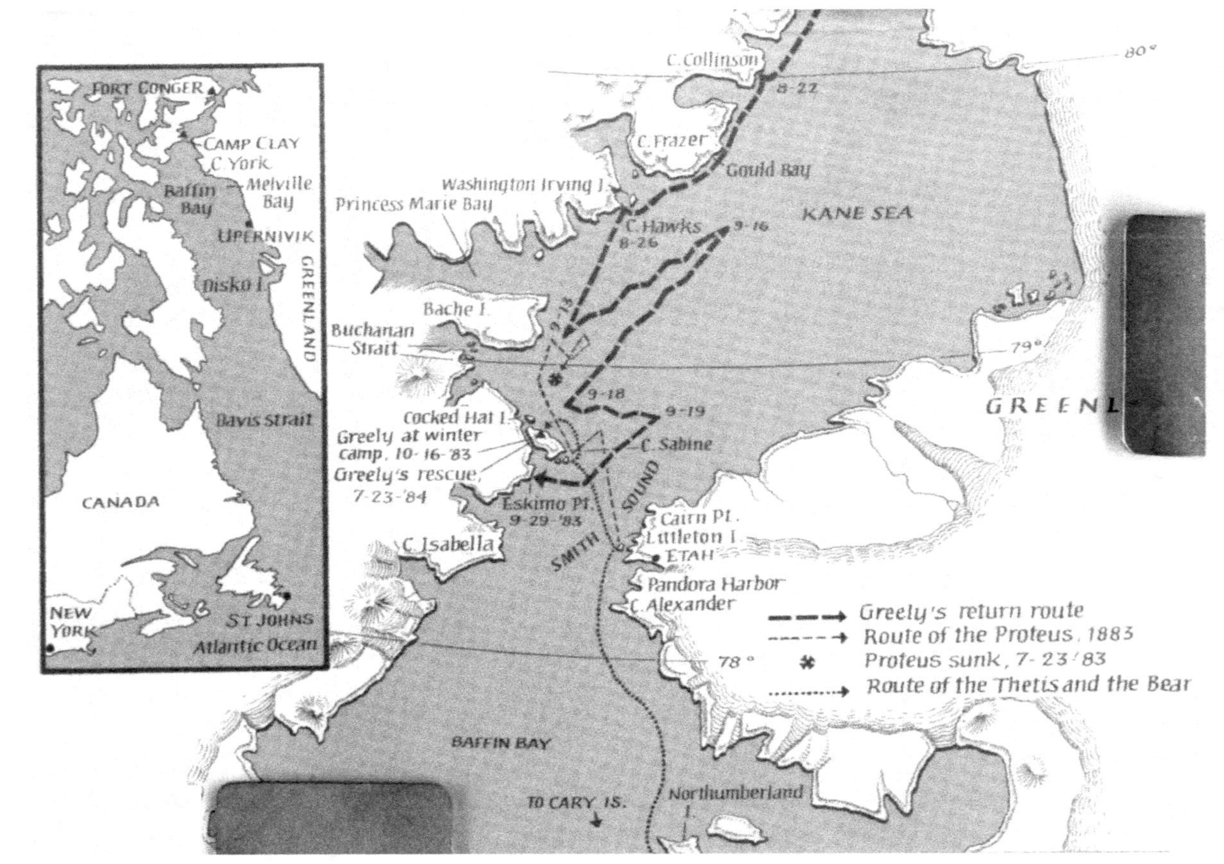

FORT CONGER
CAMP CLAY
C. York
Melville Bay
Baffin Bay
UPERNIVIK
Disko I.
GREENLAND
Davis Strait
CANADA
NEW YORK
ST. JOHNS
Atlantic Ocean
C. Collinson
8-22
C. Frazer
Gould Bay
KANE SEA
Washington Irving I.
Princess Marie Bay
C. Hawks
8-26
9-16
Bache I.
Buchanan Strait
9-13
9-18
9-19
GREENL
Cocked Hat I.
Greely at winter camp, 10-16-'83
Greely's rescue, 7-23-'84
C. Sabine
Eskimo Pt. 9-29-'83
C. Isabella
SMITH SOUND
Cairn Pt.
Littleton I.
ETAH
Pandora Harbor
C. Alexander
78°
79°
80°
BAFFIN BAY
TO CARY IS.
Northumberland I.
Greely's return route
Route of the Proteus, 1883
Proteus sunk, 7-23-'83
Route of the Thetis and the Bear

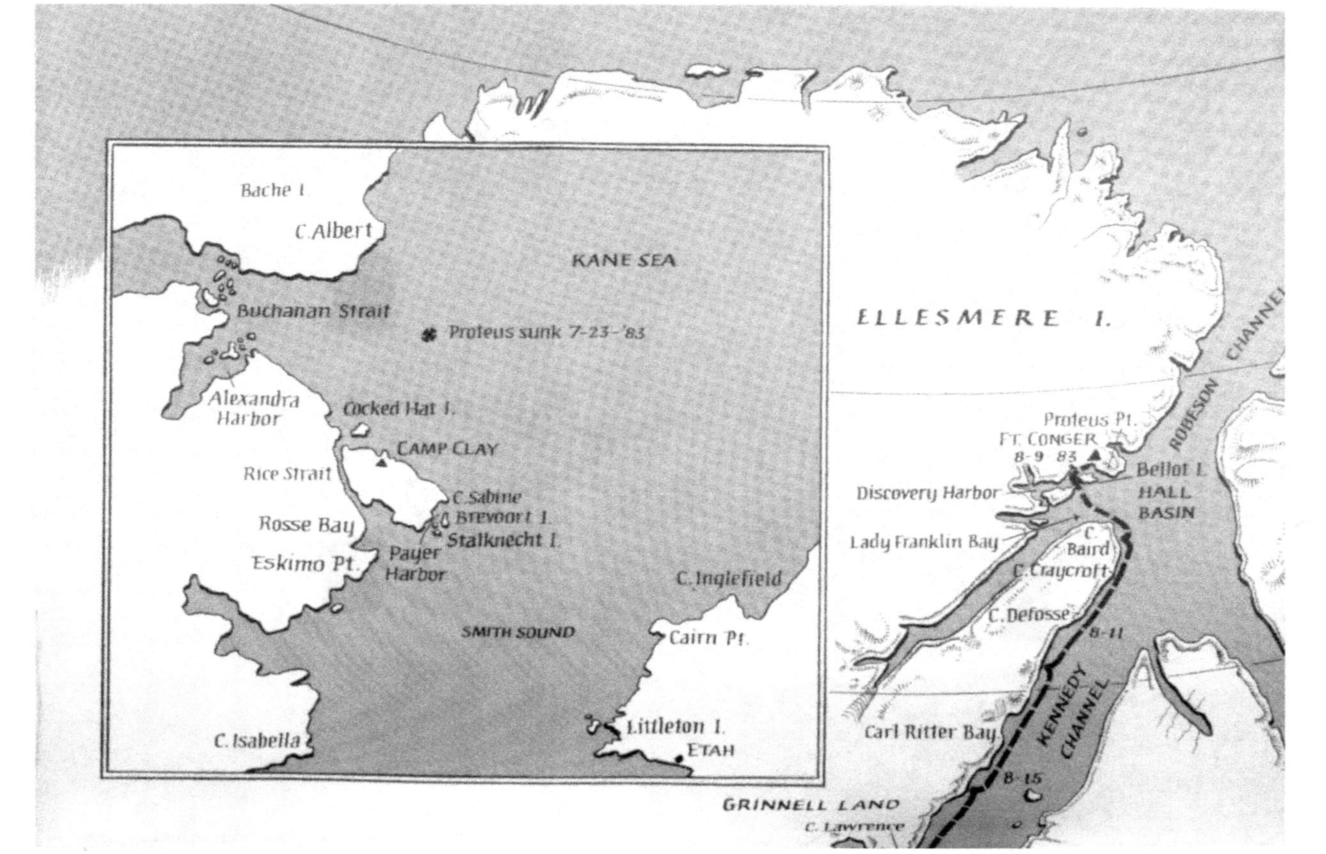

Bache I.
C. Albert
KANE SEA
Buchanan Strait
Proteus sunk 7-23-'83
Alexandra Harbor
Cocked Hat I.
CAMP CLAY
Rice Strait
C. Sabine
Brevoort I.
Rosse Bay
Stalknecht I.
Eskimo Pt.
Payer Harbor
C. Inglefield
SMITH SOUND
Cairn Pt.
C. Isabella
Littleton I.
ETAH
ELLESMERE I.
ROBESON CHANNEL
Proteus Pt.
FT. CONGER
8-9 83
Discovery Harbor
Bellot I.
HALL BASIN
Lady Franklin Bay
C. Baird
C. Craycroft
C. Defosse
8-11
Carl Ritter Bay
KENNEDY CHANNEL
8-15
GRINNELL LAND
C. Lawrence